The Callisto Myth From Ovid to Atwood

The Callisto Myth from Ovid to Atwood

Initiation and Rape in Literature

KATHLEEN WALL

McGill-Queen's University Press
Kingston and Montreal

© McGill-Queen's University Press 1988
ISBN 0-7735-0640-3

Legal deposit third quarter 1988
Bibliothèque nationale du Québec

(∞)

Printed in Canada on acid-free paper

This book has been published with the help of a grant
from the Canadian Federation for the Humanities, using
funds provided by the Social Sciences and Humanities
Research Council of Canada.

Canadian Cataloguing in Publication Data

Wall, Kathleen, 1950–
    The Callisto myth from Ovid to Atwood
    Includes index.
    Bibliography: p
    ISBN 0-7735-0640-3
    1. Callisto (Greek mythology). 2. Initiations in Literature.
    3. Women in literature. I. Title.
    PN57. C27W34 1988   809'.93352042   c88-090090-3

A version of chapter four appears in Julia M. Walker, ed.,
Milton and the Idea of Woman, Champaign: University
of Illinois Press, 1988.

For Carol Geminder Gordon
1944-1983
One of this world's tragic Callistos

Contents

Appendices:

Acknowledgments

My primary debt is to Dr. Evelyn J. Hinz, whose rigorous intellectual standards often forced me to substantiate my "hunches" and to articulate the patterns I found in my work. The questions she posed regarding my approach and my theories always helped me to address the complexities of literature more thoroughly. The effects of any fine, productive criticism stay with one for life, and Dr. Hinz has consequently helped me to become a better scholar.

I want to thank John Teunissen, Robert Finnigan, and Annis Pratt, who all gave helpful criticism when it was most needed. Valued teachers who guided me early in my career, Leo MacNamara and Lyle Powers, also deserve gratitude.

I owe a great deal to Dan Geminder, who, during the initial stages of this work, typed messy manuscripts, wrote friendly computer programs, printed out chapters, patiently ordered books I needed from interlibrary loan, and generally saved me from my own absent-mindedness.

I must also thank my daughter, Veronica, who carried books and inserted nickels in Xerox machines with astounding patience. At eight, she is an ardent feminist, quite certain of what is fair, and confident of her own capabilities. She provides me with constant, living reassurance that the principles informing this study are healthy and dynamic.

The oldest debt of all, however, is to my parents, Lawrence and Doris Wall, who always believed I could accomplish anything I undertook.

The Callisto Myth from Ovid to Atwood

Introduction

Defining the mythic patterns which accurately reflect the forms and realities of woman's experience is a major concern of feminist literary criticism. Mythic analyses of literature by and about women have revealed the inadequacies of the paradigms describing the masculine experience that have been posited by Carl Jung, Joseph Campbell, and Northrop Frye. The social restrictions traditionally placed upon women, and hence upon the heroine, result in a radical difference between the nature of her existence and that of her male counterpart, the hero. From this straightforward observation, it is but a very simple step to conclude that the myths which describe the hero's experiences could not function accurately when it comes to describing those of the heroine. Annis Pratt, in "The New Feminist Criticism," observes: "It is startling to realize that volumes have been written about the development of the male psyche as if it, in itself, defined the human soul. If there is a 'myth of the hero' there must also be a 'myth of the heroine,' a female as well as a male *bildungsroman*, parallel, perhaps, but by no means identical."[1] Carol Christ similarly observes that "the quests of heroes, from Gilgamesh and Odysseus, Apuleius and Augustine, to Stephen Daedalus and Carlos Castaneda, have been recorded throughout history. Joseph Campbell in his classic work, *The Hero with a Thousand Faces*, charted the journey of the hero in many cultures. Typically the hero leaves home, defines himself through tests and trials, and returns with a clearer understanding of himself and his place in the world. But if the hero has a thousand faces, the heroine has scarcely a dozen."[2]

Given this situation, the literary critic must undertake her or his own quest to discover the patterns which define the experiences of the heroine. Like many undertakings by feminist literary critics, my own quest began in the wilderness,[3] with a curiosity about the kinds of initiations protagonists undergo in the forest. Originally, I intended to study twentieth-century narratives that evinced similarities to the myths of Orpheus,

Acteon, and Callisto. I began by working on Callisto for reasons that I seemed almost unable to articulate: her experience felt startlingly familiar, in spite of the fact that it was literally unfamiliar. Later I recognized that seldom during my undergraduate or graduate studies had I written about a woman. Still later I realized the extent to which her experience incorporates common motifs in literature by and about women; later yet I recognized the way her rape reflects a patriarchal culture's control and definition of women's sexuality.

In my early explorations of feminist criticism, and of historical, sociological, and psychological studies of the female experience, I found the motifs that constitute the myth of Callisto – rape, troubled motherhood, forest exile, metamorphosis – were viewed by scholars as integral to the lives of real and fictional women. In the course of writing *Archetypal Patterns of Women's Fiction*, for example, Annis Pratt found that "the rape-trauma archetype recurs as one of the most frequent plot structures in women's fiction."[4] Similarly, Nina Auerbach notes that "the fallen woman, heartbreaking and glamorous, flourished in the popular iconography of America and the Continent as well as England" during the Victorian era.[5] Simone de Beauvoir's study of a young woman's initiation into sexuality in *The Second Sex* suggests that the raped or seduced woman is such a major concern, because for young women the first sexual encounter often seems like rape. Even if that encounter occurs under legally sanctioned circumstances, in the marriage bed, the first sexual intercourse symbolizes not only a man's physical possession of a woman, but his legal possession as well.[6] In *Against Our Will: Men, Women, and Rape*, Susan Brownmiller proposes that "by anatomical fiat – the inescapable construction of their genital organs – the human male was a natural predator and the human female served as his natural prey. Not only might the female be subjected at will to a thoroughly detestable physical conquest from which there could be no retaliation in kind – a rape for a rape – but the consequences of such a brutal struggle might be death or injury, not to mention impregnation and the birth of a dependent child."[7]

With the birth of that dependent child, women enter upon another experience unique to them: motherhood. Yet the main theme of Adrienne Rich's study, *Of Woman Born*, is that, potentially powerful as motherhood might seem, the patriarchy has consistently sought to undermine its "mana": "The one aspect in which most women have felt their own power in the patriarchal sense – authority over and control of another – has been motherhood; and even this aspect, as we shall see, has been wrenched and manipulated to male control ... The idea of maternal power has been domesticated. In transfiguring and enslaving woman, the womb – the ultimate source of this power – has historically been turned against us and itself made into a source of powerlessness."[8]

Another motif common to the lives of women is a special relation to nature. Sherry Ortner has suggested in "Is Female to Male as Nature is to Culture" that the single factor which most contributes to man's perception of a woman as different is her chthonic quality.[9] This characteristic is reflected in the studies of female deities: Erich Neumann's *The Great Mother* and M. Esther Harding's *Woman's Mysteries*, for example, reveal that the Goddess in all her variety is consistently a chthonic deity, tied to the fertility of nature and the fecundity of women.

The biological and cultural fact of woman's special relationship to nature is expressed in literature through the use of plot structures that consistently place the heroine in a natural setting which functions not only to express her tie to the earth, but also serves as a refuge from patriarchal control. Francine du Plessex Gray writes: "From Emily Brontë's moors to Doris Lessing's veld, women authors have turned to nature not only in search of heightened perception but also as a refuge from the patriarchal order ... Until all forms of sexual dominance are abolished, nature may be the only form of nunnery left to us, the only shelter in a desacralized world."[10] Similarly, Pratt notes that the heroine often escapes the confines and demands of society by retreating to a green world.

At this point Pratt introduces an archetypal figure that she identifies as the green-world lover, a man who is removed from the patriarchal social structure and its values, and who initiates the heroine into her sexuality. Yet the heroine's sexual experience in the forest is equally likely to occur at the hands of a rapist, a representative of the enclosing patriarchy, whom Pratt identifies with Olympian (and non-chthonic) deities like Zeus and Apollo. Pratt observes, then, that this configuration of the heroine's sojourn in the natural world has two opposite manifestations, initiation and rape, and that both are central to fiction.[11]

Another paradox in fiction by and about women is manifested in the quality of the forest retreat itself. Gray's remarks suggest that the natural world may be a place of chosen retreat – a "nunnery – " a place of companionship with other women, or, as Pratt describes it, a place of escape from the pressures of the patriarchy. But Pratt also observes that because such an escape signals a woman's rebellion against the patriarchy it frequently results in a rape which is designed precisely as punishment for her rebellion.[12] Consequently, such a retreat is as likely to end in rape as in freedom from domination. The natural world is also a place of involuntary exile. After a woman's fall, Auerbach writes, "indifferent nature simply reclaims her. Once cast into solitude, the fallen woman is irretrievably metamorphosed."[13]

Auerbach's choice of words here is significant, for metamorphosis is also part of female experience, specifically metamorphosis which renders woman part of the natural world. Pratt uses the same word to describe woman's experience in the green world: "As in many examples of 'green-world fiction' the hero not only appreciates and likes nature but, through a process of metamorphosis, *becomes* an element in it."[14]

Auerbach finds that "apotheosis" is the last element of the career of the fallen woman, as if "a woman's fall is imagined as the only avenue through which she is allowed to grow."[15] Yet if she succeeds in transforming herself and growing, that apotheosis is likely to be punishment or death. Similarly, Pratt writes that: "Woman's rebirth journeys ... create transformed, androgynous, and powerful human personalities out of socially devalued beings and are therefore more likely to involve denouements punishing the quester for succeeding in her perilous, revolutionary journey."[16]

The myth of Callisto encompasses all these motifs. A nymph in Diana's following, nature was her "nunnery" and her refuge from the patriarchal society that had defeated her father. The green-world villain is Zeus, who rapes her as she rests in the forest, tired from the hunt. Diana's band of virgins exiles her; Hera in her anger transforms her into a bear. Hence the forest now becomes the place of involuntary exile and her metamorphosis makes her part of that landscape. Because she is a bear, she cannot raise a human child; thus her motherhood is dramatically wrenched from her. The final element in her story combines both death and apotheosis: she is nearly killed, but Zeus rescues her at the last moment and enshrines her in the sky as the Great Bear constellation.

Clearly, a study of the Callisto myth's recurrence in literature in English serves to synthesize many of the motifs already observed by other critics as being integral to the experience of woman. The recurrence of this myth further indicates that it constitutes an archetype, in keeping with Leslie Fiedler's definition of the term as "any of the immemorial patterns of response to the human situation in its most permanent aspects: death, love, the biological family, the relationships with the Unknown, etc., whether those patterns be considered to reside in the Jungian Collective Unconscious or the Platonic World of Ideas."[17]

But the feminist practice of archetypal criticism necessarily differs from that of Jung's more traditional followers. Certainly Jung's ideas begin to acknowledge the feminine insofar as he views masculine and feminine qualities as "equally available for development by either sex"[18] and insofar as he recognizes the importance of feminine qualities in the masculine personality. But there are several crucial limitations to archetypal theory as it has been typically applied to women's experiences.

The first limitation is the tendency to assume an identity between archetypes of the anima – archetypes that are manifestations of man's psychological experience of the feminine – and the archetypes that emerge as descriptors of either the social or psychological dimensions of women's lives.[19] Such a limitation manifests itself in two ways. First, there is a tendency to interpret female characters in the light of male characters' experience of them, and to see the heroine primarily as an anima figure for the hero. Second, there is a tendency to read texts about women written by men without recognizing that the masculine viewpoint of the author must function as some kind of filter – not necessarily one that produces inaccuracies or fallacies, nor necessarily one that is unsympathetic or misogynistic – but a filter nevertheless. If recognition is given to the author's masculinity, the heroine is likely to suffer reduction to the role of his anima. The result is a criticism that is phallocentric and that asserts, more or less emphatically, that literature is about men: women are aspects of, or appendages to, the masculine psychology.

The second essential inadequacy of traditional Jungian criticism for feminist scholars is its tendency to view archetypes as fixed and immutable. As Naomi Goldenberg points out, by viewing the archetypes as unchanging "we run the risk of setting bounds to experience by defining what the proper experience of women is. This could become a new version of the ideology of the Eternal Feminine and it could result in structures just as limiting as those prescribed by the old Eternal Feminine."[20] Such archetypes could be used to justify socially-sanctioned, seductive but oppressive roles and behavior patterns because they are an immutable part of the feminine psyche.[21] The solution to this problem suggested by Lauter and Rupprecht in *Feminist Archetypal Theory* is to "regard the archetype not as an image whose content is frozen but ... as a tendency to form and reform images in relation to certain kinds of repeated experience; then the concept could serve to clarify distinctively female concerns that have persisted throughout human history. Applied to a broad range of materials ... it could expose a set of reference points that would serve as an expandable framework for defining female experience, and ultimately the 'muted' culture females have created."[22]

By viewing archetypes as fixed, traditional Jungian theorists ignore Jung's own exploration of the ways in which the archetypal images of the collective unconscious mirror the culture in which they arise. Similarly, archetypal images, as they rise from the Collective Unconscious to an individual's consciousness, are inevitably filtered through the experience, biases, and culture of the individual. Consequently, Lauter and Rupprecht propose a concept of archetype that "requires that we consider the experiential context in which the image occurs. A central tenet of [their] theory is that image and behaviour are inextricably linked; our images of possible behavior inform our actions, and our actions, in turn, alter our images."[23]

The purpose of this study, then, is to note not only the recurrence of the myth, but the variations which it undergoes. The configuration observed by Pratt, Auerbach, and de Beauvoir has a Janus-faced quality: the natural world may represent a retreat or an exile, the green-world man may be lover or rapist, the fallen woman's situation may end in death or apotheosis. To ignore these paradoxes would be simplistic. Consequently, the critic must also attend to what Fiedler, noting the same phenomena as Lauter and Rupprecht, terms "signature," an individual response to the "immemorial patterns": "the sum total of individuating factors in a work, the sign of the Persona or Personality, through which an Archetype is rendered, and which itself tends to become a subject as well as a means of the poem ... Signature ... belongs ... to the social collectivity as well as to the individual writer. The Signature is the joint product of 'rules' and 'conventions,' of the expectations of a community, and the idiosyncratic responses of the individual poet, who adds a personal idiom or voice to a received style."[24] These variations reflect a point or points of view on the issues which the myth or archetype addresses.

This study examines the recurrence and variations of the myth, both the archetype and the signatures, by observing its appearance in fifteen works in English. During the Middle Ages and the Renaissance, the myth was treated in translations of Ovid's *Metamorphoses* by William Caxton, Sir George Sandys, and William Golding. It was incorporated into the fabric of other works as well: Caxton's translation of Raoul Lefevre's *Recuyell of the Historyes of Troye*, William Warner's *Albion's England* and W.N.'s lyric, *The Barley-Breake, or a Warning for Wantons*. It is central, also, to John Milton's *A Mask Presented at Ludlow Castle*, but does not make a significant appearance in English literature again until the end of the eighteenth century, in Mrs Radcliffe's *Mysteries of Udolpho*. After that rather lengthy hiatus, its recurrence is frequent. Charlotte Brontë's *Jane Eyre*, Nathaniel Hawthorne's *The Scarlet Letter*, George Eliot's *Adam Bede*, and Thomas Hardy's *Tess of the D'Urbervilles* all revolve around heroines who are Callisto figures. Two major works of the twentieth century, D.H. Lawrence's *Lady Chatterley's Lover* and Margaret Atwood's *Surfacing*, provide contemporary variations of the myth. I have, perhaps somewhat controversially, included works by male authors when the myth was clearly present, under the (perhaps once again controversial) belief that women are not the only biological gender who can make observations about or attempt to grapple with a woman's experience in a patriarchal world. Whether those observations are sympathetic, misogynistic, or ignorant can only be determined by a careful reading of the text in which they appear, by attention, in short, to signature.

This is not, of course, an exhaustive list of Callisto narratives: other works which could be included range from Radcliffe's *Mysteries of the Forest* to Marian Engel's *Bear*. Some principle of selection was necessary, however, to keep this study manageable. Accordingly, the criteria consisted of a conjunction between the generic, historical, or cultural significance of a given work and the extent to which it engenders new perspectives on the myth.

The chronological order of the study and the frequency with which writers are aware of their predecessors' work might suggest that I intend *Callisto* to be a source study. Mrs Radcliffe does quote Milton's *A Mask Presented at Ludlow Castle* in *Mysteries of Udolpho*; George Eliot did read about Hester Prynne and Arthur Dimmesdale shortly before she wrote about her own Hetty and Arthur in *Adam Bede*. But a writer's conscious influence by another source (much less an unconscious one) is difficult to prove and not particularly fruitful in the context of this study. What I wish to suggest, instead, is the remarkable tenacity, persistence, and elasticity of this myth. Any chronological development points not to literary sources, but to the changing attitudes toward women that the respective variations of the myth serve to index. My use of historical, sociological, anthropological, and pyschological sources is further intended to explain the ways in which the recurrences of the myth are a reflection of their time, but I am in no way pretending to be a polymath.

Carl Jung, curious about the process that brought the unconscious, mythic configurations into the conscious realm so that they could be expressed in creative work, concluded that archetypes arise as a response to the problems of the writer's time: "Therein lies the social significance of art: it is constantly at work educating the spirit of the age, conjuring up the forms in which the age is most lacking. The unsatisfied yearning of the artist reaches back to the primordial image in the unconscious which is best fitted to compensate the inadequacy and one-sidedness of the present."[25] In this context, the frequency with which writers have reached back and found this particular "primordial image" is surely telling. As a myth about a woman's powerlessness and her rape, a myth about sexual aggression as a means of possession and control, its persistence is surely a comment upon women's lives and women's experience of their sexuality. Yet, as I shall argue, the myth has a positive, pre-patriarchal element that describes a woman's sexual initiation and her achievement of the right to self-determination. The expropriation of this aspect of the myth and our relative ignorance of the ancient women's rituals that were its expression is part of woman's dispossession, her loss of images, myths, narratives that legitimate and celebrate her strength and her complexity. Consequently, the study of Callisto's myth ought to reveal many aspects of the realities of women's experience from the Middle Ages to the twentieth century – the "inadequacy and one-sidedness" of each age. But it should reveal as well the "primordial image in the unconscious" that provides a vision of woman fully realized, fully self-possessed, fully feminine.

CHAPTER ONE

Classical Versions and Their Implications

The myth of Callisto is variously related in five extant classical works. Hesiod's *Astronomy*, written in the eighth century, BC, is the oldest source of information, but his account is quite sketchy, concerned as it is with the origin of the Great Bear constellation and not with the story itself.[1] Apollodorus, to whom *The Library* is somewhat uneasily attributed (and which is dated equally uneasily at 140 BC), dismisses the whole incident in a paragraph;[2] Hyginus (64 BC to AD 17), in the *Poetica Astronomica*, devotes only a page,[3] but both he and Apollodorus offer some of the significant variations which have developed around the essential story. Ovid's account in the *Metamorphoses*[4] (43 BC – AD 14) is the most "literary" and extended treatment of the myth in antiquity, even though a later classical version was provided by Pausanias. In his *Descriptions of Greece* (dated from the second century), Pausanias refers to the myth as a "common Greek tale"; concerned as he is with describing places rather than personages, his account is limited to a couple of sentences.[5]

Conflating these five classical redactions of the myth, one arrives at the following basic, but problematic, profile of the Callisto figure and her story. Callisto is the daughter of Lycaon, the defeated ruler of Arcadia. As a member of Diana's virgin band, she is variously described as a nymph,[6] or a young woman who "chose to occupy herself with the wild-beasts in the mountains together with Artemis."[7] Ovid's description evokes a strong, free woman, a favourite of Diana's: "This girl was not one who spent her time in spinning soft fibres of wool or in arranging her hair in different styles. She was one of Diana's warriors, wearing her tunic pinned together with a brooch, her tresses carelessly caught back by a white ribbon, and carrying in her hand a light javelin or her bow. None of the nymphs who haunt Maenalus was dearer than she to the goddess of the Crossways."[8]

Callisto is raped and impregnated by Zeus. Hesiod does not tell us precisely how Zeus manages to gain her trust, but Apollodorus reports that rumours vary on the disguise Zeus took in order to disarm her: "Some say [he took the likeness] of Artemis, others, of Apollo."[9] In Ovid's version Zeus appears in the guise of Artemis and approaches the girl exactly as the goddess might have, acknowledging Callisto as his/her favourite, and making the sort of conversation that might have been expected of the goddess herself: "'Dearest of all my companions,' he said, 'where have you been hunting? On what mountain ridges?' She raised herself from the grass: 'Greetings, divine mistress,' she cried, 'greater in my sight than Jove himself – I care not if he hears me!'"[10]

All versions agree that as soon as Diana discovered Callisto's pregnancy, she exiled the girl from her following. Shortly thereafter the nymph was changed into a bear. Hyginus maintains that Artemis was responsible for the girl's transformation: 'Callisto had not penetrated Zeus' disguise and when Artemis asked the nymph who had made her pregnant, the girl blamed the goddess. So out of anger and indignation Artemis herself is said to have metamorphosed Callisto.[11] Apollodorus asserts that Zeus was responsible for the ursine transformation – that he hoped his liaison would escape Hera's attention if his lover were no longer human.[12] Only in the later versions of Pausanias and Ovid is this metamorphosis attributed to the jealousy of Hera, a jealousy which arises not merely because Callisto was thought to be a cause of Zeus' unfaithfulness, but because Callisto had had the temerity to produce a son from the union.

The nymph's transformation into a constellation is always attributed to Zeus, and it represents a generous effort to save her from death, the causes of which are variously described. Hesiod, and later Hyginus, both tell that Callisto is captured by the Arcadians while she is "wandering like a wild beast in the forest," and is given as a gift to her father, Lycaon. Unaware of the taboos surrounding the grove of Zeus-Lycaeus, she enters the sacred compound and is hunted by the Arcadians, her son Arcas among them. Just before she is to be killed for her trespass, Zeus saves her by placing her in the sky as a constellation.[13] Pausanias and Apollodorus offer another version; both maintain that Artemis killed the girl, either as a favour to Hera or out of her own anger, and that after her death Zeus enshrined her in the Great Bear.[14] Only Ovid maintains that her son was about to kill her when Zeus intervened – thus loosely following Hesiod, who includes her son among the hunters in the sacred grove. But in Ovid's version, Arcas' inability to recognize his mother is given as the cause of the near matricide, and Callisto's loneliness accounts for her perhaps unwise efforts to approach a human while she remains a bear. Once again Zeus intervenes, preventing Callisto's death and setting both figures in the sky as constellations.

These variations suggest that there is no absolutely definitive version of the myth. Nevertheless, the account given in the *Metamorphoses* will be considered, for the purposes of this study, to be the most "authoritative" for a number of reasons. The first is the purely practical need to have a point of departure, a single configuration of the events in order to determine whether the myth does indeed inform the respective works under consideration. Second, though Hesiod may claim to be the oldest source, and Pausanias the most recent classical version, and while Apollodorus does provide variations, Ovid's version is the most extended – four times the length of the next longest – and his details give his version more weight, more significance. More pointedly, in Ovid's version we can best discern the "patriarchal signature" of the Augustan age.

Ovid's representation of Diana is not at all in keeping with what modern archaeological, psychological, and theological studies have revealed about her pre-patriarchal character, all of which point out that the virgin goddess was not originally characterized by physical virginity. Even before feminists began the task of recovering feminine deities and archetypes, Erich Neumann pointed out that Artemis, as a manifestation of the archetype of the Great Mother, was characterized by images of fecundity and was worshipped as one who could provide help for women in labour.[15] J.G. Frazer's study of Artemis also unearthed the discrepancy in the "virginity" attributed to her: "The ... word *parthenos*, applied to Artemis, which we commonly translate Virgin, means no more than an unmarried woman, and in early days the two things were by no means the same ... there was no public worship of Artemis the Chaste; so far as her sacred titles bear on the relation of the sexes, they show that, on the contrary, she was, like Diana in Italy, especially concerned with the loss of virginity and with child-bearing."[16] Both Marija Gimbutas and Barbara G. Walker note her association with child-bearing, motherhood, and cults of fertility, and they, along with other feminist scholars and theologians researching the ancient goddesses "argue that the figure of Diana/Artemis antedates Hebrews, Greeks, Romans, and Christians alike."[17] In "Spinning Among Fields," Annis Pratt notes that "this figure belongs to a period of time stretching back to about 7000 BC when goddesses were revered for a complex of qualities including generation, intellect, political power, and creativity. The virginity of the priestesses who served these goddesses, and the virginity of the goddesses themselves, was the virginity suggested by the word itself – 'a woman (gyn) like a man (vir).' Such a virgin retained at all times the right to choose what to do with her own body, whether to roam at will or stay home, whether to practice celibacy or engage in sexual activity."[18]

In *Woman's Mysteries*, M. Esther Harding likewise observes that a variety of goddesses in a number of cultures were given the epithet "virgin," and yet were noted for their fecundity, and, in some cases, for sexual promiscuity. Her noteworthy contribution to this field is the concept of psychological virginity, which arose out of her conclusion that the virginity of the ancient goddesses "must refer to a *quality*, to a subjective state, a psychological attitude, not to a physiological or external fact."[19] While Harding coined the term, she is by no means alone in noticing that many so-called "virgin" goddesses were not sexually innocent.

As a psychologist of some repute, Harding recognized the similarity between myths and psychological truths. For her, the psychological virginity of the goddess is the paradigm for that of mortal women, and refers exclusively to a state of mind. The woman who is physically virgin is physically intact; similarly, the psychological virgin can be said to be psychologically intact. A whole series of adjectives might be used to describe her. She is independent, belonging only to herself, and taking responsibility for her own life and her own fate. She is emotionally whole, mature, unfragmented, "one-in-herself."

The term may, because it contradicts the currently accepted meaning of the word "virginity," seem to indicate an irresponsible use of language. But the phrase is carefully chosen as a challenge to our concept of virginity, as an antidote to an over-emphasis upon the importance of the physically intact state. Harding deliberately wants to suggest that a woman's image of herself, her possession of those qualities of independence, strength, and wholeness, are an infinitely more important measure of her value than the intact hymen which has typically determined the way she was viewed by men. That such a term is necessary to criticism which deals with literary characters who evince these qualities is indicated by the adoption of the concept, if not the term, by a number of critics.[20]

This definition of the term "virgin" aids our interpretation of Diana's treatment of Callisto, suggesting that the goddess's moral or social condemnation of the nymph's behavior is, like the meaning of the word "virgin," a patriarchal imposition, for the matriarchal goddess of fecundity, maternity, and childbirth would not have treated her votary in this way. She would not have cast Callisto out for her loss of physical virginity. Nor would the "Opener of the Womb" have abandoned a woman about to give birth. Clearly there is another explanation of these details.

That Ovid has misconstrued the situation is also indicated by an internal discrepancy. In his version, Hera claims that Callisto, because she has been placed in the sky as a star, is a *goddess*, yet Zeus has conferred neither power nor immortality upon the young woman. Hera's claim is inexplicable unless we credit the assumption that the nymph and the goddess are one and the same, and that Callisto has been a goddess all along.[21]

Pausanias's description of the site of Callisto's grave and Diana's temple strongly suggests that Callisto was a local, Arcadian aspect of the virgin goddess. Directing us to the place he tells us, almost naively, "descending from Cruni about thirty furlongs you come to the grave of Callisto, a lofty mound of earth, on which grow trees, many of them of the cultivated sorts, and many of the kinds that bear no fruit. On the summit of the mound is a sanctuary of Artemis surnamed Calliste (the 'fairest'). I believe that Pamphos, the first poet who gave Artemis the epithet of Calliste must have learnt it from the Arcadians."[22]

William Sherwood Fox also supports this theory, using both internal evidence and information about the cult of Artemis specific to Arcadia: "In Arkadia the bear was an animal sacred to Artemis, one of whose cult-titles was Kalliste, a name which could readily be worked over into Kallisto. Kallisto, then, both maiden and bear, was none other than Artemis herself."[23] Harding similarly identifies Artemis with the bear.[24] More recent scholarship also asserts the identity of Artemis and Callisto. Barbara Walker writes that "one of Artemis's most popular animal incarnations was the Great She-Bear" and that the "Fairest One" or Callisto is the "title of Artemis as totemic She-Bear ... Of course the nymph was the virgin aspect of the goddess herself."[25] Gimbutas calls Callisto Artemis' "companion and double."[26]

It is ironic that although Ovid does not acknowledge their identity, his description of Callisto's qualities also echoes those of the goddess: he describes Callisto as one of Artemis' favourites, one of her most beautiful followers, a hunter like the goddess, and the possessor of a strong and independent nature – one who is even unafraid to defy the power of Zeus. Hesiod's description of Callisto as one who "chose to occupy herself with the wild beasts in the mountains together with Artemis" also suggests that Callisto and the Lady of the Beasts are one and the same. Artemis, as Lady of the Beasts – an aspect suggested by the bear which is sacred to her in Arcadia and which is the animal that Callisto becomes – governs the untamed side of our personalities. As Neumann explains: "Artemis has been characterized as a goddess of the 'outside,' of the free wild life in which as huntress she dominates the animal world. This is a symbolic projection of her role as ruler over the unconscious powers that still take on animal form in our dreams – the 'outside' of the world of culture and consciousness ... She is close to the wild, early nature of man, i.e., to the savage instinct-governed being who lived with the beasts and the free-growing plants."[27]

The nature of the changes imposed upon the character of Artemis by patriarchal culture also supports the theory that Callisto and Artemis are one person split into two personages, one mortal, one immortal, one virgin, one "soiled." The early Artemis, as mentioned above, was not a virgin goddess, but mother and Lady of the Beasts, patron to pregnant women, and midwife. In *The Greeks and their Gods*, W.K.C. Guthrie observes that traces of her old character are frequently preserved in later myths by allowing her a counterpart nymph who expresses her more ancient aspects: "the traces of the Mother-goddess were not obliterated in the Artemis of the Greeks ... In Greece, the memory of the past was preserved in particular in one interesting way, by attaching to her, among the nymphs who were her particular companions, some who themselves had amorous adventures which sometimes resulted in their becoming mothers."[28] Guthrie gives the myth of Callisto as one in which this phenomenon is evidenced. In *Myth, Religion, and Mother Right,* J.J. Bachofen also notes that the procedures used for patriarchal updating of an outmoded, matriarchal deity often exhibit the inclusion of the old and new aspects of the goddess within one myth: "Not infrequently new and old occur together; or the same fact, the same person appear in two versions, one prescribed by the earlier [matriarchal] one by the later [patriarchal] world; one innocent, one criminal; one full of nobility and dignity, one an object of horror and the subject of a palinode."[29]

More recent scholarship concurs with the conclusions of Guthrie and Bachofen. In her entries on Artemis, Callisto, and Ursel, Walker frequently points both to the strength of Artemis as a cult figure and to a number of attempts on the part of male deities and patriarchal institutions to undermine her power: indeed, "the ancients said Artemis the Bear ruled all the stars until Zeus usurped her place." Apollo is another male god who opposed her cult by making birth illegal on his sacred isle of Delos. Diana's cult was "so widespread in the pagan world that early Christians viewed her as their major rival." Walker suggests that dividing Artemis and Callisto in two constituted an attempt on the part of the Christians to mortalize the Goddess,[30] but the classical accounts suggest that this division occurred even earlier. It was apparently important to the patriarchy to "purify" Artemis, partly because what it would have perceived as the promiscuity of one of the primary female deities did not conform to its need for chastity in wives to ensure the purity of family lines.

The division of Diana into two discrete figures can be attributed to two developments. First, the imposition of patriarchal values upon the elements of the myth, as Bachofen, Guthrie, and Walker indicate, results in the purification of the goddess and the attribution of her less chaste, more fecundating qualities to a mortal counterpart. Thus Diana's psychological virginity comes to be thought of as literal, physical; the aspects of her character as a goddess of fecundity and pregnancy are sloughed off onto an unfortunate, pregnant girl whom the patriarchy's virgin goddess reviles.

But there is a second, equally valid, way of understanding the refraction of Diana's character into mortal and immortal counterparts: the failure to recognize the ritual which lies behind the myth. The type of myth which is the prototype for the story of Callisto is the hierogamy, or sacred marriage, and Callisto's own experience is patterned after the initiation ritual which has its prototype in the *hieros gamos.*

We can describe the hierogamy briefly as being the union of the sky god, Jupiter, and the earth or moon goddess, Artemis, the purpose of which is the renewal of a wasteland. The hierogamy has three levels of significance.

As a ritual which re-enacts creation, it has, according to the laws of sympathetic magic, a cosmic import, and can effect re-creation. These are the kinds of rituals Frazer explores in *The Golden Bough*. Caroline Merchant also notes the presence of this belief among the sixteenth- and seventeenth-century alchemists who saw the sun as the masculine principle of creation, and the moon or earth as the feminine. All of creation, certainly all of the earth's riches, were viewed as a product of the marriage of these two principles.[31] That the setting for Callisto's impregnation in Ovid's retelling of the myth is the Arcadian wasteland resulting from Phaeton's ride in his father's chariot certainly suggests that, even in Ovid's version of the myth, the implication of the sacred, renewing marriage is not lost. For the wasteland of Arcadia is indeed in need of renewal, and its renewal comes about through the reign of Arcas, son of Zeus and Callisto.

The reign of Arcas introduces the political aspect of the sacred marriage: its role in determining kingship. Both Frazer and Walker note that marriage with an earthly representative of the goddess was one of the prerequisites of rule.[32] Rule could also be passed on through the mother to her son, as is the case in the myth of Callisto, though in Ovid's version, Callisto has lost her rule long before her son comes to reign. That Arcas does indeed renew Arcadia is indicated by the fact that he was responsible for its Golden Age.

The hierogamy also has psychological significance. Insofar as Callisto is the mortal representative of the goddess, her own experiences are those of a woman initiated into the feminine mystery of psychological virginity. Harding, in *Woman's Mysteries*, reconstructs the ancient matriarchal rituals that initiated young women into their sexuality, and her descriptions of the rites correspond very closely to the events of the Callisto myth. The forest "whose trees had never felt the axe" is a sacred forest, and thus corresponds to the temple in which initiation ceremonies typically took place.[33] Callisto's devotion to Artemis, which she indicates in her greeting, is the initiate's devotion to the goddess whom she worships. Later scholars have been more able to ascertain the precise nature of initiation ceremonies conducted in the honour of Artemis, and their descriptions fit the Callisto myth even more closely than Harding's. Gimbutas writes that "well-bred Athenian girls of marriageable age danced as bears in honour of Artemis of Brauronia, and during rites of cult-initiation girls 'became' bears."[34] Walker also observes that "Hellenic writers said the Attic rites of Artemis involved young girls dressed as the She-Bear."[35] Christine Downing's view of Artemis as one who "represents a transition into womanhood that is not defined by an entrance into monogamic marriage" aptly explains why "a sacrifice to her is part of the young girl's pre-nuptial ritual."[36]

Because the ceremony represents a sacrifice of virginity to the goddess, Zeus is disguised as Artemis in many versions of the myth. Yet there must be some point in the ceremony when it becomes startlingly clear to the initiate that part of sacrificing her virginity to Artemis is having it taken away by a man who represents the god. This sudden discovery is reflected in the myth through Callisto's realization that the goddess who approached her so affectionately is a god in disguise.

The objective of the initiation ceremony is the achievement of psychological virginity. In her study, Harding concludes that "psychological virginity can only be attained through ravishment of a god, through a *hieros gamos* or holy matrimony."[37] While pondering the virginity of Isis, Harding concludes: "the *hieros gamos*, the marriage with the god creates the quality of virginity, it makes the woman one-in-herself. Through such an experience the woman comes into possession of her own masculine soul ... Thus she becomes complete, whole."[38] In the initiation ceremony, then, the initiate is like the goddess in two respects. First, she symbolically represents the goddess, playing her part in the ritual re-enactment of the sacred marriage. Second, she attains a quality akin to the nature of the goddess: she becomes virgin in the psychological sense. This interpretation of the myth accounts for another of Ovid's details. He tells us that Callisto betrayed her changed state by her blushes and her reticence, and that although the other nymphs noticed her unusual behavior, Diana, because she was a virgin, did not. Actually, however, the nymphs notice because Callisto is now different from them; the ancient, matriarchal goddess, who was by no means physically virgin, takes no notice of Callisto's state because it is like her own.

And herein lies the explanation for Diana's eventual vituperative exile of Callisto. The *tone* of her dismissal is a patriarchal addition, yet the action is not a condemnation, but a blessing that sends her forth from the temple. Once the initiate has completed the ritual, she must go back to the secular world and take her wisdom with her. Diana's expulsion of Callisto is no more than this. That the girl leaves with the qualities of the goddess now part of her very being is indicated by Callisto's transformation into a bear, the totem animal of Artemis which symbolizes the goddess' sexuality. She is like the High Priestess of Thebes described by Judith Ochshorn in *The Female Experience and the Nature of the Divine*: "Necessarily a member of one of the highest-ranking families and a virgin of great beauty, she was required to take any man she chose for a month, after which the community mourned her as if she had died. Subsequently she married and left the priesthood."[39]

The thrust of Harding's whole argument in *Woman's Mysteries* is that the ceremonies she describes were formed to ritualize necessary stages and aspects of a woman's discovery of her femaleness and her sexuality. The rituals express psychological truths: "Religious practices are based on a psychological need. The inner or spiritual necessity was here projected to the world of concrete fact and met through a symbolic act. If the rituals of sacred prostitution are examined in this light it becomes evident that the ancients felt it to be essential that every woman should once in her life give herself, not to one particular man, for love of him, that is for personal reasons, but to the goddess, to her own instinct, to the Eros principle within herself."[40]

Myth, which has often been described as the script for ritual, has the same function: its patterns express basic psychological truths about the essential events of life. Given that this myth reflects the pattern of the initiation ceremonies, its text can legitimately be examined for clues regarding the psychological experience of a woman's initiatory sexual encounter, and the feelings that follow.

The rape of Callisto need not refer to a physical violation but to a state of mind. In works of literature, particularly those written when a candid discussion or description of rape would have been discouraged, a woman's sense that she has been raped might not exclusively refer to a violent physical penetration, but to her feeling that she has somehow been violated regardless of the man's sexual behaviour. Discussing the young woman's typical ambivalence toward her first sexual encounter, Simone de Beauvoir suggests several reasons why this experience might feel like rape:

Woman is penetrated and fecundated by way of the vagina, which becomes an erotic center only through the intervention of the male, and this always constitutes a kind of violation. Formerly it was by a real or simulated rape that a woman was torn from her childhood universe and hurled into wifehood; it remains an act of violence that changes a girl into a woman: we still speak of "taking" a girl's virginity, her flower, or "breaking" her maidenhead. This defloration is not the gradually accomplished outcome of a continuous evolution. It is an abrupt rupture with the past, the beginning of a new cycle.[41]

What de Beauvoir suggests is that the first penetration by the male inevitably causes some sense of violation, however mild. Defining this experience as rape also strongly suggests the girl's powerful sense that she is changed by this encounter. Her maidenhood, a state that corresponded to the presence of her maidenhead, was a comfortable, known, free thing. But with the breaking of that maidenhead, she is thrust into a new state that is unfamiliar and frightening. Moreover, if she is at all aroused, she experiences a passion quite probably previously unknown to her.

Thus in the myth, the god appears first as Diana because certain aspects of Callisto's own passion are familiar, and thus unthreatening. But in consummating that passion she comes to know the animus – aspects of herself which have previously been unknown and unfelt. If the god takes, as Apollodorus suggests, the guise of Apollo, the Callisto figure is not initially frightened because the aspect of herself which Apollo symbolizes is neither unknown nor frightening. Apollo symbolizes Logos, which Harding defines (after Jung) as an orientation toward the objective, outer world, characterized by the logical and rational.[42] It is symbolized by the sun: "The sun as masculine principle is ruler of the day, of consciousness, of work and achievement and of conscious understanding and discrimination."[43] This does not frighten the initiate, for it is an aspect of her animus which, as a woman in a patriarchal, logos-oriented world, she has had to develop.

But when the god reveals his true identity, the struggle commences, and that struggle, like the disguise, is two-fold. In the versions where Zeus is disguised as Diana, the woman struggles with the surprise of her own, unfamiliar, passional nature. Meyer Rheinhold indicates the extent to which Zeus here symbolizes passion when he calls Zeus' disguise "the ultimate of his many transformations, in this case lust disguised as the very symbol of chastity."[44] The struggle with Apollo, however, symbolizes the woman's struggle between Eros and Logos. Eros, in contrast to Logos, is a tendency to be "more concerned with feelings and relationships, than with the laws and principles of the outer world, and hence it is preoccupied with psychic relatedness."[45] While Harding is too dogmatic about how a woman ought to be more concerned with Eros than Logos, and simplistically attributes Logos to men and Eros to women, her exploration of initiation rituals nevertheless reveals that their objective is to restore psychic balance: "Through such an experience the woman comes into possession of her own masculine soul, which is then no longer projected entirely outside herself into a man who has for her the value of a god, with god-like authority.[46] The struggle with the god becomes a struggle between the two psychic orientations, in an attempt to find balance and wholeness.

Whether the woman seeks to discover her sexual or her psychic nature, it is certain that she undergoes the process alone. Thus Zeus comes upon Callisto when she is separated from her fellows. She is alone in many parts of the myth. To begin with, she is an orphan: nowhere is there mention of a mother who might guide her through this rite of passage. Diana functions as a kind of surrogate mother; the band is a place where she might learn about her feminine nature. Yet the most significant event of this discovery takes place when she is separated from the band; her separation constitutes both vulnerability to rape and the opportunity to be initiated. It is her aloneness, in short, that attracts Zeus to her.

The outcome of the rape or initiation is an even more profound isolation: exiled from Diana's band, Callisto is effectively severed from the female world of physical virginity; transformed into a bear, she is cut off from human society altogether. These facts illustrate the primal aloneness which the young woman feels once she has been sexually initiated. The experience is powerful, and in her naïveté the young woman first imagines that an experience of such magnitude has occurred only to her. She is alone in the knowledge of her own and her lover's passion. She is sure that other young women do not feel what she has felt, and consequently in the myth she betrays herself to the other nymphs with blushes, not so much because she is ashamed of being raped but because she is awed, overwhelmed, and perhaps even shameful about the strength of her own feelings.

Not only does she feel alone, exiled from the company of virgins, but she feels bestial: her passion is an animal thing. Depending upon her sense of her own responsibility for her passion, she envisages that she has made herself animal-like, and hence in the myth her transformation is credited to the staid, proper Hera or the indignant Diana, aspects of herself, to reflect her own self-condemnation. Or it is credited to Zeus, as if the man has done this to her.

The birth of Arcas symbolizes the birth of the masculine in herself. As Harding says generally of the birth experience:

Psychologically, this child represents the birth of the new individuality, which replaces the woman's ego, sacrificed through the temple ... He is the new personality born of her sacrifice ... He is thus the "one who goes beyond," and represents the rebirth of hope and the possibility of transcending the past. Through the power of the *hieros gamos*, the complete sacrifice of egotism and of the possessive attitude towards oneself and one's own emotions and instincts which that ritual involves, is born this Hero-child, the ability to start again, even after disaster and failure and to start on a different level with new values and a new understanding of life.[47]

The mythic narrative or icon often carries both sacred and secular signification. Parallel to its sacred or psychological implications, there exists a line of secular or social import. Thus, while the myth describes the psychological realities of sexual initiation for young women, its details, especially those of Ovid's version, correspond to the truths of female sexuality under the aegis of the patriarchy. In what will be here identified as the matriarchal version or initiatory aspect of the myth, Callisto's "rape" was initially an introduction to a woman's sexuality that was patterned after the sacred marriage, and although the woman perhaps felt some surprise and even shock, it is doubtful that initiates thought of themselves as raped.

Actual rape, however, has little to do with sexuality. As Susan Brownmiller observes in *Against Our Will: Men, Women, and Rape*, rape is largely a violent act intent on establishing the man's power over his victim. Similarly, as Peggy Reeves Sanday points out in *Female Power and Male Dominance*, rape is a fact of patriarchal societies; societies in which woman is revered for her connections with a sympathetic and fecund "Mother Earth" show very low incidence of rape and are generally matriarchal.[48]

Certain facts about a young woman's experience of her sexuality under the patriarchy suggest reasons why Callisto's experience is termed rape,

reasons which reflect man's power over woman, but which do not necessarily reflect the use of physical violence to prove that power. Looking, for
example, at Zeus' attraction to Callisto, we notice that he is attracted by
two paradoxical qualities. The first is that she is not "womanly" – that is,
that she does not spin and weave, but instead hunts – and his initial desire
for her seems in part to be a desire to overwhelm the very strength which
he admires, to belittle the very quality he finds so attractive. On the other
hand, he waits until she is tired and resting before he approaches; he knows
that now she is vulnerable and he may not find her so for a long time.

De Beauvoir, discussing the young woman's sexuality in *The Second Sex*,
powerfully captures this paradox of womanhood when she observes that
the active young girl is provocative:

Beyond the lack of initiative this is due to women's education, custom makes independence difficult for them. If they roam the streets, they are stared at and ac-
costed. I know young girls who, without being at all timid, find no enjoyment in
taking walks alone in Paris because, importuned incessantly, they must be always
on the alert, which spoils their pleasure. If girl students run in gay groups through
the streets, as boys do, they make a spectacle of themselves; to walk with long strides,
sing, talk, or laugh loudly, or eat an apple, is to give provocation; those who do
will be insulted or followed or spoken to.[49]

But while the active young girl is sexually provocative, the male prefers a
mate to be a passive creature of his imaginings:

And actually, it is not by increasing her worth as a human being that she will gain
value in men's eyes; it is rather by modeling herself upon their dreams. When still
inexperienced, she is not always aware of this fact. She may be as aggressive as the
boys; she may try to make their conquest with a rough authority, a proud frankness;
but this attitude almost surely dooms her to failure. All girls, from the most servile
to the haughtiest, learn in time that to please they must abdicate ... To be feminine
is to appear weak, futile, docile. The young girl is supposed not only to deck herself
out, to make herself ready, but also to repress her spontaneity and replace it with
the studied grace and charm taught her by her elders ... There is a real contradiction
between her status as a real human being and her vocation as a female. And just
here is to be found the reason why adolescence is for a woman so difficult and
decisive a moment. Up to this time she has been an autonomous individual: now
she must renounce her sovereignty.[50]

To give oneself up to male expectations, much less to the ownership of
one's husband which legal marriage has entailed, is to be raped of one's
selfhood. The god approaches in feminine guise to reflect the girls' feminine
dreams about what love and sexuality entail; but rape by the god reflects
the social reality of sexuality and marriage in a patriarchal world. One

aspect of rape which Brownmiller points out is the negation of choice for the woman. Of early woman she writes:

In the violent landscape inhabited by primitive woman and man, some woman somewhere had a prescient vision of her right to her own physical integrity, and in my mind's eye I can picture her fighting like hell to preserve it. After a thunderbolt of recognition that this particular incarnation of hairy, two-legged hominid was not the Homo sapiens with whom she would like to freely join parts, it might have been she, and not some man, who picked up the first stone and hurled it. How surprised he must have been, and what unexpected battle must have taken place. Fleet of foot and spirited, she would have kicked, bitten, pushed and run, *but she could not retaliate in kind.*[51]

On a slightly different but still parallel plane, rape is an effect of marriage – especially of those unions negotiated by families without respect for or consideration of the young woman's wishes and feelings.

The raping male is viewed as "godly" for two reasons. First, the adjective reflects his real, transcendent power in a world where the woman is powerless, where he holds all of the social, economic and legal power, and she has none. Second, it reflects her perception of man in his maleness, about which she has mixed feelings, not the least powerful of which is adoration: "Man dazzles her, and yet he scares her, too. In order to accommodate the contradictory feelings she bears toward him, she will dissociate the male in him that frightens her and the bright divinity whom she piously adores."[52]

When Zeus is finished with Callisto, he returns to the upper air, echoing another cultural fact about male-female relations. In "Is Female to Male as Nature is to Culture," Sherry Ortner, like de Beauvoir and Sanday, points out that woman is for man a chthonic being, one closer to the natural world which he hopes to transcend through the creation and development of culture.[53] More recently, Caroline Merchant, Carol McCormack, and Marilyn Strathern suggest that this tendency to define woman as tied to nature and to view her as closer to the natural world is a basic component of western thought. Woman has variously been regarded as the passive element that, like nature, awaits man's mastery; as a nurturing mother; as a being shaped and determined by her natural biological function. Indeed "modern" science has generally supported this view of woman. Although women have been seen, at various times in history, within various cultures, as the stronghold of civilization and civilized mores, as the prime moral educators of each succeeding generation, it is clear that this latter role is assigned or taken away at the convenience of patriarchal institutions.[54] In times of political strife or great social change, women have frequently been re-associated with the natural world and defined as a chaos that must be controlled. And just as frequently, women's virtues, so indispensible in the home, were considered probable vices in the public world because women were too innocent and naïve to grapple adequately with the roughness of political or social life.[55] Thus, regardless of prevailing attitudes about women – whether they were representatives of a "good" natural world or of a natural world that was "bad", chaotic, and in need of masculine direction and rule – the control of those attitudes resided in the patriarchy, that masculine province of "ideas" that transcended woman's earthly ties.

Callisto's motherhood would normally confer upon her a great deal of power, for her child's father is, after all, a god. Moreover, motherhood is, as Adrienne Rich points out throughout her study, *Of Woman Born*, one of the more powerful aspects of womanhood. Paradoxically, it is also belittled under the patriarchy, largely because of the fear it arouses in men:

Thus in prepatriarchal life the male child early perceived that the female power of procreation was charged with *mana*. The sacred, the potent, the creative were symbolized as female ... Patriarchal man created – out of a mixture of sexual and affective frustration, blind need, physical force, ignorance, and intelligence split from its emotional grounding, a system which turned against woman her own organic nature, the source of her awe and her original powers. In a sense, female evolution was mutilated.[56]

Callisto's transformation into a bear certainly prevents her from enjoying the honours of her motherhood; her evolution is literally mutilated by her ursine metamorphosis.

Hera's transformation of Callisto emphasizes that under the patriarchy woman is paradoxically one of the strictest keepers of sexual mores. Powerful misogynistic attitudes in patriarchal cultures tend to categorize women into two exhaustive and mutually exclusive types: virgin or whore, Mary or Eve. It becomes important, therefore, for women to protect their collective image by openly denouncing any woman who trespasses patriarchal law: they denounce others in order to protect themselves. Consequently, Callisto's punishment is appropriately seen to come from two female sources: Diana and Hera. In some versions Diana is said to turn Callisto into a bear or to kill the bear as a favour to Hera, reflecting the fact that the patriarchal version of the virgin goddess proclaims all sexuality bestial. Ovid's version clearly implies Callisto's guiltlessness, but this makes no difference to Hera: an unwed mother threatens the image of all women, no matter how innocent her pregnancy might be. Diana does not inquire about the circumstances and then judge accordingly, rather she judges as she knows others will judge: blindly and uncaringly.[57]

Those versions which attribute Callisto's transformation to Hera reflect yet another phenomenon of patriarchal culture: a woman's desire to see that other women are victimized in the same way she herself has been. This is essentially an effort to legitimize her own victimization, an effort to prove that her status is something given, natural – not something imposed or which she can prevent. We can understand Hera's jealousy in this context. Hera is a victim of her ties to Zeus: he is continually unfaithful, and she is helpless to do anything about it. As Christine Downing notes, "the most accessible classical accounts of her tension-filled relationship with Zeus suggest that being a wife is singularly unfulfilling."[58] Indeed, her absence of ties to women, except to the two daughters whom she dominates, suggests that "she does not like women – or being a woman – at all."[59] Jean Shinoda Bolen, in her discussion of the Hera archetype, describes Hera's tendency to aim her rage at the other woman rather than at Zeus, thus allowing her to feel powerful rather than rejected. The tendency to be judgmental is one of the primary qualities of the archetype. Bolen notes that modern women who are Hera figures "are more critical than sympathetic toward unmarried mothers on welfare and toward rape victims."[60] This is certainly true of Hera's response toward the unwed, raped Callisto.

That Callisto bears Zeus a son is, in any patriarchal culture, the ultimate insult to the "cuckolded wife" (there is, apparently, no word to describe a woman whose husband has been unfaithful), for a male child means the granting of favours to the woman who has borne this treasure of patrilineal societies. As a consequence, Hera's power over her husband is even less than it had been. Since Callisto's power consists of her youth, her beauty, her fecundity, Hera deprives her of these qualities by changing her into a bear. This transformation refers, on a literal level, to Hera's act of pointing out and condemning Callisto's animal sexuality, a quality the patriarchy disapproves of in women. Thus, Hera makes Callisto an outcast from the society in which the nymph threatened Hera's own power.

In the third ending attributed to the myth, Callisto is threatened with death because she has entered the sacred precinct of Zeus-Lycaeus. The Arcadians had captured her in her bear form and brought her to Arcadia as a gift for Lycaon. Not knowing anything about the prohibitions, she accidentally enters the sanctioned area, where the hunters pursue her. Apparently their presence is not forbidden, causing us to wonder which aspect of Callisto – animal or woman – is the prohibited one. She is either pursued because women are not allowed in the masculine province which is deemed sacred, or because her bestial sexuality, symbolized by her ursine form, is forbidden by the patriarchy's sacred laws. In either case, her trespass into the physical area really indicates a trespass of the patriarchal law.

The epithet attributed to Zeus in this version, "Lycaeus," is very similar to the name of Callisto's father, Lycaon, and in *The Oxford Companion to Classical Literature* Sir Paul Harvey indicates that Lycaeus "appears to be connected with the word for 'wolf.' A festival, the Lycaea, was held on Mt. Lycaeus in honour of Zeus-Lycaeus. At this festival a man was supposed to undergo transformation into a wolf and he was believed to retain that form for nine years."[61] According to Edith Hamilton, Apollo is also associated with this name: "Another name for [Apollo] was 'the Lycian,' variously explained as meaning Wolf-god, God of Light, and God of Lycia."[62] The similarity in the names of all the men involved in Callisto's story is not gratuitous, but indicates the similar god-like power which both father and lover have over her. She is, as it were, surrounded by the patriarchy, and only the patriarchy has the power to rape, condemn, or legitimize her. One man is all men. Their attitudes toward her sexuality essentially represent the social force which can destroy her. At the same time – no matter which version is considered – it is always Zeus who saves her and declares her legitimate. The myth indicates in a disturbing way the overwhelming dominance of the male world and the absolute and even capricious power it has over a woman.

CHAPTER TWO

Callisto in the Medieval and Renaissance Traditions

The story Ovid tells of Callisto received several different kinds of treatment during the Middle Ages and the Renaissance in England. Three translations of the *Metamorphoses* made the work even more popular and well known than it had been in the Latin original. William Caxton made the first full translation into colourful Middle English in 1480. Arthur Golding made the first important Renaissance translation in 1567; it went through eight editions in fifty years and was *the* English Ovid during that time. At some point it even became known as "Shakespeare's Ovid," allegedly being the translation to which Shakespeare referred. Sir George Sandys published the third translation in 1621, calling it *Ovid's Metamorphoses Englished, Mythologiz'd and Represented in Figures*. Each translation has a different style, and each, being cast in a different form – Caxton writes in prose, Golding uses a long, heavily alliterated septameter line, Sandys employs iambic pentameter – results in translations whose stylistic differences are interesting in themselves, but whose attitudes toward Callisto are fairly consistent.

In addition to the translations, there appeared a number of works that make use of mythological material in a quasi-historical way. These make the "matter of Rome" – secularized versions of myths – an intrinsic part of the material and include the story of Callisto as part of Jupiter's career as soldier and king. The first published work of this nature is William Caxton's translation of Raoul Lefevre's *Recuyell of the Historyes of Troye* (1503), which was not only the first printed English book, but was particularly popular, going through a vast number of editions over the next two hundred and thirty years. Certainly the *Recuyell* influenced both William Warner, author of *Albion's England*, and dramatist Thomas Heywood who, a century later, apply their own signatures to Lefevre's version of Callisto's tale. Finally, there is an odd little narrative poem called *The Barley-Breake, or a Warning for Wantons*, written by a person who calls himself or herself merely "w.n., gent." It is a moral tale about a promiscuous girl whose father, wishing to keep his daughter pure, tells her the story of Callisto, as if this were the proper story to tell young girls who are flirtatious.

The signature, or general flavour, of the translations is thoroughly coloured by the medieval and Renaissance attitudes toward the Greco-Roman myths. Writers and thinkers of this time looked upon myths primarily as stories; if the stories could yield a moral, so much the better. Yet, because these are translations, their signature is revealed not so much in the shaping or emphasis placed on events, but in the language used to describe those events. Hence we note four common concerns in these translations. One is the elimination or de-emphasis of any sacred or psychological dimensions that the myth would have possessed for a culture that regarded Callisto's narrative as a myth. Thus all the characters seem mortal, not godlike, and Callisto's transformation into a bear, the single "supernatural" element in the myth, is downplayed or explained away.

The second aspect of the common signature is evident in the language, which is generally sympathetic toward Callisto, acknowledging her victimization. Golding spends a great deal of time describing Callisto's rape and her attempts to avert it; the description's tone and length reveal his sympathy for her:

He tooke hir fast betweene his armes, and not without his shame,
Bewrayed plainly what he was and wherefore that he came.
The wench against him strove as much as any woman could:
I would that Juno had it seene. For then I know thou would
Not take the deede so heynously: with all hir might she strove.
But what poore wench or who alive could vanquish mighty Jove?[1]

Sandys is a little more ambivalent, but by no means dogmatic, as the adjectives he uses suggest. Many of the phrases used to describe Callisto and her experience reveal an ambiguous attitude: he talks of her "violated shame," of "selfe-guilty blushes," and of the "willing rape."[2] Not only is she presented as a victim of rape, but her punishment by Hera is also perceived as unnecessarily cruel. Caxton's translation, in particular, gives their encounter the flavour of a hen-fight, and Hera is said to treat Callisto "villainously."[3] Both the Golding and Sandys translations similarly indicate that Hera reacts in an overly-cruel manner, one which does not fully comprehend Callisto's real, physical inability to fend off Zeus's rape.

A third aspect of the period signature is indicated by the language Diana uses to condemn Callisto, which is not nearly as vituperative as that of Ovid's virgin goddess. Caxton, in describing Diana's condemnation of the pregnant nymph, gives the goddess a fairly gentle tone. Rather than being told emphatically not to "defile this sacred spring," Callisto is more matter-of-factly admonished (and in the third person): "For which cause Dyane deffended her that she sholde not entre to the bayn but withoute taryeng she sholde goo wyde oute of her company." Sandys even allows his nymphs to be sympathetic, for when they disrobe Callisto and find her pregnant, they try to cover her womb with their hands to hide it from Diana. The sense conveyed by this gesture is not that they believe Callisto to be particularly shameful, but that they know she no longer belongs there.

In keeping with the intention of giving a moral flavour to this story, a fourth aspect of the signature is the consistent criticism of Jupiter. His character is that of a licentious man who is thrilled at the thought of having young, beautiful flesh for his pleasure. Caxton imbues Jupiter's thoughts about Callisto with a lecherous quality: "He thoughte that thoo was tyme or never for tacomplysshe of her hys desire and wille. And that Juno hys wyf shuld never knowe of it, And sayd to hym thus that yf by aventure she knowe of it I recche not ne sette not therby. Ffor syn I have place and tyme to doo my will, I doubte not her hate."[4] The flavour of Golding's and Sandy's characterization of Jupiter is similar. Golding's god thinks of the penalties Juno might exact for his affair, and concludes "She can but chide, shall feare of chiding make me to forslow?" (45). In the translations, Jupiter's rape is more premeditated than in Ovid's version; hence, it is more hypocritical.

Because Callisto is sympathized with, Diana's condemnation is toned down, Zeus is made to bear the full weight of his act, and Hera is presented as a jealous shrew, these translations simplify the dynamic of the myth. The main interest is in the story and in allocating the blame for Callisto's unfortunate fate, they treat myth as if it were synonymous with story, as if *blame* were the issue. But when we are dealing with myth, blame is not the issue. Myths offer a multi-faceted, multi-layered view of the world that may even contain seemingly contradictory aspects. It is, in a sense, anti-mythical to limit a myth to a single meaning in order to control its effluence. In the taking of sides, the sense of mythic proportion and symbolic significance is lost: a rape is no more than a rape, a child is no more than a child, a nymph is no more than a nymph. Essentially, issues that were once sacred have been reduced to their secular or worldly counterparts. This is perhaps most tellingly indicated by an interpolation of Caxton's in which he explains Callisto's expulsion from Diana's band by suggesting that there are politics behind it. Caxton's Diana is a powerful, rich personage, while Callisto is a poor underling who falls out of favour "for a lytel thynge." Such an explanation completely eradicates any sacred dimensions to Callisto's fate by replacing them with political or worldly ones.

One item of particular interest is Caxton's "Exposition of the Fable" which follows his translation of the myth. Once again, reflecting the medieval attitude toward myth, more specifically the euhemerist tradition of using the Greco-Roman myths as moral tales, Caxton cannot resist making clear the message we should glean from Callisto's experience. For no matter how unconsciously sympathetic his account of Callisto's fate is, his explanation of the myth's meaning identifies her as a whore: "Calysto was som tyme a ryght fayre Damoyselle & vyrgyne and ryght puyre with Dyane. Which sygnefyeth chastete. Which evyll kepte her maydenhed. Ffor whan she was perceyued by her bely she was sore sesprysed and dyfamed lytil preysed and louvd of alle her frendes & kynnsmen. They raft & put her away for her lecherye. Wherfor Calisto went to the bordel & puterye. Wher she suffred moche povrete. And there she became pale, fowle & rowhe or heery. And therefore it is fayned that she becam a beer." Similarly, Arcas is transformed into a travelling merchant who discovers his mother in her filth, is tempted to kill her, decides to abide by Christian laws that forbid such deeds, and instead reforms her. Caxton interprets Callisto's transformation into a star as an acquisition of wisdom: "Jupyter stellyfyed her. That is to saye that she becam wyse and prudente. Ffor she left & chastysed her evyll lyf. And lyved after ward honestly & holyly in gyvynge good ensample for to lyve. And therefore it was fayned that she was transfformed in to a sterre. So ther be many that lyven the moste parte of theyre age in lyvyng theyre lyf lecherously and dyssolutely in rybaudyres & putryes and after withdrawe hem fro her synne & ben ensample of alle penance & honest lyf." Caxton's express encouragement of a specific reading effectively discourages other interpretations, other readings, in an attempt to "close" the text, violating in yet another way its mythic nature.

The relative faithfulness of these translations serves as a foil to the very highly coloured version which appear in the three works dealing with the "matter of Rome." Raoul Lefevre's *Recuyell of the Historyes of Troye*, the first such work, was written in 1454, translated into Middle English by Caxton between 1468 and 1471, and published around 1474.[5] It is an extraordinarily lengthy romance cycle based upon several medieval sources dealing with the Troy Legend, principally Boccaccio's *Genealogie deorum gentilum* and Benoit de Sainte-More's *Roman de Troie*. The nature of the work – a creative compilation of material – means that great liberties can be taken with the sources, and a very definite signature is visible in Lefevre's version of the myth of Callisto. The translations were influenced by the euhemerist attitude toward myth; Lefevre's focus is also influenced by conventions, specifically those of the quasi-historical genre he has chosen. Hence one of the major concerns in his work is power, specifically political power.

The story of Callisto is given in the context of the life and adventures of Jupiter, rather than being, as it is in Ovid, a myth in its own right, connected to other myths by thematic concerns. Lefevre is far more interested in Jupiter's actions and reactions than he is in those of Callisto. Consequently, Jupiter is the centre of narrative and authorial sympathy. He is a fully-developed character, not a god with certain given, established qualities, but a great soldier who has just routed the villainous King Lycaon from Pelasgia. The Pelasgians see Jupiter as a hero; a man whom, however young, they desire to be their king – a man of true justice. In the context of this redoubtable career, his love for Callisto, Lycaon's daughter, is seen as a misfortune, for it frequently calls him away from his duties, and generally unmans him. His "herte and courage" are not completely involved in his military and political duties because he is constantly thinking about the beauty of Callisto and about his desire for her. Consequently, his lust for her and the resulting rape is presented as a misfortune for him rather than for her, because it takes his mind off the more important issues of acquiring and solidifying political power. When Lefevre does describe the rape, neither his language nor his narrative focus reveals any surprise or condemnation for Jupiter's act. Nor does he show any sympathy at all for Callisto.

When Jupiter comes upon Callisto in the tower of Lycaon's fortress, she is quite distressed that her father has been routed and naturally worried about her own fate. He attempts to reason with her, pointing out that her father was an evil man and deserved his demise, and assuring her that Lycaon's misfortune will not colour her own future. But a woman's position in feudal times was idiosyncratic, depending more on the customs of the region and the individual feudal lord than on legal codes or universal practice.[6] Consequently, Callisto's status, now that her father has been defeated, depends entirely on Jupiter's whim. It is hardly surprising, therefore, that she will not trust Lycaon's vanquisher, and resists the comfort of his proffered protection: She knows well that her poverty has made her unworthy of an important man's attentions and placed her in Jupiter's power, and prefers renouncing the world to taking favours from him.

Callisto's intention in renouncing the world is to enter a convent, Lefevre's medievalized version of Diana's band. By transforming Diana into a Mother Superior figure in a religious cloister, Lefevre not only imposes a Catholic signature upon the myth, but reflects certain facts about the position of women vis-a-vis the convent. In medieval times the convent, as well as being a home for unmarriageable gentility, was the place where "women were most free of male domination."[7] "The nun who thus found a place in the religious hierarchy ... occupied as a single woman by vocation a well-defined and nearly autonomous role that has since been lost ... The nun's life-style was more self-determining than any other available alternative."[8] Women might choose the convent not only because they felt a religious vocation, but also because they were financially and politically powerless in the marriage market or because they wanted to avoid the inevitable loss of control over their lives that came with wifehood.

Jupiter tries to discourage Callisto from entering the convent with arguments about the primary importance of marriage and motherhood for the fulfilled woman. These arguments are typical of the Middle Ages and the Renaissance, achieving their most subtle form in Shakespeare's plays and poems about marriage.[9] They arose in the Middle Ages from the attitude toward women of medieval clerics like Lefevre who felt that if women were placed on earth for any reason at all, it was to be good wives and have children. The existence of such an imperfect creature was justified only in the context of marriage and motherhood. Through marriage woman found her proper, subordinate place in the natural order, and through motherhood she could achieve grace and redeem the sin of Eve.[10]

Yet it is paradoxical that one of the things that attracts Jupiter to Callisto is her religious attitude, her devotion to virginity, just as Zeus was attracted to Callisto in Ovid's *Metamorphoses* by her strength as well as her vulnerability. Disguising himself as a maiden (being a mortal he has no recourse to magical disguises), Jupiter enters Diana's cloister in order to be in Callisto's presence. Encountering her alone one day, he reveals his true identity, tries to describe how thoroughly smitten he is with her beauty, and proposes that they have a secret affair. When she is not affected by his flattery and does not agree to that arrangement, he rapes her, declaring "Ye shall do my will and pleasir be hit be force or be hit by love. With this word Callisto began to crye with all her myght. And Jupiter began to accomplissh his pleasyr of her" (56).

Jupiter is kind enough, however, to offer to marry her after he has raped her, but she rejects his suit. It is her refusal to marry that brings about her misfortunes, for marriage would, in the social context, "undo" her rape. She would not then be condemned as an unwed mother – a woman whose status is synonymous with that of the harlot. Lefevre does not fully explain why Callisto does not choose a status that will save her the degradation she will inevitably undergo as an unwed mother. Given Lefevre's blindness to psychological motives, it seems unreasonable to assume that Callisto will not marry Jupiter because he has raped her, that she cannot forgive the emotional damage done by that act. Rather, Callisto has been characterized, however peremptorily, as a woman who does not want to submit to anyone's power, as a woman who sought out the convent precisely to escape Jupiter's newly-acquired political power in Pelasgia and to avoid the inevitable powerlessness she would suffer as both wife and conquered. Jupiter has only emphasized the power he has over her through his rape, his physical mastery of her. Given the consistency of Jupiter's quest for control and Callisto's attempts to avoid him, we can see that Lefevre has inadvertently made rape an expression less of lust than of power. It is satisfyingly ironic that a misogynistic medieval priest has characterized rape in precisely the same terms as the modern feminist.

When Diana discovers her follower's pregnancy, her wrath is expressed in a virulent tone. That her denunciation takes place in a "Chapitre" reflects the extent to which it is Christian in origin. Diana says to Callisto:

"Calisto my doughter thou hast doon fornycacōn with some man. This fornyca-
cion is not excusable
The vyrgins of this place be sory of thy synne. And haue abhomynacion of thy
shame. Ffor this cause hit is force that thou departe out of this hous.
Thou shalt be no longer theyr felawe. Thou hast maad thy self worthy to departe
by the brekyng and losyng of thy virgynyte." (58)

Nothing in the text suggests that Diana's judgment of Callisto's abomina-
tion and shame is inaccurate; Callisto herself accepts the judgment as
"trouth." Even once she has explained the circumstances of her "fornyca-
cion," she is "condempned to go out of the Cloyster" and feels such guilt that
she wanders the forest "so shamed that she wold not go to no toun" (58).

We see that Callisto's experiences are judged in terms of the severe
medieval morality that classifies an unmarried woman as either virgin or
whore, Mary or Eve; there are no intervening categories. As a typical cleric,
Lefevre implies that there is no substantial difference between being raped
and committing fornication. Certainly in the context of medieval clerical
misogyny, Callisto is at fault for tempting Jupiter with her beauty – whether
intentionally or not.[11]

Diana's condemnation is so forceful and so unqualified that it would seem
to represent one point of view of the medieval church. As Vern Bullough
notes: "Christianity was a male-centered, sex-negative religion with a strong
misogynistic tendency. The very fact that it was male-centered and
suspicious of sex would lead to a suspicious attitude toward woman as any
kind of sexual creature,"[12] an attitude here represented by Diana's
vituperative condemnation and complete lack of sympathy. Jupiter
represents the other point of view. The church discouraged virginity, except when coupled with a deeply-felt, demonstrable religious vocation. For
while chastity was considered a virtue, it was seen in some respects as a
useless one, denying as it does the one reason for woman to exist: to be fruitful and multiply.

But Callisto is deprived of even the dignity of motherhood because she
refuses to be a wife. Too ashamed to return to society, she lives in a cave
as long "as the bere holdeth hym in his denne. Wherfore the Archadiens
saynen that she was torned into a bere" (59). The child she delivers is huge
and so fierce that the wild beasts he and his mother live among do not dare
to approach him. Indeed, he is so cruel that at the age of seven, he threatens
to murder his mother. Fleeing her son's wrath, Callisto seeks protection from
Jupiter in town. Arcas calms down shortly after entering civilization and
falling under Jupiter's gaze. After Callisto identifies herself and explains the
circumstances to Jupiter, he has the boy appropriately attired and "reteyn-
ed hym in his palays. And forthon the same Archas governed hym so wele
and so wisely that at the prayer and requeste of the pelagyens Archas was
maad kynge of the contre" (60).

Lefevre's version implies that the upbringing of a child by Callisto alone is insufficient: it cannot civilize the boy. It is under the tutelage of Jupiter that the once bestial child becomes a princely young man and figures in some of Jupiter's trickiest military and diplomatic negotiations. Since Callisto will not take a husband and return to society's civilizing influence, she is a beast raising a child of bestial propensities. The aspect of Diana evoked by Callisto, huntress and bear, is the Lady of the Beasts. In this role, Diana was revered because of her strength, powerfulness, and connections with fecundity. Yet Lefevre's Callisto finds herself condemned for her animal qualities, for precisely those qualities a less patriarchal society might have admired.

This attitude toward the feminine colours both Lefevre's retelling of the myth and his use of myth in general. Lefevre uses the Roman pantheon to describe the formation of patriarchal society: Jupiter is credited with introducing people to laws and ordaining marriage so that women would not be used in common. He has a daughter named Diana who, however, does not want to be married, but wants to remain virgin and hence established the "cloistre in the wood of archade" (50). Also we note that the nymphs in the band of Diana spin and weave rather than hunt: those activities which were associated with women during the times when they were a strong force are now attributed to men.

Women in medieval literature are "pictured either as sex objects or as noble and virtuous wives and mothers nursing their children ... If they dared confront a male in any other role, they were resented and vilified."[13] Callisto's failure as a mother and her disappearance from the *Recuyell* once she has provided Jupiter with an heir in Arcadia suggest that the woman who seeks to live on her own – the woman that Harding would call a psychological virgin – is implicitly criticized. As long as she is unmarried, her sexuality constitutes whoredom. Raising her son alone means failing at motherhood. Her failure to become Jupiter's wife renders her entirely unimportant.

The narrator of the Callisto myth in William Warner's *Albions' England* (1612) similarly believes that women belong in traditional roles. In this work, the story of Callisto is an inset tale of four pages in a curious four-hundred-page verse epic which traces the ancestry of England back to the Roman heroes, thus combining the "matter of Rome" with the matter of Britain, fable and myth with history. Lefevre's version is clearly the primary source, for we have essentially the same plot: Jupiter is the conquering soldier; Callisto joins a cloister; the soldier disguises himself as a nun and joins the convent, finally finding Callisto vulnerable enough to rape her. Warner has not, however, placed the tale early in his account of Jupiter's career, but has it narrated by one of the three daughters of King Picus who are entertaining a minor rascal named Cacus while he hides from Hercules. Thus, Warner's narrator of the Callisto myth is a woman, and her version is essentially an argument for marriage, intended by Warner to be the more convincing because it is related by a woman.

Gone is the sermonizing tone of Lefevre, and in its place is a franker, more playful attitude; Lefevre's mute approval of Jupiter's act is replaced here by the narrator's express encouragement. Jupiter's treatment of Callisto is judged as thoroughly acceptable by virtue of the fact that she is his first love: "Blame Jupiter of other Loves, of this doe set him cleere./ It was his first, and first is firme, and toucheth verie neere."[14] What the narrator's motives are in granting this sympathetic approval we can only speculate.

We are told that the narrator and her two sisters spend their days dallying with Cacus, casting their dainty arms around his neck, plying him with kisses, and giving him whatever he wants. Whether she is condoning her own behaviour or describing her wishes for her own future, her situation clearly affects her attitude toward the two actors in the drama she retells. Toward Jupiter she is permissive, perhaps even appreciative of his lust. She takes delight, for example, in creating the kind of man who undresses a woman while he gazes upon her: "What viewed Jupiter this while not pleasing to his sight?/ Or what unviwed did he gesse, not adding to delight?" (50).

On the other hand, Callisto's behaviour does not seem comprehensible to the narrator. She feels that Callisto belongs at court, not in a cloister: "It greeves that natures paragon in Cloister, not in Court,/ Should loose the beautie of her youth, and he thereby his sport" (50). Furthermore, Callisto's refusal of Jupiter is seen as a denial of love, not the quest for freedom and independence to which the myth addresses itself: when circumstances are such that the disguised Jupiter finally comes upon his beloved alone and in a secluded place, the narrator comments, "Love is hardy" (51). Once raped, Callisto is fairly accepting of her situation, as the narrator thinks she should be: "That done, which could not be undone, what booteth discontent?/ As good bee pleas'd as not be eas'd: away Calista went" (51).

This narrative places no great emphasis upon the shamefulness of Callisto's experience; its permissive tone precludes any such moralizing. Diana exiles Callisto from her band, but their exchange about the girl's pregnancy is limited to curious and friendly speculations about Jupiter's ability to disguise himself so well: there is no written record of a scathing condemnation of Callisto's morals from Diana. Nevertheless, the young girl feels that she must hide herself from shame, although the narrator terms her a "silly Nymph" for taking such a serious attitude (52).

If morality is not one of the overwhelming issues here, then power is. Jupiter, by virtue of his defeat of Lycaon, has political power; nevertheless he tells Callisto: "I am [Lycaon's] Victor, but thy selfe art Victoresse of mee" (49). This cleverly flattering comment is intended to allay Callisto's natural fears of the man who defeated her father and to convince her that her beauty has more power over his emotions than his military ascendancy has over her political fate. She, however, knows the politics of marriage, knows that marriage means submission to the husband's authority, and tells him plainly that she is aware of her true status. Her insistence on joining Diana's band, like that of Lefevre's Callisto, is based upon her fear that since she brings neither financial nor political power to the contract between them, thus having no extramarital leverage, she will be unable to exercise any amount of control within the marriage. Her heart is not fit for love, she says, now that she has lost her position:

> But haplesse termes are these, quoth she, unfitting to a thral:
> Yet, in respect of that I feele, I heare them not at all.
> A friend (ah friendlesse name I Friend?) it being as it is,
> A friend I say, much more a foe, and more and worse then this,
> The sonne of Saturne should, and shall, that speed and hearing misse,
> Doe rid, ah rid mine eyes of teares, and set mine hart at rest,
> By taking life, not making Love, the former likes me best.
> Or, if that poore Calistos life shall lengthen to her wo,
> Graunt that among Dianas Nunnes a Votarie I go:
> For neither fits it now to love, or ever shall it so. (49–50)

Living exiled in her cave after Diana's discovery of her pregnancy, Callisto experiences complete destitution and powerlessness. The description of her "fallen" state suggests that the fall is more political than moral: "Long time (the daughter of a King) she lived thus in Cave, / Not wanting griefe, but wanting all that poorest wretches have" (52). So reduced that she lives in terror of her seven-year-old son, she finally returns to Jupiter. Here the feminine narrator, who perhaps wants to echo her own situation with Cacus, twists the ending. Callisto lives "lady-like" with Jupiter, becoming Juno's rival. Thus psychological virginity is also criticized in *Albion's England*, though not as damningly as in Lefevre's work. Instead, it is dismissed as a useless, if not disfunctional virtue, causing Callisto seven years of unnecessary difficulty in exile.

Although written a hundred years after the *Recuyell, Albion's England* shows the extent to which woman's role was still believed to be limited to that of breeder and wife. The protestant reformation did little to change the attitude toward women held by the misogynistic clergy, except perhaps to shift the focus from woman's moral inferiority to her weakness and irresponsibility; hence she properly belonged under the control of a father or husband.[15] Fraser's observation, that "in seventeenth-century England, neither legally or psychologically was there a proper place for an unmarried female or 'maid' ... except on her way to marriage,"[16] directs attention to the two spheres in which Callisto figures experience difficulties. In the psychological realm, we note that men are not prepared to see women as useful or fulfilling their function unless they are married – a vision of women which places the unmarried in a virtual state of non-existence, and makes very clear to the married that they exist for the convenience of men. In the legal realm, we note that the Callisto figures are very aware of and uncomfortable about their relative powerlessness; what little power they might possess is directly related to the men to whom they would ally themselves. In a world where a woman has no power on her own, she clearly must seek any modicum of power she might possess through marriage, or by renouncing the world altogether and moving outside the sphere of male influence.

Although the late sixteenth and early seventeenth centuries saw a number of improvements in the status of women, the late Renaissance was an age filled with contradictory attitudes toward the "weaker" sex. Elizabeth's cunning rule questioned old theories about the lack of intellectual powers in women (although even until the nineteenth century many held that she ruled so well and refused to marry because she was a man in disguise); at the same time, as a "career woman and virgin, Elizabeth was an affront to masculine sensibilities, and her vanity and growing paranoia seemed regal examples of feminine irrationality."[17] Yet in spite of the intelligence of her rule, at the time of her death almost everyone of both sexes agreed that female intelligence was less than that of the male. Only later in the seventeenth century was it a common argument that women were not less intelligent, merely worse educated.[18]

Attitudes toward the value of women's souls were also contradictory. The rise of neo-Platonism elevated woman's beauty to a source of divine understanding: "When a woman is loved, her lover is not only loving her but God and himself as well," Ian Maclean notes in *The Renaissance Notion of Women*. She was no longer merely a temptress, but rather her "physical beauty reflected her goodness."[19] Yet Fraser also notes that at the beginning of the seventeenth century it was generally accepted that men's and women's souls were not equal.[20]

The argument in Book III of Castiglione's *The Courtier* between the Magnifico Guiliano and Signors Gasparo and Ottaviano fairly represents the two sixteenth-century attitudes toward women. In spite of the humanism of the Renaissance, there were still strongly-held opinions about the limited capabilities, rights, and virtues of women. Arguing against attitudes like those we see in Lefevre and Warner, the Magnifico maintains that women have essentially the same qualities as men, although their different social roles demand slightly different behaviour. It was generally believed that women lacked intelligence, but the Magnifico argues that they simply lack a education, which they deserve to help develop their intellect. Women have the same virtues as men; in fact the Magnifico finds the love of virtue and desire for honour stronger in women than in men. When reminded that Eve is the world's first sinner, the Magnifico retorts that without Mary the world's saviour would never have been born. Most interesting, however, is the Magnifico's observation of a phenomenon which we have observed in the patriarchalized versions of the Callisto myth, namely that "men make different rules for themselves" regarding their sexual conduct. Moreover, if women sometimes scorn men, seek independence, and indulge in manly behaviour, it is not that "the poor creatures ... desire to be men in order to become more perfect, but in order to gain freedom and to escape that rule over them which man has arrogated to himself by his own authority."[21] The Magnifico has observed two of the important issues expressed through the Callisto myth – the double standard and woman's search for independence – and presents a more forward-looking attitude such as that found in Thomas Heywood's play, *The Golden Age*. If William Warner represents one Renaissance gentleman who felt that women were fulfilled and useful only in marriage, Heywood counters him as aptly as does the Magnifico by giving a sympathetic portrait of a woman who seeks a noble independence.

The Golden Age (1611) is a play about fatherhood and power. Uranus has died, leaving behind him two sons; the eldest, Titan, is not fit to rule so Uranus' wife, Vesta, appoints Saturn king. In order to placate Titan, Saturn promises to kill all of his own male children in their cradles. Of course Vesta and Sybilla, Saturn's wife, use trickery to secret away Jupiter, the second son. Hence motherhood is presented as fraught with difficulties; its power is secret, not allowed open acknowledgment. Callisto is a tertiary figure in the play, being Jupiter's first love, yet we find the themes of motherhood's ambiguous and questionable power re-enacted even in the portion of the play that deals with her. When Callisto and Arcas enter Jupiter's court, Arcas, having pursued his mother and threatened her life because he is angry with her, openly denounces his mother and her way of raising him: "Since she will needs be gone, be pleased, then, / Wearied with beasts, I long to live 'mongst men."[22] So in spite of the fact that bearing children was "virtuous work,"[23] the conventional virtuousness of Callisto's motherhood is completely undone by her refusal to conform to male expectations.

Not only is the power of motherhood openly ignored, so is the power of the feminine. Saturn is credited with all the qualities and powers which are usually associated with Diana or another earth goddess: "He hath taught his people to sow, to plough, to reap corn, and to scorn acorns with their heels; to bake and to brew ... Besides, he hath devised a strange engine called a bow and arrow, that a man may hold in his hand, and kill a wild beast a great way off ... Last time the King went a-hunting, he killed a bear, brought him home to be baked and eaten" (11). That bear symbolizes the goddess herself; in such a world, where the feminine is violently disregarded and where a woman's power is in eclipse (as it was in the court of James I), all that the goddess can do is to scorn the institution which gives men their most immediate power – marriage. Consequently, Diana is said to have formed her group because she has tired of anxious suitors and wishes never to marry – that is, never to submit to the power of men.

The major strength of Heywood's portrait of Callisto is the extent to which he embodies her with dignity. As in the earlier versions, Jupiter has conquered Lycaon's fortress, and so the wasteland of the myth is again a political, rather than a natural one. When Jupiter comes upon Callisto, he is "sick with passion" (24). Callisto, on the other hand, is regal and aloof, and dismisses Jupiter peremptorily: "Hence away!/ When we command, who dares presume to stay?" (24). He asks, "Are you a queen enthroned above the elements, made of divine composure" (25). Her reply indicates not only her independence, her aloofness, her inability to be swayed by flattery, but also her sense of herself: she is not a goddess, she says, "I am myself./ Uncivil stranger, you are much too rude." Asked if such a creature as herself can love, she replies, "To be alone I can" (25). When he offers her anything he can procure for her, she asks leave to go into the company of Diana and remain always a virgin.

Jupiter replies to this request with all the familiar arguments that we have seen in Lefevre and Warner about the uselessness of a woman who remains virgin:

"Women, fair queen, are nothing without men;
You are but ciphers, empty rooms to fill ...
To live a maid, what ist? 'Tis to live nothing:
'Tis like a covetous man to hoord up treasure,
Barred from your own use, and from others' pleasure.
Oh, think fair creature, that you had a mother;
One that bore you, that you might bear another."(25–6)

Heywood's Jupiter also reflects opinions about virginity similar to those of Lefevre, using a religious condemnation which the old cleric would have approved: Diana's band is "mere heresy, her sect/ A schism."[24]

Jupiter's hypocrisy is revealed in the rape scene. Callisto becomes vulnerable to Jupiter because he (disguised again as a woman) has pleaded during a hunt that he is exhausted. She takes pity on him, but he fails to take pity on her. As if to emphasize her independence, Heywood's Callisto does not even want a little friendly clasping with Jupiter while he still seems to be a woman. Her insistence that he leave her alone, both before and after she discovers that he is a man, suggests that she is sincerely desirous of maintaining not only her physical virginity, but its concomitant qualities of integrity and independence. The strength of her character completely conflicts with Jupiter's unprincipled and hypocritical behaviour; thus Heywood sympathetically develops the disparity between Callisto's view of herself as a person of integrity who desires independence and Jupiter's view of woman as a creature who exists for his convenience.

Her motherhood, in keeping with the paternalistic attitudes of the characters, is also troubled. Homer, a character who functions as a narrator, tells us that Jupiter would have treated her as his queen, and a dumb-show illustrates her expulsion from Diana's band, "Her crime thus found" (36). Like the other Callistos, she bears and raises Arcas, who is somewhat bestial, angers him one day, and runs to Jupiter when her son threatens her life. Jupiter is, of course, delighted to find his son, asks Callisto once again to marry him, and again gets a negative answer. For Callisto tells Jupiter that he has made her misanthropic:

"No, thou false man. For thy perjurious lusts
I have abandon'd human subtleties. There, take thy son, and use him like a prince,
Being son unto a princess. Teach him arts
And honour'd arms: for me, I have abjured
All peopled cities, and betook myself
To solitary deserts. Jove, adieu;
Thou proving false, no mortal can be true." (45)

Here we see Callisto choosing the role of Lady of the Beasts, preferring the animals, however wild they are, to the dishonesty of humans. Heywood has allowed his Callisto a dramatic and extreme reaction to Jupiter's treatment in the interest of exhibiting how extreme his treatment was of her. Never does Heywood explicitly sympathize with Callisto, but he depicts a woman who is independent, noble, and determined.

In spite of the three writers' differing attitudes toward Callisto, attitudes which can easily be traced to the cultural mores of their times, their depiction of her *situation* is quite consistent. By directly tying Callisto's fate to her father's defeat, they have emphasized her powerlessness in the masculine world: without the protection of either father or husband, she has only a marginal identity. As did many gentlewomen in the Middle Ages and the Renaissance, she chooses to remove herself to the convent, a place where man's rule is minimal. Thus the choice to remain virgin becomes synonymous with the desire for independence.

Her rape by the Jupiter figures is not so much an act of sexual violence as an act of power, one which is meant to illustrate explicitly their ability to overcome any resistance she might wage. That the issue is one of ownership is indicated by their proposals after their rapes: they believe that having shown their power over her, they will be able to gain possession. She foils this, however, by choosing to remain independent, in spite of her loss of virginity, and in spite of the inevitable ostracism which she will encounter as an unwed mother. That choice, with all its unpalatable ramifications – isolation, loneliness, and poverty – is presented in two of the three cases as preferable to the loss of freedom she would incur in marriage. Only Warner has her give in to the proposal, and yet in doing so he does not really contradict the general significance of the situation. Essentially his conclusion reinforces our impression of woman's powerlessness, and his Callisto, under the direction of a female narrator who feels her own equivocal situation, voices another reality: there is more political and social power in marriage, even though there is less personal freedom.

Another general conclusion that can be drawn has to do with the use of bear imagery, which is positive in the initiatory version of the myth, showing the animal strength and passion which are part of a woman's character, and symbolizing, as it often did in initiation ceremonies, a young girl's attainment of womanhood. In these redactions, however, the bear image is tied to Callisto's incompetent motherhood and to her refusal to follow male expectations. The fact that she will not marry, but chooses to raise her son alone, is linked through the bear image to a kind of natural bestiality inherent in her character. The Lady of the Beasts, respected for her strength and her fecundity, is here belittled because she does not give in to male power and the ownership inherent in marriage.

This unflattering presentation of the once-sacred Lady of the Beasts parallels another tendency in these works, which is to exorcise all the sacred or ritualistic incidents or imagery which are found in the prototypical myth. There is no sky-god to participate in a hierogamy, no divine transformation into a bear and then a constellation – indeed, the "old story" that Callisto became a bear has been debunked and explained as a withdrawal from society of the same length as a bear's hibernation.

Further, all the new embellishments suggest that these versions concern themselves with historic, not divine matters: Jupiter is a soldier, Callisto a conquered princess, Arcas a prince and diplomat because worldly power is the issue here. The wasteland which Jupiter and Callisto are meant to renew is not a charred forest but a conquered fortress, and the solution to that wasteland is not a hierogamy, but a prince; thus we see that the issues are secular and political. Callisto is concerned with her own personal power within the patriarchal institution of marriage. Certainly one of the most significant changes made to this myth between its representation in Rome and its reappearance in Christian medieval and Renaissance England is Jupiter's proposal of marriage after he has raped Callisto, a proposal which is intrinsically tied to Jupiter's desire to have control over her. Man's ability physically to overcome and impregnate a woman, to "father" a child upon her, represents his advantage, his power, and while *she* nurses the child into adolescence, *he* bestows the honours of land and position, even though these honours were once hers and would have been hers in the matrilineal society the myth alludes to. In Ovid's version of the myth, Callisto is vulnerable because she is resting in the forest; in these versions her vulnerability is directly tied to the fact that Jupiter has defeated her father, thus further emphasizing that worldly or social power is an intrinsic issue here.

In these later versions, men and women seem to be divided along pro-marriage and anti-marriage lines. Saturn and an ancient Jupiter are credited not only with the inception of agriculture, but with creating the sacrament of marriage; Diana is limited to the rather paradoxical role of resisting such constrictions and yet legitimizing them by making virginity equally sacred in the Christian context. The texts inadvertently imply that women continue to struggle against patriarchal suppression and ownership, against masculine possession of a woman's body.

What is the point of using a myth which once described initiatory rites to represent the assumption of power by the patriarchy? Before the advent of the patriarchy, when the sexes were afforded more equality, especially in the sphere of religious practices, the loss of virginity occurred in the course of a sacred ritual, and its significance was strictly religious and psychological. But with the coming of the patriarchy, and with it, marriage, the loss of virginity became a legal and social fact; it occurred not in an evening of sacred prostitution in the temple, but on the wedding night, in the marriage bed. It is perceived in the late redaction of the myth as rape because, Neumann tells us, such legal possession was perceived as a violation of the women's integrity.[25] Furthermore, the institution of fatherhood meant that by begetting a child upon a woman, the man felt he could claim *de facto* possession of her. If she refused the benefits of such possession, she was unnatural – an animal or a beast.

The Barley-Breake, or a Warning for Wantons is dedicated to "the virtuoue and chaste maiden, Mistress Eliz. C., daughter to the worshipful Robert C, esquire." Published in 1607, it is contemporaneous with both *Albion's England* and *The Golden Age*, yet it displays a very different attitude toward both the character and situation of Callisto. The poem is about a chaste, or "snowie," girl named Euphemia who keeps sheep in Arcadia with her father, Elpin. Observing that his daughter is not quite as modest as he would like her to be, and that she is not careful enough to repell the advances of a young man named Streton, Elpin sits down with his daughter under a tree and tells her the story of Callisto. Through the euhemerist tradition, Callisto's myth can be turned into a tract for chaste and modest behaviour, and such a treatment is expected here. What is given instead is one of the most sensitive accounts to date of what it must have been like to *be* Callisto.

Elpin introduces the story as if this were the appropriate story to tell in the present circumstances:

One tale (quoth he) will steale the day away,
Whilst that our flocke in shadow chew the cud:
Then of a Nymph my purpose is to say;
But not of her whom Jove bore on the flood,

Nor yet of her that caught was fetching water,
Nor yet of her whom Nessus earst did wrong,
Nor yet of her whom Jason so did flatter,
Nor of the three that Cacus kept so long:

Nor of the Queene that Carthage did inclose;
Nor will I speake of faire Lucrecias rape,
Ne tell a storie of the Albion Rose,
Nor Io yet, of Cow that had the shape.

Though all of these defloured were by men,
And each a warning to withstand disgrace,
And maides to shame occasion offered them,
By guilefull harts that beare a flattering face:

Yet of a Nimph, Calisto hight, tis she,
From whose mishap our Countrey tooke this name,
I doe intend my story whole shall be:
So note the sequell, and record the same. [26]

As in the historical narratives, power is one of the issues here. Jove sees Callisto, who is described in great detail as being of great beauty, and immediately feels that if he cannot have her, he has no power:

Am I (quoth he) the high supreme of gods,
Great King of Heaven, Neptunes elder brother?
Drown'd I the earth, made Sea-nimphes dwell in woods,
Displac'd Saturnus, was Queene Opes my mother?

Tush, tis not so: 'tis faign'd, I am no Jove:
Prerogatives yeeld unto Joue all mirth,
And may command, not humbly sue for love. (fol. B2 – B3)

The point of this speech is that Jove considers himself powerless unless he can have Callisto without too much difficulty. Power is perceived as something dependent upon being able to have any woman a man wants, under whatever conditions he wants. As we observed in the three historical narratives, power is essentially tied to sexual ownership.

There is also an illustration of feminine attitudes toward marriage, given, oddly enough, by Jove himself. When he enters Diana's band, he tells her that he is more than deserving of the protection of her Cloister because he is not only gentle born, but is tired of being pursued by suitors and wants to be part of the learned virgin life (fol. B3). That he knows the implications of forced marriage makes him even more of a scoundrel when he sexually forces Callisto.

The relative unimportance of marriage, for Jove at least, is indicated by the fact that in the very same stanza he rapes Callisto, ascends to heaven, and gives Juno a greeting kiss to cover up his adultery. Yet the author of *The Barley-Breake* knows the implications of marriage, and by putting them into the mouth of Jove creates a savagely irresponsible and cruel character. The writer's sympathy for the powerless situation of women extends to Callisto herself, whose disturbed feelings are dealt with in more detail than by any other writer of this period: two full folio pages are devoted to her situation. At the very first, she tries to hide her loss of virginity, suddenly aware that it is likely that many women who pretend to be virgins are not. But she soon realizes that she is pregnant, a discovery that the writer expresses in an fanciful trope: "the silly one, alas, / Might plaine perceive her lace come home too short" (fol. B4). Elpin takes time to describe the physical changes in her worried appearance, the waning cheeks, the failing color, and even goes so far as to mourn with her:

Poore silly soule, I moane in heart to thinke,
How she with teares her lucklesse case bewail'd,
And how from lore of patience she 'gan shrinke,
And in deepe passion on the god out-rayl'd,

And twentie times with winged shaft she threats,
Most desperately her sobbing brest to flay:
But horror of her ghostly rest entreats
To hold. (fol. B4)

The portion called "Callistos Lamentation" (fol. C) not only explores Callisto's feelings of anger and frustration at having been raped, having been forced "to beare the fruite of wanton seede," of being a victim of Jove's, and hence male, injustice, but also shows the writer's awareness of exactly what her fate will be now that she is with child. Callisto thinks of going to the gods and giving witness to the fact that Jove has raped her. But she is aware that "they will rather at his falshood winke: / Thy information they will not beleeve" (fol. C). She is also aware of what her pregnancy does to her reputation, aware that it will immediately give her "an harlot's name," whether she is blameworthy or not. Certainly her suspicions are proven true when

Diana, without asking any questions at all, cries "Strumpet, avaunt, they whoredome is descride" (fol. C2).

The inset tale of Callisto began with the mention of power, and it ends on the same note. Little attention is given to Callisto's fate after she is exiled from Diana's band. Instead, the narrator simply gives the details of the birth of Arcas and of Callisto's transformation into a bear. Of her transformation into a constellation, Elpin says:

Then Jove, to shewe his glory to the earth,
And proove him King of what the Fates had given,
He takes Calisto, to requite his mirth,
And of her makes a fixed signe in heaven. (fol. C2)

In other words, Jove's once merciful transformation of Callisto into a constellation is here expressed as a playful gesture meant to show his power over the situation.

In *The Barley-Breake* Callisto's fate is suffered by poor Euphemia. In spite of her father's warning tale, Streton manages to seduce her – not to rape her – by promising her all the romantic trappings of marriage, and indicating how envious other women will be of her situation. This puts Euphemia into an almost trance-like state that allows Streton to take his pleasure. He and Euphemia both run away, presumably to marry. Euphemia is forced to come back to Arcadia when she is ready to give birth and Streton has abandoned her, for there has been no marriage. Elpin, taking one look at his daughter, who is now big with child, dies. Euphemia, horrified at her father's death, considers, as did Callisto, committing suicide, and finally brings herself to perform the deed. At this point Streton enters, chased by a wolf and a bear. As he stops in horror to view the two corpses, many animals surround him and demand that he be hanged. He claims he has no rope, and dares them to tear him to pieces. Instead an ape suggests that he be hanged by his garters, and so he is. That this vengeance is performed by the creatures of the goddess suggests her symbolic involvement.

On one hand we recognize that W.N. is working in the genre of the moral tale: this is what happens to girls if they are not careful about their virtue. Yet there is something curiously arch and mocking about this ending that suggests that the author's purpose lies elsewhere. W.N. is worried not only about the chastity of young girls, but about the unscrupulousness of men, and is quite willing to give Streton an ignominious end in order to point out his culpability. Moreover, the complex and thoughtful sympathy toward Callisto is entirely uncharacteristic of other treatments of her during this period. The writer is unusually aware of the issues involved for a woman – aware of the damage to her reputation, whether she is responsible or not; aware of the extent to which a patriarchally-organized morality blames her for her "wantonness" while ignoring the responsibility of her rapist; aware of the ways in which men flaunt their power; and aware of the false promises of marriage – and is quite willing to indicate this awareness metaphorically in Streton's hypnotic offer to Euphemia.

The parallels between Euphemia's affair with Streton and Callisto's rape by Jove again suggest an odd relationship between marriage and rape. That Euphemia's seduction is preceded by an offer of marriage suggests that certain aspects of marriage constitute a kind of rape. Moreover, that Heywood's and Lefevre's Callistos prefer social ostracism to marriage does not speak highly of the institution. The only conclusion that can be drawn is that rape is the expression of one kind of power; marriage is potentially an institutionalization of that power.

Finally, there is no question of attaining psychological virginity: only at the risk of ostracism does Callisto dare to become a woman who will not have a husband. We see, then, that a myth, the central focus of which was the sacred initiation, and which dealt with the loss of virginity in sacred and psychological terms, has been altered by the patriarchal institution of marriage. Once upon a time, to lose one's virginity was to be forever transformed, into bear, constellation, or goddess. In the Middle Ages and the Renaissance it was to become wife or outcast.

Both Heywood and W.N.'s entirely respectful and sympathetic treatment of Callisto and their awareness of the politics of woman's treatment at the hands of men like Jupiter and Streton contrast vividly with other Renaissance versions of the myth, whose sympathy is not overt or dynamic, if it is expressed at all. If the function of archetype and myth is, as Jung suggests, two-fold, providing both a vision of the way things are and a commentary upon the failures of an age, then most of the versions of the myth discussed here fail abysmally to fulfill the second role. Not only has Callisto's rape deprived her of her integrity and her selfhood, but the patriarchalized versions, especially those of Lefevre and Warner have, in addition, deprived the myth of its integrity, its positive connotations. The bear imagery, for example, has almost entirely been explained away or eliminated, and any iconography which allies Callisto with the Lady of the Beasts is entirely negative, describing her bestial refusal to be compliant rather than her independence and strength. Callisto's motherhood is also highly criticized, again because she refuses to comply with Jupiter's expectations. In both of these matters, the virtue which is extolled by negative example is compliance, not the independence to which the myth addresses itself. Finally, placing the myth in the context of Jupiter's career negates the importance of Callisto as a central character.

A recurrent theme of Fraser's book on women in the seventeenth century is the difficulty for women living in that age to find viable role models. The Reformation effectively put a stop to mariolatry, and the post-Reformation woman was left with a pantheon that consisted entirely of her sinful "Grand-mother Eve." These versions of the Callisto myth suggest that other poten-tial members of a pantheon survived the purges, both of the patriarchy and the Reformation, though in deeply-disguised and sometimes even disfigured forms that need to be revived, examined, understood, and accepted as part of the feminine heritage.

CHAPTER THREE

A Mask Presented At Ludlow Castle: *The Armour of Logos*

Translations, or works intentionally derived from a previous source, generally deviate from the original text only to the extent that the writer can insert his or her opinions without full consciousness that these insertions might distort the intention of the original. Consequently, with respect to the Callisto myth, the three translations of the *Metamorphoses*, the two "histories" based on the "matter of Rome," Thomas Heywood's "historical" play, and *The Barley-Breake* deviate relatively little from the plot structure of the classical sources. With the exception of Jove's proposal to Callisto and the secularized settings, these seven works reveal signatures largely through language which embodies the writers' attitudes toward women – toward female sexuality in particular and sexual mores in general. One may hypothesize, however, that writers who do not acknowledge that they are working from a source – whether they are aware of the derivation or not – would exercise more freedom in imposing a personal signature.

Such is the case with Milton's *A Mask Presented at Ludlow Castle*. That the myth of Callisto informs the work has never been shown, since criticism of the masque has generally been allegorical[1] or, if mythic, has centred upon Milton's obvious employment of a reversed Circe-Odysseus plot.[2] Yet it is certain that Milton was familiar with the myth of Callisto, not only because he knew his Ovid in classical and Renaissance sources, but because it is referred to directly in his work, as Osgood has noted.[3] When the Lady's brothers begin to search for her, they wish for guidance from the "star of Arcady,"[4] the star into which Zeus transforms Arcas in Ovid's version of the myth. Even a cursory examination of the masque reveals the strong influence of the myth upon both plot and imagery.

Like Callisto, the Lady of the *Mask* is a young virgin alone in the forest who is vulnerable because she is separated from her companions. Although the Lady's companions are male – probably because Milton's commission stipulated the employment of the two young Egerton boys in the perform-

ance – the young men have decidedly feminine appearances: the Lady tells
Comus that their faces are "smooth as Hebe's" (96, l. 289). The companions
also discourse at length, and with some pretense of knowledge, upon female
virtues and vulnerabilities, as if they were indeed analogous to the band
of Diana of the myth.

Like Callisto, the Lady is sexually threatened – in this case with seduction
by Comus, a magician described as "Grandson of the Sun," who has made
his home in the wood in which the children wander. These woods seem to
belong to him, as the forests of Arcady once belonged to Zeus; there Comus
conducts his rites and performs his magic. When he hears the Lady's song,
he is immediately attracted to her; but afraid of frightening her, he adopts
a disguise, hoping to gain her trust sufficiently to convince her to drink his
magic potion, which will not only loose animal passion in her, but also
literally transform her into an animal: "Into som brutish form of Woolf, or
Bear, / Or Ounce, or Tiger, Hog, or bearded Goat" (87, 11. 69–70). When
he cannot seduce her, he "rapes" her by freezing her with his magic wand,
temporarily depriving her of control over her fate. While these correspondences identify the myth of Callisto as informing Milton's *Mask*, the
differences between the original forms of the myth and the forms given it
in the masque provide us with a sense of Milton's purposes, which are much
more sophisticated and complex than those of the writers who refer to the
myth openly. Milton is essentially interested in the dramatic dimensions
of the conflict between the various attitudes and mores that the Lady and
Comus embody.

Although Comus resembles Zeus in his control of the forest, his desire
to seduce a young virgin, his taking of a disguise, and his magical ability
to turn people into animals, there are a number of ways in which he differs
from the figure in Ovid's *Metamorphoses*. Comus contrives to look like a
harmless shepherd instead of taking on the guise of the goddess Diana. But
Milton expresses the feminine aspects of Comus' disguise by giving him a
female nature and orientation. While the mortal Joves of the histories
disguised themselves as women and *pretended* to worship Diana, Comus
really *does* worship the goddess, dancing to the moon "in wavering Morrice" (89, 1. 116), declaring himself the priest of various moon deities, and
speaking, in the goddess's stead, as a proponent of earthly fecundity. He
shuns the sun, symbol of logic, rationality, and Puritanism, but is, like the
goddess, at home in the night. Even his magic potion is said to cure the
"drouth of Phoebus" (87, 1. 66), that is, to counteract the effects of the planet
symbolic of reason and law.

Although Comus is son of Bacchus (who in his Dionysian form has a
powerful relationship to the feminine instinct) and is grandson of the sun,
the Attendant Spirit of the masque asserts that most of Comus' charcteristics
come from his mother, Circe, who, in Renaissance iconography, is the

enslaver of man's animal passions. George Sandys, in his commentary on the *Metamorphoses*, says that those who drink from Circe's cup are "men whose appetites revolt from the sovereignty of reason (by which we are only like unto God, and armed against depraved affections)."[5] But to claim that Milton's Circe can function only as a seductress because the author emphasizes only her seductive qualities is to believe that an author can fully control the effluence of a mythical figure. True, Circe turned the crew of Odysseus into swine, but she also directed Odysseus to the underworld for badly-needed instructions and warned him about the dangers of Scylla and Charybdis: her ability to direct Odysseus through the threatening elements of his homeward journey suggests that she is a guide to the dark side of the soul, both its passions and its dangers.[6]

Like the Lady of the Beasts and his mother, Comus represents the passional side of human nature. The properties of his magic liquor and the description of his following both suggest this interpretation. His magic potion is credited with the power to change men into animals, not only by transforming their countenances, but by removing the rational sides of their natures altogether. The Attendant Spirit accuses Comus of removing, with men's "human count'nance," their "express resemblance of the gods" (87, 11. 68–69). With the gain of sensuality comes the loss of rational powers. His

> pleasing poison
> The visage quite transforms of him that drinks,
> And the inglorious likeness of a beast
> Fixes instead, unmoulding reasons mintage
> Character'd in the face. (104, 11. 525-9)

Comus also considers himself a priest of Hecate and Cotytto, two aspects of the Great Goddess. The licentious orgies performed in Cotytto's names are similar to those of Comus; the rituals associated with her are performed in the interests of the earth's fertility, the cause that Comus himself professes when he argues with the Lady. Hecate is described by the Attendant Spirit as an evil witch, but she was originally the triple goddess herself, a beneficent deity in many respects, and frequently associated, like Diana, with the moon.[7]

Comus, then, is hardly associated with the sun and a rational, logical orientation. That role is saved for the Attendant Spirit, a messenger of Jove's who has come to "save" the Lady and return her to her father. The Attendant Spirit is something of a new addition in Callisto narratives: essentially he represents a different side of the Zeus figure of Ovid's myth. Like that character, he descends from "Jove's Court" to the "smoak and stirr" of the forest. And like Zeus at the end of the myth, who perceives that Callisto is in danger and saves her from death, the Attendant Spirit "stoops to her," to save her and return her safely home. In spite of his role as saviour, he nevertheless bears some resemblance to Comus in that he too takes the disguise of a shepherd, whose name, Thyrsis, connects the Spirit with Bacchus, and hence with Comus.

In a sense, then, Milton has split his Zeus figure in two, giving us the seductive and the apotheosizing components of the original figure in different characters. This act could be understood as a division of the characters into "good" and "bad" components, showing the effect of the transparent overlay of Christianity. This division may slightly alter the myth's configuration but does not undermine its meaning. Stronger than Milton's desire for moral clarity, however, is his desire to explore the implications of a confrontation between two discrete and even opposite qualities of human nature: the animal and passional, represented by Comus, and the rational and godlike, represented both by the Attendant Spirit and the Lady herself.

Whereas Harding identifies woman with the moon and with Eros, and man with the sun and with Logos, the Lady (although she evokes the moon as the symbol of chastity) is identified with both the sun and the rational. Her logical, conservative character is revealed in her opening speech, which finds her following the sounds of Comus' band, while at the same time disapproving of the "ill manag'd merriment" and the "wanton dances." She is both lost and alone, yet she is not frightened, thinking of night, in imagery both benevolent and Christian, as "gray-hooded Eev'n/ ... a sad Votarist in Palmers weed" (92, 1. 187–8). When fancies do begin to plague her imagination, she squelches them with the comforting thoughts of virtue:

> The vertuous mind, that ever walks attended
> By a strong siding champion Conscience.——
> O welcom pure-ey'd Faith, white-handed Hope,
> Thou hovering Angel girt with golden wings,
> And though unblemish't form of Chastity,
> I see ye visibly, and now believe
> That he, the Supreme good, t'whom all things ill
> Are but as slavish officers of vengeance,
> Would send a glistring Guardian if need were
> To keep my life and honour unassail'd. (93, 11. 209–19)

She comes to believe that virtue is its own reward and protection, that her own "unblemish't form of Chastity," reinforced by the appearance of the moon to light her way and give her guidance, renders her quite safe.

At this point in the masque, her entire situation – that of a young virgin lost, alone, and vulnerable – "echoes" the myth of Callisto, a myth which certainly suggests that she is *not* safe. This confusion about her relative safety is indicated in her Echo song, for she calls upon the wrong figure to help her find her brothers: Echo sought an attachment to Narcissus and could not achieve it. But the song evokes two more appropriate figures, Philomela and Callisto; the later is, unlike Echo, transported to the skies. The song reflects the ambivalence of the initiate who is the Callisto figure in the matriarchal manifestations of the myth. The initiate probably feels at least three things: she desires the impersonal love of the initiation, she fears rape, and she hopes to achieve Callisto's at-one-ness with the goddess.

Comus' own reaction to both the Lady's presence and her song reveals that the protection of chastity is equivocal. Unlike the typical Zeus figures, Comus is attracted to her not because she is beautiful, but because she is chaste, not because she is vulnerable, but because she seems so sober and self-certain. Thus he follows her footsteps because their chasteness calls him; he is entranced by her song because it indicates something holy, because it is the antithesis of the songs of licentious Circe. The Lady's song does not pull at him because it is seductive or lulling, as were the songs of his mother and her three maids, who "lull'd the sense,/ And in sweet madness rob'd it of it self" (95, 11. 259–60). Rather, her song annihilates states of insensibility like silence, darkness, and death. Comus declares that he has never heard songs quite like this: "But such a sacred, and home-felt delight/ Such sober certainty of waking bliss/ I never heard till now ..." (95, 11. 261–63). The "home-felt delight" is delight in oneself, delight in the sense that she is "self-appeasing, self-affrighting." Her bliss is sober, certain, awake, and of her own determination, coming from the independence and self-sufficiency she exhibits when she considers her lost, benighted condition. Yet that very strength is a weakness, because it attracts Comus.

The Lady's reasoning seems, in practical terms, circular; she believes that she will remain chaste *because* she is chaste. Her elder brother appears to repeat essentially the same argument, except that the image which introduces his discussion – that of his need for the Star of Arcady as guide – is an image which immediately belies his conclusion. Once chaste, always chaste is *not* the moral of Callisto's story. There seems, on one hand, a tremendous naïveté to the elder brother's declaration that she is physically safe because she is virtuous:

> but yet a hidden strength
> Which if Heav'n gave it, may be term'd her own:
> 'Tis chastity, my brother, chastity:
> She that has that, is clad in compleat steel,
> And like a quiver'd Nymph with Arrows keen
> May trace huge Forrests, and unharbour'd Heaths,
> Infamous Hills, and sandy perilous wildes,

Where through the sacred rayes of Chastity,
No savage fierce, Bandite, or Mountaneer
Will dare to soyl her Virgin purity,
Yea there, where very desolation dwels
By grots, and caverns shag'd with horrid shades,
She may pass on with unblench't majesty,
Be it not don in pride, or in presumption.
Som say no evil thing that walks by night
In fog, or fire, by lake, or moorish fen,
Blew meager Hag, or stubborn unlaid ghost,
That breaks his magick chains at Curfeu time,
No Goblin, or swart Faëry of the mine,
Hath hurtfull power o're true Virginity.
Do ye believe me yet, or shall I call
Antiquity from the old Schools of Greece
To testifie the arms of Chastity?
Hence had the huntress Dian her dred bow
Fair silver-shafted Queen for ever chaste,
Wherewith she tam'd the brinded lioness
And spotted mountain pard, but set at nought
The frivolous bolt of Cupid, gods and men
Fear'd her stern frown, and she was queen oth' Woods. (100–1, 11. 418–45)

The nymph with her arrows, "tracing the forests," is Callisto, who is not, however, "clad in compleat steel." As the younger brother points out, his elder has forgotten the simple fact of the general physical superiority of men:

But beauty like the fair Hesperian Tree
Laden with blooming gold, had need the guard
Of dragon watch with uninchanted eye,
To save her blossoms, and defend her fruit
From the rash hand of bolt Incontinence.
You may as well spred out the unsun'd heaps
Of Misers treasure by an out-laws den,
And tell me it is safe, as bid me hope
Danger will wink on Opportunity,
And let a single helpless maiden pass
Uninjur'd in this wilde surrounding wast. (99–100, 11, 392–402)

Moreover, the "old schools of Greece" contain more raped women than virgin goddesses.

On the other hand, the elder brother claims that he is describing a state of mind:

I do not think my sister so to seek,
Or so unprincipl'd in vertues book,
And the sweet peace that goodnes boosoms ever,
As that the single want of light and noise
(Not being in danger, as I trust she is not)
Could stir the constant mood of her calm thoughts,
And put them into mis-becoming plight.
Vertue could see to do what vertue would
By her own radiant light, though Sun and Moon
Were in the flat Sea sunk. And Wisdoms self
Oft seeks to sweet retired Solitude,
Where with her best nurse Contemplation
She plumes her feathers, and lets grow her wings
That in the various bustle of resort
Were all to ruffl'd, and sometimes impair'd.
He that has light within his own cleer brest
May sit i'th center, and enjoy bright day,
But he that hides a dark soul, and foul thoughts
Benighted walks under the mid-day Sun;
Himself is his own dungeon. (98–9, 11. 365–84)

It is impossible *not* to see the Platonic image of the feathered soul embedded in this description; the fact that self-knowledge and chastity are juxtaposed is precisely the point. Exploring the Platonic echoes in the *Mask*, John Arthos concludes that Milton's concept of chastity is similar to the kind of self-knowledge implied by Plato's "sophrosyne," which Ficino describes in the epitome to his translation of *The Charmides* as "the light that drives out darkness and helps us to escape the potions of Circe that would transform us into beasts." Arthos points out that "Socrates ... develops the meaning [of sophrosyne] stage by stage, as reverence, as working for oneself, as doing good, and finally, as knowing oneself."[8] Such self-knowledge is consonant with that implicit in psychological virginity. In this masque, self-knowledge is frequently expressed in terms of the light from the stars and moon – the symbolic planets of the Callisto myth. On one hand those planets bespeak her vulnerability, yet in the myth's matriarchal versions they also bespeak woman's becoming one with the moon goddess through achieving the goddess-like quality of psychological virginity.

But the moon is not the only protector of virginity in the masque, for the Lady, arguing with Comus, invokes the "sun-clad power of Chastity." The sun is not usually associated with chastity, but rather with knowledge, with Logos. The Lady suggests that her chastity is not, then, merely a physical entity but a matter of knowledge, a frame of mind. Hence the brother's speech is not, on this level, quite so naive. Milton's concept of chastity is consonant with Harding's notion of psychological virginity in that one's psychological orientation is as important as one's physical state.

Certainly allegorical critics of the masque have failed to provide any fixed notion of chastity in the work. Allegorical criticism of the *Mask* understands "the sage/ And serious doctrine of Virginity" (114, 1. 785-6) to be coterminous with some aspect of Christian doctrine. This has generated a good deal of peroration regarding the exact meaning of the Lady's chastity. John S. Lawry calls it "fidelity to both reason and God."[9] A.S.P. Woodhouse, in "The Argument of Milton's *Comus*," an article which has been the initial stepping-stone to further conclusions about the nature of chastity in *Comus*, tells us that the doctrine of virginity "becomes in the poem the illustration and symbol (but not the complete synonym) [for] Grace." Given these definitions and their limitations, the doctrine of chastity would seem but a bettered, Christianized version of temperance and continence. The Lady's chastity, Woodhouse says, rather than being a merely passive denial of vice, is "not mere abstention from evil but an active pursuit of good."[10]

E.M.W. Tillyard, in one article, would like to excise any religious or mystical sense from the word "chastity," and so tells us baldly, "We must remember that chastity had a wider meaning in Milton's day than in ours. It meant monogamy as well as virginity."[11] Yet in another essay devoted to the issue of chastity in Milton, he notes that "the doctrine as stated in *Comus* is that chastity gives supernatural powers" – more specifically, the "means of hearing the celestial music."[12]

Just what chastity represents in an allegorical reading of the masque is not the point here. What is the point is that the meaning of chastity has not been and cannot be pinned down as tidily as it should be if the masque is only allegorical. If, on the other hand, we understand chastity in the terms of the Callisto myth, we can account for the paradoxical nature of the elder brother's arguments, his naïveté about his sister's physical safety and yet justified belief in the power of his sister's chaste frame of mind. We also see more clearly how it is that the Lady can refute Comus' attractive arguments, for Comus is not questioning some abstract religious doctrine but is challenging the woman's very concept of herself as her own person, not a bit of beauty to be "us'd."

The argument between Comus and the Lady corresponds to Callisto's struggle with the god, a struggle which, as has been suggested, often represents the clash of two attitudes, Logos and Eros, attitudes which must come into balance if the initiate is to achieve psychological virginity. Zeus' disguise as Diana is echoed here by Comus taking on the typically feminine attitude, arguing for Eros, relatedness. The Lady, in her logical replies, represents Logos. That these two orientations are in question is indicated at the opening of their discussion. Comus threatens to "rape" her with his phallic wand; she replies "Thou canst not touch the freedom of my minde"

(110, 1. 662). He then feels it necessary to remind her that she has a body as well and that she must not treat it harshly by forbidding it the "refreshment after toil." She shifts the argument back to the mental sphere by confronting him with his dishonesty and arguing that if he is false, so are the gifts he offers. He replies by appealing to her senses and by arguing that the whole natural world is there only in relation to us, wanting us to use it, and, by analogy, that her beauty and virginity also have meaning only if they are used.

One of the critical exercises performed on Milton's *Mask* is the analysis of these arguments of Comus and the Lady. Comus sounds very much like the Jupiter figures of *Albion's England* and *The Golden Age*, evoking the now-familiar argument which suggests that women exist only in relation to the men who possess them. Comus' logic is highly questionable: nature is not always bounteous, and even if she were, virginity is not. Hence the argument from analogy, which is invariably logically incorrect, is certainly so here. Her staid frame of mind, Logos, and logic are definitely the Lady's tools: she argues for a logical, if somewhat cold and unresponsive, use of nature, and, to cap her arguments about nature and virginity, invokes "the Sun-clad power of Chastity." Neither Comus nor the Lady are right. In an aside Comus admits his falsehood openly: "I must dissemble, / And try her yet more strongly" (115, 11. 804–5). The Lady has been unsympathetically criticized for her "prudery,"[13] her unyielding allegiance to her principles and equally unyielding refusal to acknowledge Comus' attractiveness.

At this point, the issue of the genre of *A Mask Presented at Ludlow Castle* illuminates Milton's reasons for attributing these qualities to the Lady and Comus. Angus Fletcher, discussing the hotly-debated issue of whether *Ludlow Castle* is a masque at all, describes the work as a "visionary ritual" which explores the conditions of rebirth within the community.[14] In Milton's *Mask* the "themes of chastity and virginity give structure to the concern for freedom" as well as to the "Pagan temptation"[15] which we are witness to. Fletcher's comments suggest that the masque form in general, and Milton's *Mask* in particular, present us with a ritual initiation. Rituals, however, need a script, a myth: the script for this particular ritual/masque is the myth of Callisto. When Callisto represents not the victim of a rape but the subject of an initiation, the outcome is psychological virginity – a quality associated with balance, especially the balance of Logos and Eros – and independence.

The question becomes more complex, however, when we take the idea of initiation out of its timeless realm of myth and place it in historical time. Such placement is often achieved through signature alone. But in *Comus* the characters are meant to correspond to real people. Milton wrote the masque for the Egerton family to celebrate an important political appointment for the Earl. The poet was somewhat constrained by the Earl's request that his two young sons and adolescent daughter, Lady Alice, be given important parts in the masque, and that the plot reflect the occasion of the children's joining him in his new position. Thus the situation – young people on their way home to join their father and restore the *political* wholeness of his new realm – emphasizes the influence of real, historical time even more. Certainly the youthful cast precludes any literal application of the myth, beyond giving Comus a wand with which to freeze the Lady. In Milton's *Mask* our sense of whether the Lady is a prude or independent-minded, our conclusion about whether or not she has achieved real psychological virginity, must take history into account. What if the Lady *had* given in to Comus' arguments, as those who term her "prudish" suggest she should have?

Chastity was important in the Renaissance: without that one virtue, all a woman's other virtues were as nothing; with it, a shrew might be thought a good wife.[16] The consideration of Renaissance men was, of course, a practical one: only a chaste wife can assure a man that his heirs are really his own. Still suspected because of Eve's unreliability, Renaissance woman was expected to prove her virtue through her chastity. In this respect, the chastity of Lady Alice is doubly, if not triply, important; a scandal in the not-so-remote corners of the Egerton family which came to the fore at about the time of the Earl's appointment made it politic to assert Alice's purity.[17] Thus, the masque's audience is meant to understand that Lady Alice's virtue withstands all temptations; the masque becomes, in a very real sense, a ritualistic celebration of her virginity, complete with initiatory trials.

This initiation is usually seen in Christian terms. Robert Wilcher describes the Lady as someone who must "'sally forth and meet her adversary,' armed with the confidence that heaven will protect her, but aware that the responsibility for meeting her 'trial' rests on her own powers of argument."[18] Similarly, Fletcher remarks that "We might call this action a rite of passage, at the end of which the children have 'grown up.'"[19] Both comments suggest that the Lady is seen to have experienced only a moral initiation, that she is now "a young woman on the threshold of adult life who comes to realize that she has her part to play in the universal battle between good and evil."[20]

It is true that the Lady, unlike Ovid's Callisto, remains physically chaste. Comus freezes her with his wand, but in doing so makes her as untouchable "as Daphne was, / Root-bound, that fled Apollo" (109–10, 11. 660–1). Such chastity, Fletcher tells us, "can be said, at first, to be the power to remain unmoved, unseduced, unmetamorphosed, undeflowered, uninitiated, unchanged. For the virgin to remain chaste requires all these kinds of stability."[21]

Even if the Lady could have seen her way clear to – or been duped into – drinking from Comus' sensual cup and had experienced the transformation into a animal, could she, in the context of Renaissance society, have achieved Harding's version of psychological virginity? The inevitable answer is no: she has been so indoctrinated into the patriarchal notion of *sun-clad* chastity that she cannot conceive of any other. The sun, of course, symbolizes the patriarchal orientation she exhibits in her arguments, the patriarchal concept of *physical* chastity which replaces the older, matriarchal notion of psychological virginity. In a sense, she does the best she can by remaining, as Fletcher says, unmoved and independent in that sense, by being her own person even if that person does not acquire, as she might have in another context, the wholeness indicative of a virgin in the matriarchal sense.

When the Lady rashly tells Comus that he cannot, whatever he does to her body, touch the freedom of her mind, she *professes* that mind is more important. But the transformation of Callisto shows this to be untrue. When Zeus or Hera changes Callisto into a bear, her mind is left untouched and free. Yet it is Callisto's supposedly free mind which causes her to wander toward Arcadia in search of human company. What she meets instead is her death. Clearly the message is that in a patriarchal culture, physical virginity is important. The positive matriarchal symbolism of the bear, Diana's totem animal, is not powerful enough to overcome man's fear of the animal in himself and in fellow humans, whether the creature is met in the sacred precincts or in the forest. As if aware of Callisto's fate, the Lady does not – in spite of the professed importance of a free mind – allow Comus to have her body, for she is aware of her culture's real priorities as opposed to those it professes. Moreover, she wants, as did Brownmiller's rock-flinging female Homo sapiens, the right to choose when and to whom she will "sacrifice" her virginity.

Comus, on the other hand, seems to be more interested in making the Lady's body part of his revelry, yet he does not, like the typical Zeus figure, simply take what he wants. He does not want to rape her, he wants to *initiate* her, to persuade her to choose his matriarchal vision over her patriarchal one. His very alliance with Circe, Cotytto, and Hecate shows him as a priest of the ancient goddesses – one quite fit to perform the initiation ceremonies Harding describes. The Lady is unable to give in to the experience because of her very "masculine" patriarchal frame of mind, one which she cannot transcend. Consequently Comus must find some other way to achieve the desired result – an initiated woman – without the usual means: sexual intercourse. Comus' wand, an appropriately phallic prop, freezes the Lady, putting her beyond his control. Harding says, after all, that the object of initiation is to free a woman from her *need* of a man, and this is precisely the effect his wand has. It even puts her beyond rescue by the Attendant Spirit. By having Sabrina rescue her, Milton forces the Lady to depend upon the feminine for guidance.

The masque's ending is the complete turn-about of the myth: instead of being reviled and exiled, the Lady is rescued, not by a male Zeus figure but by Sabrina. Sabrina is, perhaps like the pre-patriarchal Callisto, a local aspect of the Great Goddess. She is noted somewhat paradoxically (but in a way often characterizing patriarchal goddesses) for her physical virginity and for her contribution to fecundity among the local shepherds who pay tribute to her. Instead of denouncing the Lady, as Diana did Callisto, Sabrina brings from her stream a virginity-renewing liquor.

The Lady is, in effect, saved by the feminine, not destroyed by it, because she has adhered to the rules enforced by women to protect themselves from the disdain of the patriarchy.[22] Also, the Attendant Spirit's inability to save her, in spite of what he knows, indicates that it is the feminine quarter from which the Lady must draw the strength and knowledge to achieve wholeness. Comus' rape with the phallic wand forces the Lady to look to the feminine for help, and it is this which gives her as much wholeness as she can achieve in the Renaissance context.

Being saved by Zeus typically indicates the extent to which a woman's status is bestowed upon her by a man, and this is reflected in the masque. For the fact remains that the Lady inhabits a patriarchal world, so that while Sabrina saves her, the Attendant Spirit presents her to her parents, repeating the situation of Jupiter refining Arcas, although it is Callisto who has raised him. Since her maidenhead is intact he credits her with having withstood temptation.

What is curious is that the Lady has nothing to say once the spirit has "rescued" her. It would seem that, in a position where she had to fight her own battles, she was more than adequately equipped with strength, courage, language, but that these qualities are repressed once she is returned to the normal world. Her experience with Comus has allowed her to test her own strength. Her wordlessness suggests that her strength is, however, not much use to her in the patriarchal world; that it is, in fact, either demanded or taken for granted.

We ultimately see that the two versions of the myth are part of the dramatic conflict of the masque. Not only is Milton exploring the conflict of Eros and Logos embedded within the myth, he is contrasting its matriarchal and patriarchal manifestations. Comus intends to offer the Lady an initiation, but the Lady is too afraid of being raped to allow herself the opportunity. She is not being precious, she is being practical, but Milton nevertheless views her practicality as a limitation.

The Attendant Spirit, in contrast, offers the Lady an entirely different vision of any eventual union she should make – for we must remember that the real Lady Alice is doubtless meant for a more reasonable relationship: marriage.[23] Those "happy climes" toward which the Daemon flies contain the "golden tree" given to Hera as a wedding present. The golden apples of that tree tempted Atalanta to give up her virgin freedom and marry Hippomenes. Like both Diana and Callisto, Atalanta was a great huntress who was militant about her virginity. Her determination to remain virgin is reflected in her consultation with the Delphic Oracle on the subject of a husband. Apollo, Ovid tells us, responded to her question by saying: "You have no need of a husband, Atalanta. You should avoid any experience of one. But assuredly, you will not escape marriage, and then, though still alive, you will lose your own self."[24]

The parallels between Atalanta and Callisto are strong. Both virgin hunters, they are metamorphosed into animals, a lion and a bear, respectively, when men dominate them. The difference is that Atalanta agrees to marry Hippomenes after he wins the race by diverting her attention with the golden apples. Atalanta's experience has a message for the Lady who, like both Callisto and Atalanta, values her virginity, has been threatened with transformation into an animal, and is probably bound for marriage.

Atalanta gives in to her husband when he is moved by an "untimely urge" to make love to her. In effect, she allows him to control her sexuality and does indeed lose her self as a result. She functions as a monitory image for the Lady who might take the Christian notion of chastity too literally and unwillingly allow a husband the favours which she would not allow Comus. To do so would be merely to repeat the very experience she refused with Comus. The context of marriage does not make the giving up of one's volition any less a loss of self and integrity.

The myth of Atalanta is related by Venus to Adonis in the *Metamorphoses*; shortly afterwards, Adonis is wounded by the boar. Here one encounters one of those uncanny correspondences characteristic of myth, which Jung called "synchronicities," when one realizes that the Daemon's next reference to myth in the epilogue of the *Mask* is to Venus and Adonis. Hence we see both the appropriateness of allowing the Hesperian tree to recall Atalanta's story, and the implied relationship of the Atalanta and Venus myths. Let us assume that, like the myth of Atalanta, that of Venus and Adonis is about the dangers of a permanent union, for Milton has changed the original myth to suggest permanence: her Adonis waxes "well of his deep wound." Venus told Atalanta's story to Adonis as a warning to avoid "every kind of wild beast which does not turn tail and flee."[25] But of course he does not avoid them, and so receives the wound which, in the masque, merely saddens the Assyrian Queen rather than resulting in his death, as in the *Metamorphoses*. The animal imagery suggests that Adonis' animal passions ran wild, rather than being governed by the superior knowledge of Venus. This is true to Renaissance thought in a very prosaic way: women, when they were not being damned for their unchasteness, were credited with a superior, guiding virtue. So while the Atalanta myth describes a woman's loss of self via the submission of her sexuality to the

demands of the male, the myth of Venus and Adonis shows a future relationship not quite so grim: Venus loses control over Adonis only temporarily, and while she is saddened and deeply affected by his wound, she loses
nothing of herself.

The final scenario from mythology presented by the Attendant Spirit as
he ascends to his home is the myth of Cupid and Psyche, the myth of
"woman becoming individual, self-responsible, taking her own initiative."[26]
Psyche does not originally know who her lover is, but accepts a lover she
cannot see and therefore does not know. This lack of knowledge, Erich
Neumann suggests, symbolizes Psyche's acceptance of the sexual domination of Eros:

For with all its rapture is this existence in the sensual paradise of Eros not an unworthy existence? Is it not a state of blind, though impassioned, servitude, against
which a feminine self-consciousness – and such is the matriarchal attitude of the
feminine – must protest, against which it must raise all the arguments that are raised
by the sisters? Psyche's existence is a non-existence, a being-in-the-dark, a rapture
of sexual sensuality which may be fittingly characterized as a being devoured by
a demon, a monster. Eros as an unseen fascination is everything that the oracle of
Apollo ... has said of him, and Psyche really is his victim.[27]

The myth suggests that real love, the kind of love that will inspire the
undertaking of impossible tasks, comes only through knowledge, for we
are told that only when Psyche sees her lover does she fall in love with Love.
This moment of knowledge also marks the change from passivity to activity
in Psyche's attitude. Neumann further suggests in his "Commentary" that
Psyche's helpers, insofar as they symbolize or indicate the masculine aspects
of her character, show that she comes to know the masculine side of herself.
Such knowledge, Harding tells us, allows her to be one-in-herself; only then,
in this myth of marriage, is Psyche willing once more to subordinate herself
to the male god.

The ascent of the Daemon which is paralleled in these three references
to myth is not, as Woodhouse points out, a movement from the area of
nature to that of grace,[28] and Tillyard's observation that it introduces a new
theme, that of marriage, is only partially correct.[29] Instead, the three
myths – that of Atalanta, evoked by the Hesperian tree; that of Venus and
Adonis; and that of Cupid and Psyche – represent the range of experience,
in ascending order, which the Lady may find when she marries.[30]

This ascending sequence is part of the updating of the Callisto myth for
Renaissance woman. Psychological virginity, along with the philosophical
orientation that it implies in Milton's work, is still the goal for the independent woman, yet being one-in-herself is largely an intellectual quality, as
it is embodied in Lady Alice's ability to argue so logically and persuasively.

But just as such virginity cannot be achieved through anything even re-motely similar to a night of sacred prostitution in the temple, so it must include the reality of marriage. The age demanded chaste brides; it also demanded that women marry. As Ruth Kelso points out, the Renaissance lady was educated for marriage; outside that social structure she had no identity.[31] The woman who would retain her inner independence in the con-text of marriage must not follow in the steps of Atalanta, a Callisto figure whose fate is not any different for her marrying. To do so is to repeat the experience with Comus within the legalities of marriage.

In a sense, then, Milton offers the Renaissance woman two workable prototypes. For the married woman there is the example of Psyche. For the unmarried maiden there is his disguised Callisto, whose mind and virtue protect her body and who nearly achieves psychological virginity through her masculine exercise of logic and reason, her sun-clad chastity. Callisto has, in a sense, been patriarchalized. Completely feminine and completely whore in the works of Lefevre, Warner, and Heywood, her transformation by Milton into a receptacle of patriarchal virtues renders her virtuous in the masculine sense, but deprives her of the fullest knowledge of her own femininity.

CHAPTER FOUR

Mysteries of Udolpho:
Mysteries of the Forest

When Milton wrote *A Mask Presented at Ludlow Castle,* he explored the possibility of psychological virginity in the context of Renaissance mores. His shaping of the myth, aside from all its complexities, essentially constitutes a response to a social and cultural imperative: rape victims and unchaste girls can hardly be employed as heroines. Milton had to find a way of allowing his heroine to achieve some modicum of psychological virginity without actually losing its physical counterpart. The result is a work that essentially defines psychological virginity in Renaissance terms and that ignores the spiritual and psychological gains hypothesized by Harding, trading them instead for a more realistic set of virtues. The psychological virgin is a woman whose strong conviction about who she is enables her to choose and direct her own fate. Her limitations, however, are not ignored by Milton, for he perceives her as somewhat masculinized.

Milton's *Mask* is the last work until the late eighteenth century that is informed by the myth of Callisto: one could speculate that the "Age of Reason" was not conducive to exploring such an "irrational" virtue as psychological virginity. The Gothic novel, however, with its forests, its preoccupation with "sensibility," and its threatened orphan heroines, provides a perfect background against which to re-enact Callisto's story. But like Milton's Lady, the Gothic heroine must also remain virgin. Maureen Duffy, in her comments upon the Gothic novel, remarks that "the aspiring middle classes ... had no titles to confer, but could improve their connections if they had money by marrying their daughters into the aristocracy as long as the daughters were perfect, unsullied, and pleasing objects."[1] Consequently the Gothic novelist must also define psychological virginity for her heroine in a way that is again somewhat at variance with Harding's definition.

Forests and orphan girls and seductions inevitably call Mrs Radcliffe's *Mysteries of Udolpho* to mind. To see that *Mysteries* falls into the pattern of Callisto narratives, we need only observe the courtship of Emily and Valancourt and the attendant patterns of sun, forest, and moon imagery. Their first meeting comes during St Aubert's decline, much as Jupiter and Callisto met as Lycaon was being driven from his fortress. Like the Jupiter figures in the medieval and Renaissance works, Valancourt is described as having a chevalier-like air; indeed, we later find that he is, like the secular Jupiters, a soldier. After St Aubert is conquered – that is, after he has died, and Emily has returned to La Vallee – Valancourt pursues her there, meeting her frequently among the oaks and plane trees which the estate boasts. Under Emily's favourite plane tree, Valancourt asks for permission to court her, permission which Emily grants only hesitantly because of her anomalous, unprotected status. Here they are interrupted by Madame Montoni, who functions in the novel both as Hera and Diana. As Diana, she "protects" Emily from what she perceives to be the improper attentions of Valancourt and exposes her to the dangers of exile when she forces Emily to accompany them to Venice. She also functions as Hera in that she later slanders Emily by accusing the heroine of impropriety in her truly accidental meetings with Valancourt.

Emily, like Callisto, tries to keep Valancourt within the proper bounds, but finds that if she roams the natural world – the gardens and the forests – she will inevitably encounter him. In fact, we rarely see Valancourt inside; he seems, instead, to be part of the natural world which surrounds Emily. When they must part, he leaves not the typical lover's momento, but entreats her to recall him when she sees the sun set. Their chance encounters, which move Madame Montoni to question and rebuke Emily, are, with the proposal to elope and escape the dictates of Montoni, the closest the gentle Valancourt ever comes to raping Emily. Given Madame Montoni's active tongue, however, and a world so morally formalized and idealized, suggestions of impropriety would have had an effect on Emily's reputation not unlike that of having been raped. Moreover, asking Emily to marry him without the complete approval of both Emily's family and his own is to put her in a position in which she cannot control her own life, because devoid of family support and money, Emily has no power.

Aside from Emily's relationship with Valancourt, there are other aspects of her career which are reminiscent of Callisto's. Called a "nymph" and "goddess" by Du Pont, Emily finds herself abandoned after her mother's death, and deprived of feminine companionship and guidance, much as Callisto was separated from Diana when Zeus raped her. That she typically invokes her mother on moonlit nights is another indication of Madame St Aubert's mythic function. Like Callisto, Emily is generally most comfortable in the company of women: with Maddelina or Annette, for example. The convent also serves in this novel, as in the medieval and Renaissance works, as a kind of updated, Christianized version of Diana's band. Here Emily frequently retreats, or hopes to retreat, to protect herself from the undesired attentions of men – not merely from M. Du Pont but also from the pressures of Montoni and the attentions of his officers.

One assumes that a young woman joins a convent at least in part because she is not comfortable with her sexuality, or not ready to deal with it. Similarly we see Emily anxious to avoid the overtones of sexuality in her relationship with Valancourt; this is the purpose of the almost laughably formalized conversations between Emily and Valancourt. Although Radcliffe is too discreet to allow us a direct view of Emily's repressed sexuality, her heroine's amorphous and unexplained fears of even encountering Montoni's watchmen suggest that Emily is uncomfortably aware that she can be seen as a sexual being. Furthermore, she attributes her apprehensions about the second, unlockable door to her chamber and her distance from the rest of the family, to a fear of being robbed. Yet we must realize that the only thing this penniless orphan can be robbed of is a mongrel dog, a few books, her drawing materials, and her virginity.

When threats to her virginity do arise – when, for example, Morano attempts to carry her off, or Valancourt presses her to marry him hastily – we find Emily, like the Lady in Milton's masque, quite capable of logical arguments. That Radcliffe knew *Comus* is indicated by her use of quotations from Milton's masque as epigraphs or songs in four chapters. In each case the excerpt is appropriate enough to suggest that she recognized parallels between her work and Milton's. In the first case, the benighted Laurentini sings the Attendant Spirit's description of the Lady's song to Echo, Philomela, and Callisto, while in the background St Aubert and La Voisin discuss the fate of the Marchioness. Laurentini and the Marchioness serve as two monitory figures for Emily, just as Philomela and Callisto do for the Lady. In the second case, the speech quoted comes from the elder brother's description of the evil soul; the chapter describes Montoni's villainy. In the third instance, Radcliffe quotes the brothers' request for some guiding light; in that chapter Emily believes Valancourt is near, and this conviction "guides" her behaviour toward Montoni. In the final epigraph, Radcliffe quotes the beginning of the Attendant Spirit's departing speech which begins his references to marriage; in that chapter Emily and Valancourt marry.

In showing her familiarity with Milton's masque and quoting it appropriately, Radcliffe demonstrates that she is aware of the similarities between Emily's situation and the Lady's. A closer look at *Mysteries* reveals that both the myth and the literary tradition surrounding it as represented in Milton's *Mask* are informing patterns for the whole novel. Like Milton, Radcliffe must create a character capable of coping with the threats to her integrity and of maintaining her virginity. Moreover, her audience, like Milton's, expects the villain and the hero to be two different characters. The

Zeus figure who legitimizes the heroine by marrying her, as Zeus legitimized Callisto by placing her in the sky, cannot be synonymous with the Zeus figure who attempts to rape her. Milton divides his Zeus between Comus and the Attendant Spirit, between the man who would possess her virginity and the man who would ensure that she is legitimized and acknowledged.

Radcliffe's division likewise falls into camps. There are, of course, the lovers: Valancourt, Morano, Du Pont, and Verezzi, among whom the latter is probably the only one interested in literal rape. Morano wants Emily passionately, but, like Comus, focuses his power – even during the abduction – on persuasion, not force. On the other hand, St Aubert, Montoni, and the Count de Villefort, all of them patriarchal figures, are interested in control of the woman – of her emotions, her destiny, her choice of a husband, her property. Radcliffe's use of sun and forest imagery, as well as the patriarchal attitude of the men who seek control of Emily, reinforces our suspicions that Emily confronts more than one Zeus figure in this densely-forested novel.

More to the point is the fact that each of these men damages Emily through the misuse of his power. Rape can be viewed as control of a woman's sexuality and her life, a control which damages her psyche or her integrity. Looked at in this way, St Aubert's effort to protect Emily from her own feelings and from the experiences of womanhood constitutes emotional and psychic rape. Montoni's intention to sell Emily in marriage, deprive her of her inheritance, and leave her prey to the sexual attentions of Verezzi and his other officers is similarly a form of rape. The Count de Villefort's hasty denunciation of Valancourt and his edict, "Leave me to understand your heart,"[2] in that his concern is to control Emily's life and emotions, is another example of metaphorical rape. In addition, the setting, the circumstances, and the outcome of each encounter reflect the Callisto paradigm. In each case the paternal benefactor appears in the Apollonian disguise noted by Apollodorus; in each case, the man attempts, in a fatherly way, to make Emily more reasonable.

St Aubert is associated with his favourite oaks and his much beloved plane tree at La Vallee as well as with a favoured, ancient chestnut on his ancestral estates. His health, we note, typically declines with the setting of the sun. These images provide only a skeleton key, however, to the extent to which Emily's father functions in the novel as a kind of Zeus figure in Apollonian disguise. At La Vallee, the death of Emily's mother leaves both St Aubert and Emily grief-stricken. The loss of her mother renders Emily prey to what her father perceives to be false conceptions of her own feminine sensibility, which he, in the guise of teacher, seeks to extinguish. Determining that Emily is too sensitive to live a placid life without a rational armour, St Aubert endeavours to teach Emily the benefits of rational self-control. His lessons backfire in a number of ways.

First, they provide Emily with a prototype for behaviour which she cannot always meet, and hence which becomes the source of constant self-reproach. Emily often observes at her leisure that her conduct is not up to her father's standards. But in the midst of the fray, during many of the real tests, she is saved by her own innate dignity, not by taking the time to consider what her father would expect of her under the circumstances. Her rebellion against Montoni, her ability to break the hold of the amorous officer with only the "strength of indignation," her perennial dignity, do not have their source in her father's teachings but rather in a feminine conviction regarding who and what she is, and who and what she intends to remain.

Second, she justifies her rejection of Valancourt's proposal to elope and her refusal to accept him in his fallen state, with considerations based on "all the precepts, which she had received from her deceased father, on the subject of self-command, to enable her to act, with prudence and dignity, on this the most severe occasion of her life" (518). Such actions might, on the surface, seem noble and even wise. Yet their effect suggests tremendous ambivalence on Radcliffe's part; the first refusal puts Emily in Montoni's power; the second refusal causes both Emily and Valancourt great and needless pain. Emily herself questions the value of her restraint: "And what have I gained by the fortitude that I then practiced? – Am I happy now?" (584).

Mary Poovey, in "Ideology and *The Mysteries of Udolpho*," places the cult of sensibility which St Aubert teaches Emily in its social context. She observes that it did indeed function to oppress women subtly, and that Radcliffe was in some ways aware of this. The ideology of sensibility "rationalized the economic and political powerlessness of women; it also constituted the basis for their peculiar but undeniable power. In the course of the eighteenth century, sentimental virtues were increasingly identified as feminine virtues, until, by the end of the century, authors of conduct books for 'women of rank and fortune' consistently described women's 'natural' characteristics as a variation of sentimentalism."[3]

Although St Aubert attempts to strengthen Emily's sensibilities with reason, perhaps in an effort to free her from some of the passivity which sentimentality inculcates, he provides her with no armour against men like Montoni, men who are persuaded neither by virtue nor by logic. He fails to teach her resistance or defiance, and leaves her to imagine a world which does not require these powers in a woman. Yet he holds in his possession the proof that these characteristics are necessary: the history of his sister, the Marchioness de Villeroi.

Believing that Emily is unable to cope with information about the fate of her aunt, St Aubert makes Emily promise to burn his documents concerning her aunt's life, which she does in spite of a curiosity which Radcliffe terms "necessary" (103). By doing so, St Aubert withholds from Emily the realization that women are married off by their "protectors," and the knowledge of what happens to women who allow themselves to be manipulated in this way, as well as important information regarding her ancestry, information that could have saved great confusion. When Emily later discovers herself in the same position as her aunt – offered by Montoni to Count Morano in a profitable match – she finds the fortitude to refuse his demands. Yet this refusal leaves her feeling isolated and forsaken. The knowledge of her aunt's situation might have provided her with a sense of solidarity with other women. In this case, "divide and conquer" might be considered the motto of the patriarchy, a motto reflected in the fact that Callisto is raped by Zeus only when she is separated from her fellows.

That separation, depending upon the cultural and social context, opens the Callisto figure to either rape or initiation, and often it is difficult to distinguish between the two. Such is the case here, for it is difficult to decide if Emily's innocence about her aunt's fate results in experiences which damage or rape her, or in experiences which test her and in so doing endow her with strength. Our inability to decide suggests Radcliffe's own ambivalence. On the one hand, we feel that there is strength in solidarity. On the other, we know that a woman's isolation from the experience of other women was a cultural reality of the times in which Radcliffe wrote. Consequently, Gothic novels are, as Maureen Shechan Jacobs points out, singularly lacking in images of "healthy, whole adult females."[4]

Rather than fully acknowledging the benighted and potentially harmful influences of St Aubert, Radcliffe somewhat disguises them. As Poovey observes, she "does not abandon sentimental values; instead, she retreats from the terrifying implications of her discovery and simply dismisses the threat [Montoni] that sentimentalism cannot combat. Rather than proposing an alternative to paternalistic society and its values, she merely reasserts an idealized – and insulated – paternalism and relegates the issues she cannot resolve to the background of her narrative."[5] An examination of the metaphorical "rapes" by Villefort and Montoni may help to clarify Radcliffe's position, and suggest both that St Aubert is one of those who violate Emily's integrity, and that, despite whatever damage he does, he is a more or less beneficent member of his class.

Emily leans heavily on the Count de Villefort in making her decisions about Valancourt. She is overly inclined to depend upon the advice of her sympathetic and loving heart; in contrast, Villefort is overly inclined to depend upon what he knows. The struggle with the god, the struggle between Eros and Logos, is thus replicated in their encounters. In one of their conversations in the forest, the Count gives Emily incorrect information about Valancourt's decline (while meaning well, of course), and encourages her to dismiss Valancourt with only the briefest of meetings. Emily's belief in the Count causes her to take his information without hesitation, thus preventing her from questioning Valancourt more closely. Such questioning would have revealed the true circumstances of Valancourt's minor debauch in Paris, and would thus have rendered him once again worthy of her esteem, and therefore of her love.

Moreover, the Count is continually drawing Emily away from the maternal support of the convent Abbess, maintaining, like Lefevre's and Heywood's Jupiters, that she belongs in the real world. When Du Pont calls at the chateau, Emily feels the need to retire to the convent, a need for which the Count reproves her, insisting that only in the outside world will she recover from her sense of emotional loss. He feels, moreover, that his superior knowledge and experience make him more able to judge her situation than she. As Emily proposes to retire again, in an effort to regain her tranquility, the Count argues that he knows the only way to restore her emotional health, and utters his refrain: "Leave me to understand your heart" (494).

His control over her is such that she fears that if she stays in the convent after she has been invited to Chateau-le-Blanc, there will be "an appearance of caprice in her refusal, which she could not persevere in, without offending the friends, whose esteem she valued." (564). This situation reveals two important facets of her relationship to the Villefort family. First, her worry about seeming capricious reveals the extent to which she knows they expect her to conform to their wishes. Second, it reminds us of the helplessness of her orphan state. Without the protection of the Count, she cannot move about in the world outside the convent with any freedom or appearance of propriety.

To a certain extent, the Count takes advantage of her friendless situation, much as Zeus took advantage of Callisto's separation. His meritorious advice is inevitably given on their forest walks. While there is obviously no sexual encounter involved, his efforts to control her feelings and her future – efforts benighted by both his lack of knowledge of the facts of Valancourt's "fall" and of the ways of a woman's heart – do temporarily damage her.

Like both Villeroi and St Aubert, Montoni seeks control of Emily's sensibility. His edicts to her are an amplified version of her father's. When she asks Montoni the cause of their sudden departure from Venice, he observes that he is not in the mood to answer questions, and suggests that such questions would be unnecessary if she were more sensible: "I recommend it to you to retire to your chamber, and to endeavour to adopt a more rational conduct, than that of yielding to fancies, and to a sensibility, which, to call it by the gentlest name, is only a weakness." Thus she is forbidden to inquire about her own fate. Similarly, when she discovers a second unlocked door to her room and asks for a new chamber, he again attacks her "sensibility": "If you will not release yourself from the slavery of these fears ... at least forbear to torment others by the mention of them. Conquer such whims, and endeavour to strengthen your mind. No existence is more contemptible than that, which is embittered by fear" (244).

These exhortations are exaggerations of the sermons of St Aubert and the Count de Villefort, evoked here in circumstances which show all of the autocracy of their originators. After all, Emily has a right to know whether or not Montoni still expects her to marry Morano, as well as a right to protect herself from possible rape by Montoni's unprincipled fellow banditti. These demands that she be more rational are based upon a notion common to all three men and the age in which they live: that women need firm guidance in everything, and this is man's duty to give such guidance. While this notion underlies all of the advice of St Aubert and Villefort, it is articulated fully only by Montoni. It is as if only the villain can acknowledge the villainous truth regarding his real opinion of women.

Emily is continually represented by Montoni as a typical member of her sex, lacking "sincerity and uniformity of conduct" (210), which are, along with obedience, "virtues which are indispensable to a woman" (270). He expects, of course, that these very "virtues" will enable him to perpetuate two metaphorical rapes of Emily. The first is, of course, the "sale" of Emily to Count Morano, the price being Emily's estates in Gascony. The second is his attempt to defraud Emily of property she should inherit from her aunt, Madame Montoni. Having Emily safely captive in the forest-surrounded Udolpho, where he is threatened from without by a veritable wasteland of debt and intrigue, and where he disguises his purposes insofar as possible through deceit, Montoni attempts first to flatter Emily by telling her that she possesses "an understanding superior to that of [her] sex; and that [she] has none of those contemptible foibles, that frequently mark the female character – such as avarice and the love of power, which later makes women delight to contradict and to tease, when they cannot conquer" (380). When this fails, he tries, like Comus, to reason Emily out of her aunt's estates. Like the Lady, however, Emily is well-armed with logic: she knows "the laws on the subject" (280), and, moreover, defeats Montoni's whole argument by proposing that if the estates are legally his, he certainly does not need her signature to release them.

She complies with his wish only when threatened with rape by Verezzi or any of Montoni's unprincipled officers. Aware that the price of her aunt's estates will be her honour, she signs them over to him, thus securing his protection from the amorous attentions of his men. One kind of rape replaces another. Thus while Montoni himself evinces no sexual attraction to Emily, part of his control over her consists of sexual threats by his representatives.

Morano is, of course, also a sexual threat, and is, at the same time, another of the Zeus figures – not one of those in the Apollonian disguise, but a man who is madly in love with Emily – implying, but only implying, sexual passion and desire. Like the Jupiter in the medieval and Renaissance works, Morano meets Emily at court, in Venetian society, where she has no sympathetic protectors. Caught in the wasteland of his passion and his gambling debts, which he hopes to pay off with Emily's estates, the Count presses Montoni to make a deal.

When the arrangement for the sale of Emily is cancelled because of the discovery that Morano has disguised himself as a wealthy suitor and has no intention of signing over Emily's estates to Montoni, the Count tries to take her from Udolpho by force. He fails partly because, like Comus, he would rather have Emily choose him than force her, and his arguments delay him long enough for Montoni to rout his party, much as the brothers rout Comus and his party. And much as Milton's Lady began to achieve the Renaissance version of psychological virginity, we begin here to see Emily exhibiting her own unusual strengths and resolves, as if the tests do indeed expose unexpected virtues.

Morano has his noble counterpart in M. Du Pont, who finally does "abduct" Emily from Udolpho. Du Pont appears to Emily in a number of disguises: she sees him as an apparition which she supposes first to be the ghost of Laurentini and later the spirit of her aunt, whom she presumes dead. These "disguises" give him the appearance of women who serve as Diana figures, figures of guidance, in Emily's career. His second disguise is instigated by the songs he sings in the quiet evenings, songs which are familiar to Emily, and which she concludes come from Valancourt. Their mutual escape frees both of them from the wasteland of Udolpho.

Each of Emily's encounters with men has some aspect of the Callisto myth underlying its structure, and its imagery as well. To see *The Mysteries of Udolpho* as a Callisto narrative is primarily to see that rape includes certain acts and attitudes which are not usually associated with either sex or violence. The desire of St Aubert, Montoni, and Villefort to confine Emily's feelings to a certain acceptable range is a kind of rape; Montoni's intention to take advantage of Emily's helplessness and force her to marry a man she does not love, and his subsequent attempts to deprive her of her inheritance constitute rape; Villefort's careless judgments, which he considers to be based upon superior knowledge and experience, and forces on Emily, are rape; and Morano's attempts to arrange a marriage with a woman who does not love him are also rape.

By seeing these examples of typical patriarchal control as rape, we see them in their full seriousness. In a sense, Radcliffe appends her signature to the myth by telling us that these are the kinds of rape which violated the integrity of eighteenth-century women and kept them from being fully independent. Until a woman is economically independent, until she is free to choose her husband, free from being forced into "matches," free to determine her own fate, free to make her own judgments, and free from paternalistic control of her emotions, questions regarding the sexual aspects of psychological virginity are almost beside the point.

The notion of rape reflects those means by which eighteenth-century men controlled women. When Montoni, for example, cites sincerity, uniformity of conduct, and obedience as virtues which are indispensible to a woman, he is merely reiterating the expectations of his society. Woman must conform. Even Emily's aunt, Madame Montoni, demands that Emily conform. To obey the edicts of her father is, moreover, to comply with his prescription of psychic health. To follow without questioning the advice of Villefort, to visit Chateau-le-Blanc when requested, so as not to seem capricious, are other versions of submission.

The sense which we frequently have of Emily as excessively weak and passive rises from our misperception of her docile behaviour. We mistake passivity for powerlessness. The fate of Callisto suggests that the demands of the patriarchy constitute a kind of social rape, and that to resist that violation is to risk exile. To displease the Count de Villefort is to be exiled from her only protection; to fail to live up to her father's standards is to be exiled from his esteem, one of the most vaunted values of the novel. We see in the section that takes place at Udolpho that to rebel has its very real physical dangers. To disobey Montoni is to be exiled to the east turret or to be prey to the animal passions of his fellow banditti.

In *Love, Mystery, and Misery*, Carol Ann Howells points out that Emily is powerless: "She cannot influence her environment in any way and indeed the outside world is unresponsive to her at very crucial times. It is from this sense of Emily's powerlessness that we derive our image of her as a victim of circumstances and perhaps it is her own awareness of it that generates her deep melancholy and frustration."[6] The extent to which the passivity of the perpetual victim is inculcated in her is expressed in one of her verses which deals with a pilgrim attacked by a robber. As he dies, "his spirit knew no vengeful care, / But, dying, for his murd'rer breath'd – a sainted pray'r!" (415).

Emily's powerlessness is also indicated by her financial dependence. Notes Mary Poovey, "money, in fact, lurks behind every turn of *The Mysteries'* plot. Emily's hysteria within Udolpho is ultimately a consequence of her legal dependence on Montoni; as an orphan, she is penniless and powerless; as a female she has no legal rights."[7] It is Emily's financial dependence that puts her in the position of being raped – both metaphorically and literally. For Montoni to possess estates that are rightfully Emily's is really to do no more than the typical eighteenth-century husband.[8] If he cannot browbeat and threaten her into submission, he suggests that rape, by Verezzi, will. Either act would produce the same results: "In a society in which a single woman's value is intimately tied to both sexual purity and endowed property, the consequences of sexual and economic exploitation are effectively identical: either would curtail Emily's chance of attaining social identity through the only avenue open to her – marriage."[9]

While the threats to Emily's economic and emotional stability represent one kind of rape, they are a kind of violation that can be undone. In spite of being forced by Montoni to sign over her estates, Emily finally regains them after his inglorious death. Regardless of her father's criticism of her oversensitive behaviour, she endures the threats of defeat, death, despair, and loss. And even though the Count convinces her to renounce the unworthy Valancourt, she regains him once his true worth is proven.

What cannot be renewed is physical virginity; it and its psychological counterpart can be maintained only if the heroine is able to choose her mate. The Callisto myth in this respect is a myth about choice. When Montoni tries to force Count Morano on Emily, when Du Pont is substituted for Valancourt, Emily's right to choose is threatened.

Emily's powerlessness in the face of St Aubert, Villefort, and Montoni is not only a function of a dependent position which makes her prey to their various kinds of control, but is also exacerbated by her isolation from women who can help her. The heroine as orphan is a heroine without a mother who can instruct her in her femininity; without her mother's guidance, she is left, like Callisto, to discover the implications of being a woman for herself. In this respect, the myth suggests that under the patriarchy there is no ready or willing guide to the experiences of womanhood. The one figure who might have protected Emily from Montoni's greed and Morano's lust is Madame Montoni. Yet like Hera, subject of so much humiliation from Zeus, Madame Montoni is so much a victim of the patriarchal values that she becomes their advocate. Consciously unaware of the extent to which she has been "raped," that is, fooled into a marriage she believes to be more beneficial to herself than to Montoni, Madam Montoni exerts what power she has over Emily. Only after Montoni begins to demand the resignation of her own estates does Madame Montoni come to sympathize with Emily and to realize that they are fellow victims. But at this point Montoni's desires have become so extreme that the only lesson Madam Montoni can leave Emily is to resist at the risk of death.

The two other women involved in Emily's career, the Marchioness de Villeroi and Laurentini, represent two extremes of femininity, one too passive, the other too aggressive. The Marchioness, in effect, teaches Emily the fate of those who conform. Having obediently married a man she did not love and who did not love her, she almost passively submits to her husband's poisoning. Laurentini, on the other hand, illustrates the fate of the woman who refuses to meet all the conventions of feminine propriety, and who, seeming too willful to her lover, forfeits the possibility of a legal union with him.

Significantly, Emily learns the full story of both women and her relationship to them only from the convent Abbess. That which her father has withheld, that which remained a mystery at Udolpho, is explained by another woman in a location removed from the male world, one of the few places where the patriarchy does not rule. The patriarchy seems to conspire against such a discovery: St Aubert, while trusting the Abbess with the information regarding his daughter's relationship with the Marchioness, asks her to withhold it, while the Count would have Emily eschew the convent altogether.

The patriarchy prefers that women remain ignorant; this imposed ignorance becomes the means by which men metaphorically effect the disguise Zeus takes in the myth. Consequently, we realize again and again that Emily's credulity is her worst enemy. In almost every case of rape, it is either ignorance or innocence which makes her vulnerable. In her innocence, she allows her father to shape her femininity; in her ignorance, she allows Villefort to influence her wrongly about Valancourt. Had she trusted her feminine judgment more, she would have been less likely to allow these paternal teachers to influence her to such an extent. Similarly, had Callisto known more about the feminine, which the goddess symbolizes, she might have realized that the person who approached her was merely disguised as a woman and might have been able to prevent her own rape.

Nevertheless, everything suggests that in spite of her apparent weakness, in spite of the conspiracy of the patriarchy, Emily does achieve a measure of psychological virginity. The acquisition of a sanctioned but weakened husband, the circumstances which finally allow her to exercise her choice in marriage, the acquisition of fortune and family, all point to a strengthened Emily whose marriage will represent the true beginning, rather than the end, of her power as a woman.

When Valancourt is finally proven worthy of Emily's love, we see that her intuitive sensibility is validated. In spite of all the arguments of Villefort and the attractiveness of Du Pont, Emily's feelings for Valancourt remain absolutely constant, even though she knows that according to the precepts of her father she ought to have been able to will her heart into relinquishing its love for him. Even while her head "knows" that Valancourt is unworthy, her heart cannot stop instinctively returning to the notion that an unworthy Valancourt is an impossibility. By remaining true to her own perceptions in the face of all those who would question or negate them, she achieves that certification of her female nature and knowledge which identifies her with the psychological virgin. Such validation, however, does not come from without: no one acknowledges that her faith in Valancourt was well-placed. Instead, she experiences only a sense of relief that Valancourt has proven true, and remains wholly unaware of the way in which her "feminine" intuition has triumphed. Thus she continues to believe that the validation of her inner worth must come from without.

She displays more awareness of her triumph in holding out against Morano, Verezzi, and Du Pont. But Emily's most obvious strength is displayed when she resists all of Montoni's threats, largely because she understands them as insults to her dignity or views them with moral contempt. In turn, Madame Montoni and her husband think of her as a foolish girl who is ignoring the "excellence" of the match with Morano, and who insists stubbornly on some ideal marriage with her beloved Valancourt. What she insists upon, however, is as much her right to *choose* as her love for Valancourt.

A more subtle aspect of Emily's insistence on choice is expressed in her two refusals to marry Valancourt. Choice determines not only whom to marry, but also when to marry. She refuses him both times because to marry him at that juncture would not fully validate her as wife. If one of Emily's goals is the "social identity" achieved through marriage, then her marriage cannot be clandestine, one which society does not approve of or does not acknowledge. At the point at which Valancourt suggests elopement, neither he nor Emily possess the fortune or the approval of their respective families needed to give their marriage social validity. In another time, a Callisto figure may possess the inner strength to dare to make a marriage of which society does not approve; in another time, a Callisto figure may not need to depend upon her identity in marriage to validate her self. Emily possesses neither the inner strength nor the milieu to make what we might perceive to be the "right" decision regarding the elopement with Valancourt, so she must undergo further strengthening tests.

As it is, their marriage comes not only after Valancourt is proven worthy, but after Emily has acquired two means of power in French society: a fortune and a family. These powers are bestowed upon her after Valancourt's innocence is mentioned to Villefort but before it is mentioned to Emily, and before her marriage to Valancourt – not with it, as is typical of middle-class heroines who marry well. So she becomes a force in the world without the appendage of husband, becomes a woman with the power to gain or maintain psychological virginity even under the aegis of wedlock.

While her fortune comes only by virtue of Montoni's death, and her relation to Villefort is an accident of birth, these things are not unearned. She does, after all, outlive Montoni essentially by outwitting him. And her steadfastness at the bedside of sister Agnes, her unwillingness to withdraw until she has heard all Agnes has to tell, earns her the right to hear the rest of the story from the Abbess.

Other circumstances seem to conspire to make Emily the strong partner in the union. Although Valancourt's brother sees to it that part of his "rich domain" goes to Valancourt, the rest to descend to the younger on the elder's death, Emily's fortune is, for the time being, the greater of the two; it is to her estates that they retire to live their unsullied life.

We must realize, too, that the behaviour of Valancourt in Paris, while not as despicable as it had been painted, was not wholly honourable. While he was gambling, however naively, in Paris, Emily was continually withstanding not mere temptation, but frightening threats. She remains, as it were, in a much stronger moral position than Valancourt. His relative weakness is perhaps best symbolized by his being shot as a common thief by Emily's gardener: he is Zeus made quite mortal.

It becomes evident, then, that the Callisto figure acquires a host of things which Harding would not necessarily associate with psychological virginity. First, she gains a certain knowledge of herself, a certain strength of will which is indicated by her determination to marry the man she loves and no one else. She also gains two very practical means to power in the social world: family connections and family money. Finally, the lover that she marries, by the time she marries him, no longer resembles the god of the myth but has been revealed as quite mortal through his faults. Although she may not have achieved psychological virginity through ravishment by the god, she has achieved power, and that, for Radcliffe, seems an acceptable substitute.

CHAPTER FIVE

Jane Eyre: *Even Plain Jane Can Be a Nymph*

Jane Eyre is one of the nineteenth century's literary oddities, for it is a novel of considerable power written by a relatively inexperienced young woman. In attempting to account for this paradox, critics have generally resorted to source studies, the ingenuity of which has largely been limited to combing the obscure works of the Gothic era in hopes of finding a precursor for *Jane Eyre*. Oddly enough, none of these studies has suggested *Mysteries of Udolpho* as a possible source, although there are great similarities in plot: Jane and Emily are both orphans; both display an almost heroic effort to be their own persons; both young women undergo a series of trials in their efforts to gain their beloveds on their own terms; and both finally inherit fortune and, with fortune, family, just before they marry their suitors. That *Mysteries of Udolpho* is a source for *Jane Eyre* is not being argued here; what is being argued is that the power of *Jane Eyre* has to do with its evocation of the same myth which informs *Mysteries of Udolpho*.

The sharp outlines of the myth are certainly present in the plot of *Jane Eyre*. Jane is an orphan who, like the Callistos of the Renaissance tradition, recognizes her powerlessness and begs to be sent away to school. The all-girls school at Lowood functions precisely as Diana's band, and is headed by a beautiful young woman who is frequently associated with the moon. Later Jane becomes governess at Thornfield, a hall renowned for its ancient trees. Rochester, who variously disguises himself as a gypsy and an unmarried man, proposes to her in the garden, but that proposal is seen to be a kind of rape once Rochester's wife is revealed. Jane's departure from Thornfield parallels Callisto's exile in that Jane's appearance, that of a lady, belies her state, that of an indigent, and thus she cannot get help from the villagers around her.

These few details suggest that Brontë's novel derives its power not from obscure literary sources, but from mythic ones. Yet an additional power comes from Brontë's ability to wed the material of myth with that of history, reflecting the situation of women in the nineteenth century with an accuracy which frightened her contemporaries: Brontë not only evokes the archetype but engraves on it a signature which demands and rewards close attention.

Jane's father, not a defeated general but a dead minister who had been haunted by poverty, nevertheless leaves his daughter in the same situation as Lycaon left Callisto – powerless and dependent on others. Helene Moglen describes the situation in terms which emphasize both the debilitating connection between Jane's low status and her sex, and her valiant attempts to overcome her powerlessness: "Orphaned, poor, and plain, faced with the pressures of making her own way in a world which measured the likelihood of her success by the degree of her marriageability (her familial connections, her economic status, and, above all, her beauty), Jane tests the limit of social, moral, and psychological possibility, discovering the kinds of power which are, in fact, available to a woman."[1] Brontë has admittedly given us in the young Jane the ultimate portrait of powerless woman; with no family, no money, no beauty, she has no claim to love, affection, respect, or self-respect. Moreover, she is aware, as were the medieval and Renaissance Callistos, that to have no socially-defined status is to be vulnerable. In asking to be sent to school, Jane chooses, again like Callisto, the company of women who are her peers. But whereas the medieval band of Diana was composed of ladies of rank who sought to escape the attentions of men, the girls in the school to which Jane is sent are her equals in their dispossessed position in society.

In corresponding to the virgin band of the myth, Lowood School constitutes the environment wherein Jane may learn the lessons required of nineteenth-century women. Brontë, in exploring this phase of her heroine's career in greater detail than other writers of Callisto narratives, gives us a very concrete view of the preparations for womanhood in Victorian England. Far from teaching "woman's mysteries," Lowood instead inculcates some very disturbing – but obviously functional – virtues in its inmates, while providing them with the practical accomplishments necessary to their status as "unconnected" women. There is a biting irony in the comparison of a collection of would-be governesses to Diana's virgins, for the common fate of these women who were half servant, half lady was to remain unmarried, though hardly by choice. The "myth" of the nineteenth-century governess was that she either died a spinster or was seduced by her employer.[2]

In the medieval and Renaissance redactions of the myth, Diana's band is spoken of with contempt for its heretical insistence on remaining outside the patriarchy's control; in *Jane Eyre*, the girls remain within society's control, but are still treated with the same contempt, for somehow failing, although through no fault of their own, to possess the qualities which the patriarchy attributes to respectable women. Hence the myth's virgins are transformed here into women who are not validated by the patriarchal institutions of family or money. As a result, these women are victims of a tremendously cruel double standard which Brocklehurst enforces. Described in overtly phallic imagery and essentially an intruder at Lowood who likes to play god, he "rapes" the girls by stifling any outer expression of their femininity. He purposefully starves their "vile bodies," giving his patriarchal religion as justification: "'Madam,' he pursued, 'I have a Master to serve whose kingdom is not of this world: my mission is to mortify in these girls the lusts of the flesh, to teach them to clothe themselves with shamefacedness and sobriety, not with braided hair and costly apparel; and each of the young persons before us has a string of hair twisted in plaits which vanity itself might have woven: these, I repeat, must be cut off.'"[3]

That his standards are hypocritical is demonstrated by Brocklehurst's inconsistent taste in hair. Julia Severn's natural curls are to be cut off because Lowood's precepts are conformity to grace, not nature. Yet Brocklehurst obviously has no objections to his wife's wearing a *"false* front of French curls" (97, emphasis mine).

Brocklehurst's intention in educating these girls is to enable them to make their own way in the world, yet the scene with Julia Severn's curls illustrates that he defines, as society's representative, what that way must be. Hence Jane learns at Lowood that she has the capacity to be financially and morally independent, but that within the context of this independence she must repress her desires and expect to encounter severe limitations. This paradox colours all of her tenure at Lowood as the lessons on the practical skills she will need are alternated with object lessons about the status of indigent women in a patriarchal world.

Her studies will enable her to be an independent woman in the tradition of the pre-patriarchal virgin band, as her intellectual education provides her with skills with which she means to maintain herself. In her first French class she learns to conjugate the verb *etre*, and consequently, her first French phrase will be *je suis* – I am.[4] This lesson is, in a sense, a synecdoche for her whole education: it will enable her to claim a legitimate existence.

Jane also learns the virtues of self-respect from the women around her. Maria Temple, as is suggested by the pagan associations of her last name, her position as superintendent of the school, her superior intelligence and beauty, and her frequent appearances in moonlight, is the goddess Diana of Lowood School. Like the goddess, she is all forms of woman: "Mother, governess, and latterly companion" (116). By assuring Jane that the students' assessment of her depends only upon her own behaviour, Miss Temple teaches Jane that she can control what is thought of her and that respect can be earned.

Helen Burns also contributes to these lessons through the example of her own self-containment. When Jane protests that she cannot be content without the approval of others, Helen reminds her: "If all the world hated you, and believed you wicked, while your own conscience approved you, and absolved you from guilt, you would not be without friends" (101). Helen refers only in part to the comfort Jane should take in a heavenly Father's approbation; she also alludes to a kind of self-respect that will grow in Jane and render her capable one day of saying "*I* care for myself."

Helen Burns also serves as a monitory example to Jane, illustrating the dangers of passivity. The fact that she "lives in calm, looking to the end" (91) seems inextricably tied to the fact that she dies. Like the Marchioness de Villeroi, she teaches that the wages of passivity is death. While she seems admirably endowed with the strength to "bear what it is [her] fate to bear" (88), that which Helen calls her fate is partly determined by her own refusal to take any active control over her life. She tells Jane, supposedly in comfort: "By dying young I shall escape great sufferings. I had no qualities or talents to make my way very well in the world: I should have been continually at fault" (113). We know that Helen has great intellectual capacity, so her sense that she should be "at fault" is derived not only from the habit of passivity but also from her sense that she cannot conform, as a proper orphan should, to the expectations of a world which demands certain behaviour of her because she is unconnected to wealth or family.

Like Helen Burns, Miss Temple has only a limited capacity to teach Jane. Her first name, Maria, indicates that she is a Christianized Diana figure, one shaped by the patriarchal forces in her environment. Her ability to guide and protect her pupils from Brocklehurst's practices is limited by his power as director of the school, though she invariably does what she can to circumvent his dicta. While she quietly endures the sermon about feeding the girls an extra meal of bread and cheese, the "coldness and fixity" (95) of her expression speaks of her repressed rage and rebellion. When he demands the barbering of Julia's curls and the other girls' topknots, Miss Temple must smooth away with her handkerchief an "involuntary smile" (96), knowing, along with Jane and perhaps the other girls, that whatever he "might do with the outside of the cup and platter, the inside was farther beyond his interference than he imagined" (96). Yet when he accuses Jane of lying, Miss Temple asks Jane to give her own version of her history and, independent of Brocklehurst, checks its veracity with Mr Lloyd.

The position that Miss Temple has attained as head of the school suggests that she offers an example of one rather successful means of dealing with the patriarchy: the compromise of repression. Consequently she can and does teach Jane practical ways of coping with the circumscriptions of womanhood. Along with useful accomplishments, Maria Temple teaches her pupils that servitude is inevitable and that one means of dealing with the patriarchy's expectations is frequent resort of repression of one's own desires. She teaches camouflage and resignation. These are useful tools: we cannot, much as we might now regard them as submissive, criticize their usefulness for a governess in Victorian England.[5]

So in Lowood School, Charlotte Brontë's version of Diana's band, Jane learns the lessons of nineteenth-century womanhood. She learns the necessity of disguise and evasion in the face of the patriarchy, lessons which will be useful to her in her manoeuvres with Rochester; she learns the fate of the passive; she learns as well that she need not always be nourished by the love or respect of others, but that she can feed herself on a diet of self-respect.

Yet under the tutelage of Miss Temple, Jane has disguised, even from herself, her need for adventure and change – it is as if the repressive habit adopted from Miss Temple applied to all things. When Maria marries and leaves Lowood, Jane becomes aware that her teacher has provided only an attitude of acceptance and resignation. Her own desires emerge; she longs to surmount the limits which Lowood has imposed, although her willingness to settle for "a new servitude" reflects quite faithfully the limited expectations which Lowood has instilled in her. When Jane notes "any one may serve," that "anyone" means *even* Jane Eyre.

So once alone in the "low wood," Jane goes hunting for experience in the real world by engaging herself as a governess. The first few weeks at Thornfield do not represent a drastic change: Thornfield, with its huge trees, replaces the low wood, and she is still surrounded only by women – Mrs Fairfax, Adele, Sophie, Leah, Grace Poole, and Bertha Mason. That this sample of womanhood includes only orphans, servants, and wives, and that their respective social positions are relatively equal, is perhaps indicative of the fact that the status of women is so low that the gradations within the group are meaningless.But even in the context of the real world, and a real job, Jane cannot resign herself to the constricting definitions of womanly behaviour. So she haunts the upper floors, pacing back and forth where her rebellion against the fetters of womanhood is seconded by mad Bertha's slow "ha! ha!":

Women are supposed to be very calm generally: but women feel just as men feel; they need exercise for their faculties, and a field for their efforts as much as their brothers do; they suffer from too rigid a restraint, too absolute a stagnation, precisely as men would suffer; and it is narrow-minded in their more privileged fellow-creatures to say that they ought to confine themselves to making puddings and knitting stockings, to playing on the piano and embroidering bags. It is thoughtless to condemn them, or laugh at them, if they seek to do more or learn more than custom has pronounced necessary for their sex. (141)

It is out of the frustration she feels here that Jane makes the walk to the village that ends in her meeting with Rochester. Jane's desires here are so powerful that the reader has the uncanny sense that her need for adventure has almost literally caused him to materialize, or at least that he has appeared at this point in the novel because Jane needs him. Stifled by the version of femininity which she has been given and the quiet nature that is expected of her, Jane seeks to discover some other aspects of her nature and of life. So on this evening, as Jane watches the "rising moon; pale yet as a cloud, but brightening momently" as it "looked over the Hay ... half lost in the trees" (143), she sees Rochester for the first time.

There is a distinct reversal of the myth here, for it is Jane who seeks Rochester, not the other way around, and thus she defies the conventions of the myth and of her time. The suggestion implicit in this active search for experience is that she seeks initiation; this fact is also indicated in that her romance with Rochester is conducted entirely within the context of the company of women at Thornfield, just as a woman's initiation occurs within the context of worship of the goddess.

Although there is a reversal of myth at the beginning of their romance, the rest remains true to form. The imagery that is applied to Rochester is alone enough to assure us that he is playing Zeus to Jane's Callisto, for he is frequently associated with the sun, and hence the sun god of the myth. "How joyless will sunshine be if he is absent" (178), Jane thinks to herself at one point. His affection seems to "warm ... one like a fostering sunbeam" (216); and she surmises that his wife will "be the very happiest woman the sun shines on" (216). When she returns from the interlude at Gateshead, she basks in the "real sunshine of feeling" which he sheds over her. Finally, when she flees Thornfield, she takes "a road which led from the sun" (351).

The wasteland which Rochester seeks to renew by marrying Jane is a psyche charred by his ghastly marriage to Bertha Mason. As if to underline the extent to which the myth informs this work, the scorched world which Zeus is trying to restore when he meets Callisto is echoed twice when Bertha sets fire first to Rochester's bed, and later to the whole of Thornfield.

Jane's rescue of Rochester on the evening of the fire is part of a pattern of similar rescues. In fact, Jane is first attracted to Rochester because he seems to need her: having fallen from his horse, he needs her as a prop; he needs her company to divert him from his miseries; he needs her to nurse Mason; and finally he needs her to refresh his own life. Jane's apparent ability to heal the scars through a union with Rochester is illustrated in a number of ways. On a concrete, practical level, Jane's cool-headedness and her intelligence make her a person who reacts calmly in the emergencies which arise. But Rochester's allusion to Jane as a "disguised deity" (168) who will bring a "regeneration of life" (247) when she marries him suggests that her power extends beyond the practical to the cosmic. This imagery suggests that Jane, rather than being the innocent victim of rape, is more akin to the

Kalliste who was Diana's local aspect in Arcadia, and who, as the Great Goddess, could join with the sky god in a sacred marriage that would regenerate the earth. When this regenerative union cannot occur, Jane speaks of its failure in natural terms: "A Christmas frost had come at midsummer; a white December storm had whirled over June; ice glazed the ripe apples, drifts crushed the blowing roses; on hayfield and cornfield lay a frozen shroud; lanes which last night blushed full of flowers, to-day were pathless with untrodden snow; and the woods, which twelve hours since waved leafy and fragrant as groves between the tropics, now spread, vast, wild, and white as pine-forests in wintry Norway" (323). This imagery recalls the natural wasteland of the myth, while referring to Jane's and Rochester's inability both to effect a cosmic regeneration of the world at Thornfield, and to renew the waste of Rochester's personal life.

Rochester has turned to her because he believes that she can renew the psychic wasteland which he inhabits. But *Jane Eyre* addresses itself to the limits of power for women, and Brontë does not allow herself to be seduced into giving Jane a goddess-like power greater than that which her social status would afford her. Consequently, while establishing the possibilities for regeneration, Brontë also carries on with those aspects of the myth – the god's disguise and his seduction – to explore the ways in which Jane is *not* like the goddess.

Rochester comes to Jane in a number of literal disguises: she first believes he's the Gytrash; later he dresses as an old gypsy to tell Jane's fortune. His most significant disguises, however, are of his marital status and his supposedly egalitarian attitude toward the "poor, plain, disconnected governess" whom he is to marry. Jane is initially seduced by his regard for her as an equal, by her ability to be his equal in the banter, and by his forgetting that she is a paid subordinate.

She seems deliberately to ignore the fact that he wants to play the part of a Zeus-like initiator. While she claims the moral superiority of innocence, he is well aware of the practical leverage which experience gives him, and warns her, "You have no right to preach to me, you neophyte, that have not passed the porch of life and are absolutely unacquainted with its mysteries … By what instinct do you pretend to distinguish between a fallen seraph of the abyss and a messenger from the eternal throne – between a guide and a seducer?" (167–8). This language not only reminds us of Zeus' ritualistic role in initiation, but strikes us as false candour, yet another disguise. Rochester's account of his affair with Celine Varens similarly strikes us as disingenuous. But Rochester has so accurately assessed Jane's sympathies that he knows she will view him as the disappointed lover, badly in need of purification and affection, or renewal. His whole behaviour during the courtship is a series of disguises. He pretends to court Blanche Ingram, for example. On more than one occasion he speaks ambiguously to Jane: after she has rescued him from his bed he departs by saying, "My cherished preserver, good night!" (182), leaving Jane suspicious, but not entirely sure of his feelings, much as Callisto is not sure of "Diana's" true sex and intentions.

Because of the prolonged nature of Jane and Rochester's courtship, two other images which are part of the myth's iconography repeat themselves: the struggle with the god and the seduction. Jane's struggles begin when she first suspects that Rochester cares for her in some special way – a suspicion which causes her to admit that she cares deeply for him.

Her struggle is manifested in two ways. First, her overwhelming awareness that she is poor, plain, and disconnected makes her realize that a union with Rochester is inappropriate to their relative social statuses. His social and economic standing is but a functional version of Zeus' godliness, and Jane, in contrast, feels very much the helpless, inferior mortal. What is disturbing is the way in which this perception of their inequality causes her to denigrate herself: she is "a dependent and a novice ... governess, disconnected, poor, and plain ... indigent and insignificant plebeian" (190–1). She is preoccupied with the differences in their respective stations, and these differences haunt their entire courtship. Disturbed by the fact that he is "a gentleman of family and a man of the world" and she a mere "dependent and a novice" (190), Jane wages a battle within her own soul between the forces of "imagination" and "common sense," between "sentiment" and "self-control" (190–1).

A second struggle is more literally represented when Rochester grasps the beloved who he knows will soon leave him. The passage is worth considering for the fiery imagery that recalls the mythic original and the body-soul dichotomy found in Milton's masque: "He crossed the floor and seized my arms and grasped my waist. He seemed to devour me with his flaming glance: physically, I felt, at the moment, powerless as stubble exposed to the draught and glow of a furnace: mentally I still possessed my soul, and with it the certainty of ultimate safety" (344).

While Jane is trying to figure out what to do about their differences in station, her psyche is trying to cope with the forces of Eros and Logos within herself in order to arrive at a true and whole balance. E. Margaret Fulton also notes this conflict in Jane, although not in the context of the myth, and describes Jane's task as one which will "bring into balance the logical, rational, reasoning, or so-called masculine side of her being with the intuitive, instinctive, spiritual, or so-called feminine side."[6] Logos reminds her of the laws (common sense and self-control) to which their relationship is subject: laws of class, laws of church and state, economic laws. But at the same time, Eros urges her love for Rochester. Jane can become a psychological virgin only when these two qualities are balanced within herself. At the same time, it is clear that she needs, like Milton's Lady and like Emily St

Aubert in her arguments with Montoni, a preponderance of logic for self-defense.

That her awareness of her social position relative to Rochester's is an impediment to their love is most strongly displayed in the actual seduction scene. Here the mythic overtones are evinced by the setting of Rochester's proposal to Jane, which occurs, like so many of their encounters, in the orchard, when "sunset is thus meeting with moonrise" (277). There the two struggles, psychic and political, meet as Jane's "emotion, stirred by grief and love within [her] was claiming mastery, and struggling for full sway, and asserting a right to predominate, to overcome, to live, rise, and reign at last: yes – and to speak" (280–1). The emotion with which she speaks tells of the rise of Eros; it is this rise, significantly, that allows her to be "raped." Brontë suggests, therefore, that a woman who allows herself to be ruled by her feelings for another is more vulnerable to various kinds of violation.

But Jane's impassioned manifesto of spiritual equality evinces her preoccupation with a worldly inequality which is the only impediment to their love:

"I tell you I must go!" I retorted, roused to something like passion. "Do you think I can stay to become nothing to you? Do you think I am an automaton? – a machine without feelings? and can bear to have my morsel of bread snatched from my lips, and my drop of living water dashed from my cup? Do you think, because I am poor, obscure, plain, and little, I am soulless and heartless? You think wrong! – I have as much soul as you – and full as much heart! And if God had fitted me with some beauty and much wealth, I should have made it as hard for you to leave me, as it is now for me to leave you. I am not talking to you now through the medium of custom, conventionalities, nor even of mortal flesh: it is my spirit that addresses your spirit; just as if both had passed through the grave, and we stood at God's feet, equal – as we are!" (281)

In the psychic struggle, Eros has won, but Jane is still aware of the impending worldly battle, so that when Rochester obliquely declares that he will marry the woman who is his spiritual equal, the social inferior continues to wrestle with the situation. Rochester's words – "'My bride is here ... because my equal is here, and my likeness'" – speak of a union based on equality. But the equality is *only* spiritual, and the subsequent events of their courtship seem to say that spiritual equality is not worth a whit unless it is seconded by a worldly equality of class and fortune.

Jane's realization of this fact begins the next day when Rochester sends for the family jewels and tries to buy her half a dozen dresses in colours that would outshine her own plain exterior, thus making her cheek "burn with a sense of annoyance and degradation" (297). When Jane asks permission for Adele to join them on the shopping trip and Rochester refuses, Jane almost loses "the sense of power over him" and even though he finally allows Adele to join them because the "sunshine is gone" (294) from his Jane, she certainly realizes that her influence over him depends entirely on his willingness to be swayed. So aware is she of her dependent position that she makes a financial arrangement with Rochester which both openly acknowledges her dependent situation and enables her to rise above it. By remaining Adele's governess, she argues, she will earn her keep and thirty pounds a year to furnish her wardrobe, thus needing nothing but Rochester's "regard" (298). Then she tells him, "If I give you mine in return, that debt will be quit" (298).

The threat to Jane's integrity comes about as a direct result of financial dependence: as Moglen observes, "economic and social status seem after all to be minimal conditions of sexual equality. These would at least lend support to the sense of self which makes love possible in a patriarchal world."[7] Thus, in *Jane Eyre*, the worldly struggle with the god manifests itself as a power struggle between Jane and Rochester that has two dimensions. She is aware that her influence over Rochester is limited to her ability to manipulate him. She is also aware that her own poverty places her in an anomalous position. Jane is, unlike Emily perhaps, aware of the extent to which she must continually parry for power with her beloved.

Bertha Mason is obviously the literal impediment to their marriage, but we must not fail to see that Jane's unwillingness to remain in an economically dependent position causes her to write the letter to her uncle, thus setting off the chain of events which reveals Bertha's existence. Much has been made of Bertha Mason: she is most frequently seen as a monitory figure, warning Jane about the dangers of unlicensed passion.[8] In more recent criticism she is perceived as Jane's shadow, a dark doppelganger who acts out Jane's anger and frustration.[9]

It is important here to see why, in the context of the myth, Bertha is the appropriate impediment in the confluence of archetype and signature. As Rochester's wife, she is a Hera figure, avenging her husband's infidelities by burning him in his bed when he relates the tale of his affair with Celine Varens and by rending the governess' wedding veil but a few nights before the wedding day. She is not merely a woman who has let passion loose, she is a woman of profound anger. As Adrienne Rich points out, Rochester condemns her as "at once intemperate and unchaste," but his criticism of his own affairs is quite in accordance with the Victorian double standard: minimal.[10] Karen B. Mann has observed that Bertha's rage is not so much passion as "the outward expression of malevolence bred by a system which denies her a separate will and imprisons her in a marriage that is primarily a monetary bargain."[11]

We know that one role of Hera is to punish the girls to whom Zeus has taken a fancy, which is understandable, given her powerlessness over the god and her inability to force him to remain faithful to her. But she is also "essentially the goddess' representative of women, especially as wives, and *protectress* of marriage."[12] If Bertha is a monitory figure, she warns Jane not only about the dangers of female passion, but about the truths of female powerlessness. Bertha is no threat to Jane; what she tears up is the expensive wedding veil which represents, as Mann has suggested, the "riches Rochester intends to bestow on Jane."[13]

By tearing the veil, Bertha utters a Hera-like warning to Jane about her anomalous economic and social position. A woman's social status in the nineteenth century was almost entirely dependent upon her ability to marry well: she was defined, socially and legally, by her husband. It has been difficult enough for Jane to accept that, "unconnected" but nevertheless a "lady" in behaviour and education, she cannot transcend the role of a governess – a dependent – without marrying. But Bertha's existence makes it clear that Jane cannot, in her present condition, transcend her status *even by marrying*. The implication is that as long as woman gains social definition only in marriage and only by a definition bestowed by the husband-patriarch, she really remains mistress and dependent. She is certainly *not* self-defined, much less a psychological virgin.

We may sympathetically condone Rochester's handling of the situation, feeling that his inability to divorce a mad wife justifies his plan to marry Jane without morally endangering either of them. But he has been short-sighted about the practical effects of the situation. Even supposing that Bertha's relation to him might remain secret throughout his life, Jane's position would be extraordinarily insecure when her older husband dies. He has admitted that Bertha will likely live longer than he, and Jane is twenty years his junior. We might hypothetically consider what happens after his death when matters at Thornfield Hall are looked into. Rochester, in agonizing over the morality of the question and in considering it from that point of view, camouflages the real damage that he would do to Jane. Marriage promises definite status; in marrying her bigamously he would do exactly the reverse, and would place her in the thoroughly ambiguous position of kept woman.

Jane's protection from such a rape is again Logos, as if the only way for a woman to protect herself from the male is to allow masculine qualities to come to the fore. When Rochester assures her that he did not intend to make Jane his mistress, she replies: "Sir, your wife is living: that is a fact acknowledged this morning by yourself. If I lived with you as you desire – I should then be your mistress: to say otherwise is sophistical – is false" (331). Like Emily, who recalls the teaching of her father when she refuses Valancourt, Jane realizes that "if [she] were so far to forget herself and all the teaching that had ever been instilled in [her] ... to become successor to these poor girls, he would one day regard [her] with the same feeling which now in his mind desecrated their memory" (339). Also like Emily, who denies her feeling for Valancourt because of what she owes herself,[14] Jane denies her love and pity for Rochester by saying "*I* care for myself" (334). This is Jane's manifesto of psychological virginity.

Indeed, Rochester is very aware of her untouchability in a way that recalls Comus:

"Never," said he, as he ground his teeth, "never was anything at once so frail and so indomitable. A mere reed she feels in my hand!"(And he shook me with the force of his hold.) "I could bend her with my finger and thumb: and what good would it do if I bent, if I uptore, if I crushed her? Consider that eye: consider the resolute, wild, free thing looking out of it, defying me, with more than courage – with a stern triumph. Whatever I do with its cage, I cannot get at it – the savage, beautiful creature! If I tear, if I rend the slight prison, my outrage will only let the captive loose. Conqueror I might be of the house; but the inmate would escape to heaven before I could call myself possessor of its clay dwelling-place. And it is you, spirit – with will and energy, and virtue and purity – that I want: not alone your brittle frame. Of yourself you could come with soft flight and nestle against my heart, if you would: seized against your will, you will elude the grasp like an essence – you will vanish ere I inhale your fragrance." (344–5)

The physical woman is, then, a minor concern. What Rochester wants is her soul, and he wants it, significantly, with her psychological virginity intact.

Jane Eyre was always strongly in possession of her soul, and the temptation to "marry" Rochester, to submit to his "rape," is the ultimate test of Jane's true independence, her ability to be autonomous in spite of the whole world forsaking her. But Brontë's narrative also tells us once again that spiritual independence is nothing without the backing of economic independence and financial connections. Consequently Jane sets out in search of these.

Jane's journey to Moor House recalls the exile of other Callisto figures: without money or social position she has no means of fulfilling her own needs. Having left her purse in the coach, she is penniless; since she is dressed like a lady, her begging is not perceived as sincere. Like Callisto, the distance between outward appearance and inward reality renders her completely in exile from civilization. This experience is not altogether different from what her fate would have been had she married Rochester, except in degree. Jane is put through the ultimate test and succeeds only by virtue of her indomitable will to live, her resistance to the passive attitude.

Her reward is, like that of Emily St Aubert, both family and fortune. Jane's uncle dies the same month that Bertha Mason jumps to her death. Unknown to Jane, she becomes heiress and cousin; at the same time, and also unknown to Jane, the literal obstacle to her marriage with Rochester dies. This coincidence is a very subtle detail of the novel which stresses the way in which Bertha symbolizes Jane's economically and socially disenfranchised position, in addition to being a real impediment. Once she is a rich heiress and Bertha is dead, nothing remains to prevent her marriage with Rochester.

In both *Mysteries of Udolpho* and *A Mask Presented at Ludlow Castle*, the passionate Zeus is given an Apollonian complement. St John Rivers, as the word incarnate in both his name and character, is the representative of Logos in *Jane Eyre*. His overemphasis upon this aspect of his own personality, and his insistence that it reign in Jane, force her to re-balance herself. What St John's logic demands of her is the patriarchy's version of womanhood: complete passivity in the face of his demands. He denies her femininity altogether, expecting her willingly to submit to a marriage with a man who tells her that she is "formed for labour, not for love" (428). In the face of this kind of attack, Jane re-learns the feminine, reclaims the necessary freedom of heart and soul, the need to have "recesses in [her] mind which would be only [hers], to allow the fire of passion to burn truly" (423). When she expresses the passion with which she feels her feminine nature and feminine needs being threatened, Rivers declares her words "violent, *unfeminine*, and untrue" (438, emphasis mine).

Rochester, in trying to seduce Jane into marrying him, is attempting "physical rape" by undermining Jane's social position. But St John attempts what Inga-Stina Ewbank significantly terms a "more grievous spiritual rape" when, in an effort to get Jane to marry him, he clearly demands that she give up her essential femininity.[15]

What she then needs is to regain a sense of her own womanhood. Diana and Mary Rivers are instrumental in this. Their names suggest the primary pagan and Christian female deities, but in this phase Diana is always the stronger of the two, as Mary/Maria was stronger earlier in Jane's life. And significantly, it is Diana who, learning of her brother's proposal and its terms, proclaims it "insupportable – unnatural – out of the question!" (441). Here Jane re-learns the validity of feminine intelligence and feminine strength, both through the examples of Diana and through the supportive affection both sisters have for her, an affection which once again gives her strength and security.

As it is Diana Rivers who supports her in her quest for independence, it is also the Great Mother, the Moon Goddess, who, with the "mysterious call through the Night ... saves her and prevents what would have been total loss of her own self."[16] In the final battle for her soul, Jane listens for "God's will" (444), to determine her fate. What she hears instead is Rochester's voice inspired by moonlight – the first thing he has really seen since being blinded – carried by nature. In returning to marry him in the forests at Ferndean, Jane completes the cycle of the myth.

The changes in their relative status exemplify the myth's matriarchal manifestation that had been suggested by the earlier regenerative imagery. Much has been made of Jane's superiority over Rochester at this point in the novel: Richard Chase refers to Rochester's loss of hand and eyes as a symbolic castration.[17] Other criticism also runs along these lines, suggesting that a relationship which had once been that of daughter and father is now transformed to that of mother and son. What is important is that Rochester has been undeified: he is no longer god and idol, no longer proudly independent, no longer only giver and protector (470). Instead, he needs Jane's love and aid. His maiming is not a comment on Rochester's sexuality, which seems to be still strong: Jane tells us that his "athletic strength" could not be quelled, nor his "vigorous prime blighted" (456). Nor does it indicate the terrible punishment he must undergo to subdue his fiery passion. Rather it tells us to what man must be reduced in order to bring his power to the level of woman's. Jane, an "independent woman as well as rich," is now Rochester's financial equal; connected with one of the oldest, most respectable families in Morton, she is his social equal. Even so, in order for them to be true equals, Rochester must be blinded and crippled. Rochester's maiming is a powerful comment upon the lack of sexual equality in the nineteenth century.

Charles Burkhart has noted, as have other critics, the ways in which the "sun, the creative male principal, has been associated with Rochester, just as the moon, arbiter of the female cycle, has been linked with Jane ... Sun and moon meet at Ferndean."[18] Several critics, including Adrienne Rich, Barbara Rigney, and Robert Heilman, have noted the persistent presence of the moon, "symbol of the matriarchal spirit and the Great Mother of the night sky,"[19] but without seeing Jane's very specific mythic relationship to her. Indeed, this celestial body accompanies virtually all of the important rites of passage in Jane's career: her departure from Gateshead; her meeting with Rochester; and the evening of Rochester's proposal, when she orders him to turn his face to the moon so that she can determine his honesty. It appears in shifting guises on the uncertain eve of Jane's wedding, as well as taking part in her decision to leave Thornfield; it follows her in exile and accompanies the faint sound of Rochester's entreating voice, when, seen through the trees at Ferndean, it encourages him to call out. Finally, Rochester maintains, the "honeymoon will shine our life long: its beams will only fade over your grave or mine" (475).

The moon and the goddess she symbolizes are also associated with the women who have served as models of womanhood for Jane. She associates "the disc of the clearest planet" (99) with Helen Burns; on the night Helen dies, Jane intuitively seeks her out, guided only by the light of the moon. Miss Temple is also associated with the moon on the occasion when she searches for the humiliated Jane to give her comfort. Bertha Mason howls on a night when the moon is blood red (335), and Jane is awakened by moonlight just before Bertha attacks her brother. Blanche Ingram, we are told, is molded like Diana; Diana Rivers, whose strong, independent qualities Jane admires, carries the goddess' name.

For Roger Heilman, who approaches the moon imagery in *Jane Eyre* via Robert Grave's *The White Goddess*, but without the aid of Erich Neumann's *Great Mother*, the moon symbolizes – particularly on the night Bertha Mason attacks her brother – "disorder" and intuition.[20] Other than realizing that the references to the moon in Brontë's work "turn on the note of divinity," he is not fully sure of its significance: "For the simple naming of authority she substitutes a symbolic presence – concrete, pictorially exciting, stimulatingly rich in its undefinedness and in its undeniable suggestion of independent animalistic forces and indeed of the pagan."[21] Adrienne Rich's excellent feminist interpretation of Jane's experience leads her to conclude that the references to the moon, particularly in the scene where the goddess orders her "daughter" to flee temptation, show that Jane is "in touch with the matriarchal aspect of her psyche which now warns and protects her against that which threatens her integrity." Noting that "Jane can become a wife without sacrificing a grain of her Jane Eyre-ity," Rich suggests that Jane achieves something akin to psychological virginity.[22] Barbara Rigney's comments upon this same scene go one step farther:

The moon here undoubtedly represents, in accordance with long literary tradition, primarily chastity. Yet Brontë's images are never quite so simple. For example, a similar moon often precedes the apparition of the nun in *Villette* whose mysterious life had included some sin, presumably sexual, against her vows. Perhaps Brontë would be more in accord with the Jungian psychologist M. Esther Harding, who devotes her study *Woman's Mysteries* to an analysis of the moon-mother in ancient and modern cultures. Various moon goddesses, says Harding, have represented fertility as well as chastity; they are universally autoerotic, "one-in-themselves," belonging only to themselves. If one can assume such a complexity for Brontë's image, it is possible to conclude that the moon-mother is the voice of the feminist consciousness, a kind of inner voice of sanity which, unlike the traditional patriarchal God to whom Jane frequently pays lip service, affirms self-respect and not self-denial, sexual or otherwise.[23]

Clearly this pattern of moon imagery belongs in the novel because it is demanded by the myth which informs the work – the myth of Callisto. Observing the presence of the myth makes apparent the connection which Rigney observes between the moon imagery and Jane's search for psychological virginity. Indeed, the moon's presence, in many of the scenes, seconds Jane's preference for change over the status quo, for activity over passivity. It is present when she leaves Gateshead because she has chosen to leave the known and explore the unknown, because her rebellion against the stifling atmosphere at Gateshead has won her "freedom." It is present when she walks to Hay and back because that walk results directly from Jane's refusal to accept the circumscription of Thornfield and her inactivity as governess. She hunts for activity and change, and finds it when Rochester's horse slips.

Similarly, we can envision the "temptation" which the moon exhorts Jane to flee as the temptation of passivity, for to remain where you are is always easier than to leave. What she avoids is the powerlessness of a typical Victorian marriage which is here emphasized by the fact that should she "marry" Rochester, she will find herself in the submissive position of wife without even the small leverage which legal status might give her.

Jane's ultimate act of passivity would have been to marry St John Rivers: his direction of all Jane's activities, his sense that she exists only for his purposes, could have provided Jane with a permanent escape from her human journey to selfhood. To go to India and die under the too-hot sun is a passivity not unlike starving to death. Adrienne Rich notes that what Rivers "offers Jane is perhaps the deepest lure for a spiritual woman, that of adopting a man's cause or career and making it her own. For more than one woman, still today, the felt energy of her own existence is still diffuse, the possibilities of her life vague; the man who pressures to define it for her may be her most confusing temptation. *He* will give shape to her search for meaning, her desire for service, her feminine urge toward self-abnegation: in short – as Jane becomes soon aware – he will *use* her."[24] Under St John's pressure, Jane is "tempted to cease struggling with him – to rush down the torrent of his existence, and there lose [her] own" (443). Into this mood of abnegation comes the moonlight. The moon brings with it not only Rochester's voice, but a sense for Jane that "it was [her] time to assume ascendancy. [Her] powers were in play and in force" (445). Jane thus brings about her own apotheosis with the help of the Great Goddess.

The moon seems, then, to play a part in many of Jane's struggles against comfortable passivity in the face of the patriarchy's demands that woman be still, serene, and accepting. The moon comes, in this context, to symbolize the matriarchal force that must be exerted to overcome the inertia of Victorian femaleness; only a woman's urge to become one-in-herself saves her from the oblivion of her own femininity.

Although the novel moves inevitably toward Jane's marriage with Rochester, it places certain conditions on that union, mainly requiring that it be a meeting of equals. Similarly, we must note that the endless turns in the plot of *The Mysteries of Udolpho* all work toward creating a picture of a completely disenfranchised young woman who gains, after much to-do, a fortune, family connections, and a respectable husband. Both women acquire their fortunes and connections *before* they wed; both marry husbands who have been humbled and, as a consequence, we feel that their marriages are not such that they will sink into them obliviously. Rather we sense that they will have some real control over their lives.

It has been said that Radcliffe conforms to many of the typical plot patterns of her day, especially with respect to her orphan heroines. But orphaning a heroine is merely one way of embodying woman's powerlessness. The orphaned Callisto figure who retreats to a convent or a school for girls merely reflects the disenfranchisement of woman in a man's world. She is deprived not only of status in the patriarchy, but of an authentic, *female* definition of her womanhood. The patriarchal authority figures impose upon her rules of conduct which meet their needs: conformity, acquiescence to authority, or, in Montoni's words, "sincerity, uniformity of conduct, and obedience." Although the words may come from the villain of one novel, they are the implicit standards by which Mrs Reed, Mr Brocklehurst, and St John Rivers judge Jane Eyre. St John's own words might likewise fit Emily St Aubert: "Jane, you are docile, diligent, disinterested, faithful, constant, and courageous; very gentle, and very heroic" (429).

Seeking more authentic definitions of womanhood in the company of women, both Jane and Emily are given two monitory examples which circumscribe the perilous journey through womanhood: the mad Laurentini and the dark doppelganger, Bertha Mason, function at least in part to illustrate the fate of a woman who does not meet the submissive definition of femininity. On the other hand, Helen Burns and the Marchioness de Villeroi die through an excess of passivity. Between these two extremes there must be a safe route, and Maria Temple and Madam St Aubert show that it is possible to circumvent the dangers, though not without making compromises.

But like Diana in the myth, neither Miss Temple nor Madame St Aubert continue to guide their respective Callisto figures during the perilous meeting with the god in the forest. On one hand, we know that each woman encounters her femininity alone, and that this is what the myth intends to convey when it separates Callisto from Diana's band. But this aspect of the myth also reflects truths about womanhood under the patriarchy: Madame St Aubert cannot see Emily safely through this encounter because she has sacrificed her own life while nursing her husband back to uncertain health. Miss Temple is hindered in her attempts to aid her students by the rigid controls of Brocklehurst. In these works the patriarchy would appear to conspire against a supportive community of women.

Both Emily and Jane encounter not only physical struggles with unacceptable men, but inward struggles with their own emotions, reflected in the myth by the female nature of Zeus' disguise. When Valancourt suggests that Emily elope with him, the heroine must carefully weigh the emotional advantage of remaining with her beloved against the practical advantages of marrying him with the approval of family and friends. A similar conflict comes about when she and he are both free, but he is found to have "debauched" himself in Paris. When Jane finds that "common sense" and "imagination" rival with one another for control of her feelings – when she later finds that Rochester is married, but her love unchanged – Logos and Eros struggle, just as the initiate struggles with the god. The psychological aspect of the woman's struggle with the god is the conflict between Eros and Logos in her own psyche. The implication here is that when Eros wins out at the wrong time, the woman is vulnerable to rape.

There are no literal rapes in either of these novels. Rape is, instead, presented metaphorically, and in both novels its main effect is to deprive woman of her individual integrity in very practical, expedient ways. Emily is variously deprived of her right to her own sensibility, her right to choose both who and when she marries, and her economic status. Rochester's intention to "marry" Jane while Bertha Mason lives would deprive her of economic, legal, and social status; marriage to St John would destroy Jane's femininity altogether.

Both women ultimately have the strength to say no: Emily continually asserts both her right to choose whom she will marry and her desire for economic independence. Emily and Jane even say no to the men they love; love and marriage are not worth the various kinds of disenfranchisement which accompany the emotional ties. They are willing and able, although both ultimately marry their beloveds, to assert the value of their personal integrity over the comforts of love, and this willingness and ability constitute the final achievement of psychological virginity. The rewards are, oddly enough, financial and social: the direct result of denying the rape is, for both Jane and Emily, the acquisition of fortune and family.

The novels suggest that, once achieved, psychological virginity is not destroyed by marriage *if* it is accompanied by the social and economic guarantees which the heroines have won. To further insure this, both lovers are humbled: Valancourt's pristine reputation is slightly tarnished, Rochester is blinded and maimed. These facts have their social and mythic implications. On a social and economic level, the maiming illustrates to what extent man must be reduced in order to be equal to a woman. His superiority, which exists merely by virtue of his sex, can be undermined only by a drastic diminution of his being. Only maimed is he truly equal to woman in eighteenth-and nineteenth-century terms. That Jane and Rochester live sequestered at Ferndean, and Emily and Valancourt live isolated at La Vallee, suggests that real equality is not acceptable in society.

The maiming of the god-lover also renders him mortal; the man who seemed to Jane a god is now a blind Samson, a mere hero. This reminds us that, like the marriages which end both novels, the experiences of the heroines have constituted not the primordial paradigm which is the prototype for the respective plots, but ritual, enacted not between gods and goddesses, but between mortals. The novels which provide the verbal score are the mythic script for the heroines' achievement of psychological virginity.

The Scarlet Letter:
The Power of Society's Sacred Sanctions

Nathaniel Hawthorne's fascination with myth is obvious from his two books for young people, the *Wonder Book* and *Tanglewood Tales*. Both offer lovely, original versions of the Greek myths, each with a new tone imparted by their common narrator, Eustice Bright. In the introduction to *Tanglewood Tales*, Hawthorne remarks that myths are "indestructible" and that "the inner life of the legends cannot be come at save by making them one's own property."[1] This is precisely what he has done with the Callisto myth in *The Scarlet Letter*. By finding its "inner life," Hawthorne has let the myth speak for itself; at the same time, making the myth his property has meant appending his own signature.

Hawthorne's inclusion of the Custom-House chapter in the volume makes it clear that for him finding the balance between the myth's life and the writer's property was a difficult process. Speaking of the "divided segment of the writer's own nature,"[2] he alludes throughout the chapter to the various and conflicting points of view which are manifested in the novel. On one hand, he presents his narrator as one who comes from the distinctly patriarchal tradition of the Custom-House. The tradition is exemplified by the exclusion of women from the premises, by the frequent use of the word "patriarch,"[3] by his colleagues' relation to one another through a "common Uncle," and by the respect he has for their clear-cut, unimaginative, dutiful existences. The narrator's sympathy with their ways is suggested by his assertion that it is good for his "moral and intellectual health" (22) to be among them. The other branch of the patriarchal family tree to which he feels himself, however shamefully and helplessly, allied is inversely suggested by his desire to explain – to his Puritan ancestors and to us – that being a mere storyteller is not a worthless occupation. On the other hand, the whole creative act which produced the novel is associated with the feminine – not only with the power which Hester conveys through the letter even sixty years later, a power which is reiterated by the similarities between Hester and the narrator,[4] but also with the moonlit realms where fancy and imagination can move freely.

Hawthorne's narrative attempts to explore the middle ground between these two traditions:[5] the novel itself is located "somewhere between the real and fairy-land, where the Actual and the Imaginary meet, and each imbue itself with the nature of the other" (35). Consequently, Hawthorne professes no moral, but instead presents the mingling and meeting of the two traditions to which the narrator belongs: the patriarchal, with its emphasis upon law, logic, reason, and its allegiance to the Judaeo-Christian tradition, and the matriarchal, with its alliance to nature, intuition, and the feminine.

The novel also expresses this tension in its treatment of the Callisto myth itself. Those versions of the myth which present Callisto as a representative of the goddess in the sacred marriage, and those which treat her as a mortal woman of uncertain morals, are not neatly distinct from one another in this novel. One way in which Hawthorne heightens the dramatic conflict between the two aspects of the myth is to leave behind the metaphorical versions of psychological virginity explored in *Jane Eyre* and *The Mysteries of Udolpho* and to provide us with a heroine who, like her prototype, Callisto, bears a child out of wedlock and must face the public consequences for a very private act. Hawthorne's narrative, because it begins with Hester's punishment rather than with Pearl's conception, places the emphasis of the novel on the public dimensions of the Callisto-figure's career. It is possible that in doing so he was following the directives of Sir Charles Anthon, whose *Classical Dictionary* he owned. Anthon's Victorian treatment of her story de-emphasizes Callisto's rape and instead focuses upon her trespass of the sacred enclosure of Zeus (see Appendix F). Similarly, a major aspect of Hester Prynne's struggle lies in her attempts to come to terms with the public judgments of her private life, and throughout her tenure in Puritan Boston she is made to feel as if she, too, has trespassed the "sacred enclosure" of the patriarchy's morality.

Hester's punishment at the hands of the Puritan community in Boston echoes almost exactly that incident in the myth when Callisto meets Hera and undergoes both condemnation and transformation. The dark prison in which Hester gives birth is analogous to the cave in which Callisto spent her confinement. Upon stepping from her prison, Hester is greeted by a group of Hera-like matrons who vehemently argue that wearing the scarlet letter is not the severe penalty she deserves, and who propose that branding would be a more appropriate punishment. Like Hera, they demand a more literal transformation, a lasting destruction of her beauty. Just as Hera laments to Tethys that Zeus has put Callisto beyond her influence and undone her vengeance, they complain that by putting Hester upon the scaffold, the patriarchs have put her punishment out of their hands and that the penalty itself enhances her reputation rather than ruining it. As the angry but repressed victims of misogyny which the Hera figure represents, they articulate one of Hera's major objections to Callisto's looseness: "This woman has brought shame upon us all, and ought to die" (49).

Another public dimension of the myth is suggested by the setting of Hester's punishment and the rhetoric of the authorities who castigate her. The scaffold where she is to be displayed "stood nearly beneath the eaves of Boston's earliest church, and appeared to be a fixture there " (52). The elders of the church, in condemning the "vileness and blackness of [her] sin" and her "grievous fall" indicate that her main fault in their eyes is the trespass of their sacred, patriarchal laws.

Callisto's transformation into a bear is echoed in *The Scarlet Letter* by the change in Hester which comes about when she begins to wear the letter. In the matriarchal versions of the myth, the connotations of the metamorphosis are largely positive: the initiate's figurative transformation into a bear, the totem animal of the goddess, symbolizes her achievement of psychological virginity. The scarlet "A" frequently does this for Hester. The letter itself, for example, is endowed with the power to see her through her public condemnation in a way that almost suggests Callisto's apotheosis: "It had the effect of a spell, taking her out of the ordinary relations with humanity, and inclosing her in a sphere by herself" (51). It sets her apart from other women, and people who do not know the history of the letter invariably mistake it for a sign of preferment (99). Even those who do know what the letter is meant to symbolize allow it to accrue other meanings as Hester's life in the community goes on blamelessly. The "A" comes to stand for "Able; so strong was Hester Prynne, with a woman's strength" (155). It even brings Hester into association with a venerable figure of virginity in the Christian clerical order, the nun: "the scarlet letter had the effect of the cross on a nun's bosom. It imparted to the wearer a kind of sacredness, which enabled her to walk safely amid all peril" (157). The letter has the power to protect her reputation, allowing her to talk to the seaman of questionable morality with "less result of scandal to herself" than the "matron in town most eminent for rigid morality" (226) would have incurred in the same situation. Finally, her badge symbolizes her freedom: "The tendency of her fate and fortunes had been to set her free. The scarlet letter was her passport into regions where other women dared not tread. Shame, Despair, Solitude! These had been her teachers, - stern and wild ones, - and they had made her strong" (193).

As the symbol of the bear indicates that the initiate has achieved psychological virginity, so Hester's scarlet letter and the transformation she undergoes when she begins to wear it symbolize Hester's achievement of these qualities: at those particular moments when the letter is endowed with its positive powers, she is truly autonomous. Yet it is immediately obvious that this is not all the letter signifies; the patriarchal interpretations of the ursine transformation must also be contended with. That Callisto is considered a creature of bestial propensities is embodied in her bearness; that Hester is a creature of sinfulness is indicated by the scarlet letter, which the clergy point out "and in which they might vivify and embody their images of woman's frailty and sinful passion" (74). Hawthorne has expressed all of the implications of the transformation by allowing the letter to accrue the connotations appropriate to both versions of the myth. Yet he attributes the negative aspect of her rebirth not to her experience or to the letter which symbolizes it, but rather pointedly to the community's judgment:

The effect of the symbol – or rather, of the position in respect to society that was indicated by it – on the mind of Hester Prynne itself, was powerful and peculiar. All the light and graceful foliage of her character had been withered up by this red-hot brand, and had long ago fallen away, leaving a bare and harsh outline, which might have been repulsive, had she possessed friends or companions to be repelled by it. Even the attractiveness of her person had undergone a similar change. It might be partly owing to the studied austerity of her dress, and partly to the lack of demonstration in her manners. It was a sad *transformation*, too, that her rich and luxuriant hair had either been cut off, or was so completely hidden by a cap, that not a shining lock of it ever once gushed into the sunshine … Some attribute had departed from her, the permanence of which had been essential to keep her a woman. … She who has once been woman, and ceased to be so, might at any moment become a woman again, if there were only the magic touch to effect the transfiguration. We shall see whether Hester Prynne were ever afterwards so touched, and so *transfigured*. (157–8, emphasis mine).

The language in this passage, which deals with transfigurations and transformations that result in a "bare and harsh outline" and a loss of femininity, powerfully evokes the transformations of Callisto into a bear and Hera's intentions to deprive her of the feminine beauty which attracted Zeus. Yet Hawthorne makes it clear in this passage that the character of transformation is not due to the experience itself, but to society's evaluation of it. Moreover, it is Hester's acceptance of that evaluation which results in her self-imposed adoption of the severe and unfeminine dress. Also self-imposed is Hester's exile from the community. The "forest-land" becomes "Hester Prynne's wild and dreary, but life-long home" (75), much as the forest became the home of Callisto after her metamorphosis. But Hester chooses her separateness; even once the kindness and goodness of her night-time visitations have been acknowledged by the community, she forbids public thanks by daylight; once her reputation is deemed spotless, she refuses to take off the scarlet letter. She is strong enough, it would seem, to enjoy the freedom which the exile gives her. She is one-in-herself just so long as she is one *by* herself and does not attempt to be part of society.

If the scarlet letter effectually functions as Callisto's ursine transformation, Pearl is Hawthorne's version of Arcas. When Callisto's pregnancy is discovered, she confesses to Diana that Zeus is the father; likewise when Hester is exhorted to reveal the name of her child's father, she replies that her child "must seek a heavenly father" (65). There are several more obvious parallels. Arcas, for example is taken from his mother when he is small; the Puritan elders consider taking Pearl from Hester, except that the godly Dimmesdale acts a little sooner than Zeus did in the myth to keep the two together. Finally, near-tragedy is brought about in the myth because Arcas, now grown, refuses to recognize his mother. Pearl similarly refuses to recognize her mother on the day when they are in the forest to meet Dimmesdale. Hawthorne has, however, given us an interesting reversal of the myth. Arcas does not recognize Callisto because she is a bear – that is, he refuses to acknowledge her sexuality. Pearl, on the contrary, does not acknowledge Hester because she has taken off the scarlet letter. Leland Person's study of the myth of the Divine Child in *The Scarlet Letter* describes the prophetic role which Pearl plays in this scene, suggesting that Pearl knows that "only by asserting the 'deep meaning' of her nature within a social context, can [Hester] discover her full humanity."[6] Pearl effectively demands that Hester acknowledge her achievement, regardless of how painful that process has been.

This difference between Pearl's acceptance of her mother's sexuality and Arcas' rejection of it is related to another more essential way in which Hawthorne has deviated from the myth. Pearl is not, like Arcas, a boy. It will be recalled that, according to Harding, the birth of a son signals a woman's symbolic achievement of the masculine within herself and thus of wholeness. That Hester gives birth to a daughter provides symbolic evidence that "wholeness" or "completeness" has been precluded.

Yet finding the masculine aspect of herself is certainly part of Hester's transformation. Hawthorne describes her turning to the masculine ways of thought: "A woman never overcomes ... problems by exercise of thought. ... If her heart chance to come uppermost, they vanish. Thus Hester Prynne, whose heart had lost its regular and healthy throb, wandered without a clew in the dark labyrinth of mind ... At times, a fearful doubt strove to possess her soul, whether it were not better to send Pearl at once to heaven, and go herself to such futurity as Eternal Justice should provide. The scarlet letter had not done its office" (160). That "the scarlet letter had not done its office" refers to its failure to transform her fully into the woman she has the capacity to become. Hawthorne again emphasizes the extent to which society precludes this feminine wholeness, for what she ponders is the impossibility of happy, satisfied womanhood in the Puritan context. Thus Hawthorne implies that society determines to an unduly large extent the way in which Hester experiences her female nature.

Although her charitable acts make others think of her as a person "strong with a woman's strength," Hester's womanhood blossoms fully only once. Her womanly energy, strength, and "magnetic power" (190) are given voluntarily only to Dimmesdale. During the forest scene when she and Dimmesdale talk of leaving Boston together, they re-enact the passionate love-encounters which produced Pearl.[7] In her joy at the prospect of escaping Boston's confines with her beloved, Hester takes off the scarlet letter and the severe cap which confines her hair. Here she undergoes the rebirth which ideally would have occurred in the earlier encounter:

There played around her mouth, and beamed out of her eyes, a radiant and tender smile, that seemed gushing from the very heart of womanhood. A crimson flush was glowing on her cheek, that had been long so pale. Her sex, her youth, and the whole richness of her beauty, came back from what men call the irrevocable past, and clustered themselves, with her maiden hope, and a happiness before unknown, within the magic circle of this hour. And, as if the gloom of the earth and sky had been but the effluence of these two mortal hearts, it vanished with their sorrow. All at once, as with a sudden smile of heaven, forth burst the sunshine, pouring a very flood into the obscure forest, gladdening each green leaf, transmuting the yellow fallen ones to gold, and gleaming adown the gray trunks of the solemn trees. (196)

As if to remind us of the cosmic undertones of such a renewal, the natural world becomes young and gay along with her. But the point which is to be made is that the flash of sunshine and cheer is the outcome of their plan to *leave* the society which has given its own definition to the letter and to the experience. That plan is ultimately thwarted because Dimmesdale himself accepts society's definition.

There is one final, drastic difference between Hester and Callisto: although Hester gives birth to a child out of wedlock, she is not "raped." Even if we give rape the gentler name of seduction and attribute Zeus' role to Dimmesdale, we encounter another problem: that Hester is not virgin at the time of her sexual union, but a married woman. In examining her relations with both men, it becomes clear that each, in his various ways, possesses the qualities and plays the role of Zeus.

As her lover and as father of Pearl, Dimmesdale seems at first glance the more likely candidate for the Zeus figure. His disguise is feminine insofar as he presents himself to the community as one who has a special sympathy for the feminine psyche: when asked to speak "to that mystery of a woman's soul, so sacred, even in its pollution" (63), in order to exact from her the name of her child's father, he is hesitant, feeling "that it were wronging the very nature of woman to force her to lay open her heart's secrets in such broad daylight, and in presence of so great a multitude" (62). Yet while his sympathy with the feminine strikes us as true, it must be noted that his real motive is not the desire to defend the feminine psyche but to protect his own reputation, perhaps even his own life. His sympathy with Hester's motherhood, his extolling of her "instinctive knowledge" of Pearl's nature thus serves as another example of his feminine disguise.

He is also termed by Mr Wilson a "godly youth," and his Jove-like transcendence is expressed in a number of additional ways. The most obvious is his goodness, which manifests itself not only in his words and deeds, but in the "fasts and vigils of which he made a frequent practice, in order to keep the grossness of his earthly state from clogging and obscuring his spiritual lamp" (114). Like Zeus, he is an Olympian being, characterized by light rather than earthiness, by the patriarchal logos-oriented qualities – intelligence and reason. He is distinctly aligned to culture rather than nature, and his reward is a powerful, almost godly, position within the Puritan community.

Yet Dimmesdale hardly resembles the raping god of the patriarchal versions of the myth. When he and Hester meet in the forest she maintains that "what we did had a consecration of its own" (188), implying that there was some kind of sacredness in their love. In that same scene Hester momentarily achieves womanhood, so that for a brief moment she attains psychological virginity. This, along with the fact that some of the effects of her affair with Dimmesdale were positive, suggests that he has not raped but initiated her, and that through her love for this godly young man she has come as close as possible to achieving feminine wholeness and autonomy as Puritan society allows.

In this same scene, however, Chillingworth is said to have "*violated*, in cold blood, the sanctity of the human heart" (188, emphasis mine), suggesting that he is the one who has committed rape, at least of a metaphorical kind.[8] He too carries many of the qualities of the god who rapes Callisto. He is said, for instance, to "drop down, as it were, out of the sky" (115). In a lovely, Hawthornian irony, however, he emerges from the forest not to find a virgin nymph, but to find his wife proven guilty of adultery. He might be said to enter the myth not really at its beginning, but at its end, where Zeus discovers that Callisto has broken sacred law and is threatened with death. At that point in the myth Zeus shows his compassion; Chillingworth, however, is quite willing to leave Hester prey to whatever punishment the Puritans choose, hiding his involvement with her through the agency of his disguise. Although he might be personally compassionate about Hester's adultery, he in no way endeavours to convince the community that she is not entirely culpable.

Chillingworth's disguise is literally expressed in his hiding the secret of his identity. But in another scene, he admits to having taken a less literal disguise which has done violence to Hester's character and to her fate. "Mine was the wrong," he tells her, "when I betrayed thy budding youth into a false and unnatural relation with my decay" (71). Later he similarly confesses that his marriage to her has damaged her almost irreparably by stifling her youth and her vitality: "Thou hadst great elements. Peradventure, hadst thou met earlier with a better love than mine, this evil had not been. I pity thee, for the good that has been wasted in thy nature!" (167). The implication is that Chillingworth had attempted during their engagement to fool Hester into believing him – an old, scholarly man – to be a fit husband for a beautiful young woman. She, in turn, struggled against his metaphorical rape: "Thou knowest that I was frank with thee. I felt no love, nor feigned any" (70). Like Zeus, he leaves her once he has secured what he wanted and only comes back when convenient.

In this particular assignment of roles which makes Chillingworth the rapist, there is an implicit questioning of the Christian scheme of things. In spite of the fact that Chillingworth and Hester are joined by the *sacred* vows of Christian marriage, it is Chillingworth who does violence to her being; and although she and Dimmesdale are joined out of wedlock, it is he with whom she performs the sacred, consecrated act.

Yet if Chillingworth is said to have "violated the sanctity of the human heart," we are forced to recognize that he has raped not only Hester, but Dimmesdale as well. Closely examined, the minister – regardless of his sex – can be seen to possess a number of qualities in common with both Hester and Callisto. Although his particular use of his feminine sympathies constitutes part of his disguise, the sympathies in themselves are quite real. Unlike his fellow clergymen, for example, he speaks to his congregation through his heart, and it is this sympathy rather than his intellect which distinguishes him in Boston. Like Hester he wears the scarlet letter, and like her he is transformed by their union in a metamorphosis which is expressed largely in his declining health. Like Hester, he undergoes a voluntary exile, remaining within the community to perform his ministerial duties, but refusing every other connection.

Dimmesdale resembles Callisto in that he is associated with the star of the myth: on the evening when he mounts the scaffold for a night-time confession of his adultery, a meteor blazes in the sky. In the myth, Zeus' placement of the star in the sky marks Callisto's apotheosis; in the *Scarlet Letter* the star falls, and Dimmesdale's mounting of the scaffold is, if anything, an ironic apotheosis. Coming as it does just after the presence of Pearl and Hester gives him the energy to resist confessing his sin, the falling of the star suggests his own failure to achieve his ennoblement. Yet that such an apotheosis is dependent primarily upon his ability to square things with his own conscience is indicated by the various interpretations of the meteor's significance. It can obviously be understood in a number of ways, and one's frame of mind, the narrator suggests, has a great deal to do with one's interpretation. Dimmesdale believes that the A stands for adulterer, and the narrator considers this a "symptom of a highly disordered mental state" (149), suggesting perhaps that Dimmesdale's judgment of himself is overly harsh. Like the Callisto of *The Recuyell of the Historyes of Troye*, he accepts society's judgment as truth.

He also resembles Hester in that he is renewed by the prospect of leaving behind the society which so powerfully and righteously condemns their love for one another. When Hester reiterates her plan for them to leave Boston together, it has an "exhilarating effect – upon a prisoner just escaped the dungeon of his own heart – of breathing the wild, free atmosphere of an unredeemed, unchristianized, lawless region. *His spirit rose*, as it were, with a bound, and *attained a nearer prospect of the sky*, than throughout all the misery which had kept him grovelling on the earth. Of a deeply religious temperament, there was inevitably a tinge of the devotional in his mood" (195, emphasis mine). Even here, the suggestion is that the sacred act is the one performed with love, even though it is performed out of wedlock.

There is not a great deal of difference between Dimmesdale's rising spirits or Hester's radiant beauty in the discovery of their "newly born" love, and the passage carries, for both of them, echoes of the Callisto myth. Nevertheless, the similarity of their private rebirth here in "wild, heathen Nature of the forest, never subjugated by human law" (196), contrasts with their very different experiences in the marketplace. By tinging both characters with the qualities of Callisto, Hawthorne is now free to contrast as well as compare their respective fates as that character: differences occur mainly because he is male and she is female, because he is a reputable, productive member of society, and she is a woman. While the forest rebirth is similar for both, the apotheosis in the marketplace is radically different.

When the Zeus of the patriarchal versions of the myth places Callisto in the sky, he legitimizes both her experience and her person. While Hester is continually placed "above" the people – on the scaffold, for instance – the object is not to legitimize her but to make sure that her behaviour is recognized as illegitimate. The narrator's description of her life and of the opinions of her fellows re-enacts a similar, distorted version of Callisto's apotheosis. Hester, for example, is continually given goddess-like qualities that are then either undercut by the narrator or the Puritans. If she is the image of "Divine Maternity," it is only so that the narrator can then add by way of critical comment: "Here, there was the taint of deepest sin in the most sacred quality of human life, working such effect that the world was only the darker for this woman's beauty" (53). In spite of the respect which she has gained through her dignity, her uprightness, her charity, her comforts to the sick and dying, she is subject to the rude stares of her fellow-citizens while Dimmesdale gives the election-day sermon.

The extent to which society meddles with Hester's apotheosis, which has private dimensions as well as public, is expressed in her own sense of her limited achievements:

> But, in the lapse of the toilsome, thoughtful, and self-devoted years that made up Hester's life, the scarlet letter ceased to be a stigma which attracted the world's scorn and bitterness, and became a type of something to be sorrowed over, and looked upon with awe, yet with reverence too. And, as Hester Prynne had no selfish ends, nor lived in any measure for her own profit and enjoyment, people brought all their sorrows and perplexities, and besought her counsel, as one who had herself gone through a mighty trouble. Women, more especially, – in the continually recurring trials of wounded, wasted, wronged, misplaced, or erring and sinful passion, – or with the dreary burden of a heart unyielded, because unvalued and un-sought, – came to Hester's cottage demanding why they were so wretched, and what the remedy! Hester comforted and counselled them as best she might. She assured them, too, of her firm belief, that, at some brighter period, when the world should have grown ripe for it, in Heaven's own time, a new truth would be revealed, in order to establish the whole relation between man and woman on a surer ground of mutual happiness. Earlier in life, *Hester had vainly imagined that she herself might be the destined prophetess, but had long since recognized the impossibility that any mission of divine and mysterious truth should be confided to a woman stained with sin, bowed down with shame, or even burdened with a life-long sorrow.* (253, emphasis mine)

Hester has, in a sense, accepted their Christian judgment of her as a valid one, has failed to recognize that those old patriarchs who proclaimed her a woman stained with sin are quite incapable of "sitting in judgment of an erring woman's heart, and disentangling its mesh of good and evil" (61). Hawthorn implies, then, that the Puritans cannot judge Hester, and that she is perhaps wrong in accepting their judgment of her. Certainly we can see that any apotheosis such as that which Callisto undergoes is allowed Hester only in diminished form. She becomes the adviser of woman, but is not allowed to be the representative of the Great Goddess.

Dimmesdale, on the other hand, is allowed a full public apotheosis. Flinging himself with added fervour into his spiritual duties, he acquires a saintly, spiritual quality which his followers choose to attribute to an unworldly goodness. While we grant his hypocrisy, we must also admit that the congregation refuses to accept the implications of what he says, just as they refuse to acknowledge the possible meaning of his glove on the scaffold or the significance of the falling star and scarlet A which appears in the sky on the night of the Governor's death. The most obvious example of this is their interpretation of what happens on the scaffold just before he dies. The narrative and the quoted dialogue suggest that Dimmesdale quite directly confesses his sin and exposes a scarlet letter that is imprinted on his own flesh. There are, however, those who refuse to grant this as truth and who would insist that he was always and only the saintly man that he seemed:

It is singular, nevertheless, that certain persons, who were spectators of the whole scene, and professed never once to have removed their eyes from the Reverend Mr. Dimmesdale, denied that there was any mark whatever on his breast, more than on a new-born infant's. Neither, by their report, had his dying words acknowledged, nor even remotely implied, any, the slightest connection, on his part, with the guilt for which Hester Prynne had so long worn the scarlet letter. According to these highly respectable witnesses, the minister, conscious that he was dying ... had desired, by yielding up his breath in the arms of that fallen woman, to express to the world how utterly nugatory is the choicest of man's own righteousness. After exhausting life in his efforts for mankind's spiritual good, he had made the manner of his death a parable, in order to impress on his admirers the mighty and mournful lesson, that, in the view of Infinite Purity, we are sinners all alike ... Without disputing a truth so momentous, we must be allowed to consider this version of Mr. Dimmesdale's own story as only an instance of that stubborn fidelity with which a man's friends – and especially a clergyman's – will sometimes uphold his character; when proofs, clear as the mid-day sunshine on the scarlet letter, establish him as a false and sin-stained creature of the dust. (249)

Thus Hawthorne illustrates the tendency to excuse sin where "reputation" seems to warrant it, and to condemn where it does not. Dimmesdale and Hester have committed the same "sin" but she is condemned for it, while the community avoids subjecting Dimmesdale to a similar condemnation in every way it can. Hester has, of course, that problem common to many seduced women: there is tangible proof in the child that she is no longer a virgin, proof which cannot, like a man's death-bed repentance, be misunderstood or denied. On the other hand, Hawthorne is frankly interested in pointing out the discrepancy of their respective treatments by Boston society. He introduces this idea with a statement which dismisses, from the point of view of the Boston Puritans, the possibility of any similarity between the two: "The sainted minister in the church! The woman of the scarlet letter in the market-place! What imagination would have been irreverent enough to surmise that the same scorching stigma was on them both?" (238). In this statement, Hawthorne expresses the unthinkableness, from the community's point of view, of considering Dimmesdale an adulterer. But at the same time it slyly alludes to the folly of their blindness. Two pages later he again deals with this contradiction in a way that suggests that Dimmesdale weathers the adultery unpunished because he is a man, but that Hester is more vulnerable to punitive treatment not only because of the tangible proof, but because she is considered, as a woman, less worthy, less important:

Thus, there had come to the Reverend Mr. Dimmesdale – as to most men, in their various spheres, though seldom recognized until they see it far behind them – an epoch of life more brilliant and full of triumph than any previous one, or than any which could hereafter be. He stood, at this moment, on the very proudest eminence of superiority, to which the gifts of intellect, rich lore, prevailing eloquence, and a reputation of whitest sanctity, could exalt a clergyman in New England's earliest days, when the professional character was of itself a lofty pedestal. Such was the position which the minister occupied, as he bowed his head forward on the cushions of the pulpit, at the close of his Election Sermon. Meanwhile, Hester Prynne was standing beside the scaffold of the pillory, with the scarlet letter still burning on her breast. (240)

This very issue is, of course, raised in the myth. Callisto is raped, yet because she is mortal – less powerful – and a woman, she is punished. Zeus, who commits the rape, who is unfaithful to his wife, but who is godly – more powerful – and male, goes unpunished. By casting Dimmesdale in the two mythic roles, by comparing him to both Zeus and Callisto, Hawthorne emphasizes that both Hester and Arthur have committed the same deed, that both are mortals, but that society's refusal to acknowledge that fact elevates the male to the status of a god.

All through the novel there has been a tension between the mythic and the moral, the cosmic and the historical, and much of the criticism of *The Scarlet Letter* has been an attempt to divine Hawthorne's position. Yet because Hawthorne was a man who loved myth and who spoke of the delight of appropriating it and making it his own, one suspects that he has no definable moral position. He is more interested in the "life of the legend," the process of placing Callisto's mythic experience in a historical context and observing the lively interactions. It is for this reason that we notice in the novel a whole series of interlocking or even parallel conflicts, of which head and heart,[9] and "the empirical, daylight faculty of Reason and the nocturnal magical power of Imagination,"[10] are but two. Hester's "antique" beauty, her independence and wondrous strength echo back to matriarchal times and even evoke the goddess herself.[11] Yet she lives in a decidedly patriarchal society that fears her qualities. As Nina Baym notes in "Hawthorne's Women: The Tyranny of Social Myths," "she represents warmth, imagination, intuition, and love; identified with nature and the heart, she also implies the non-rational complexities and mysteries of the self. The male prefers to live in an orderly, rational, moral world, and in the course of structuring such a world around himself he inevitably rejects the woman." Her experience is "pre-lapsarian; it predates patriarchal religion altogether,"[12] yet she finds that her innocent initiation is judged by Christian standards.[13] Her love for Dimmesdale is private; its results earn her public vilification. These are the very conflicts of the myth: as Callisto struggles with all that Zeus symbolizes, Hester struggles with these contradictory aspects of her own life. In Hawthorne's exploration of this myth, he asks how women weather these contradictions.

Using Dimmesdale as a masculine foil to Hester, Hawthorne observes how much simpler (though perhaps no less painful) it is for man to resolve the conflicts between his private experience and the mores of his society. Although Dimmesdale undergoes, in his return from the forest, an agonizing period of questioning, wondering how "Heaven should see fit to transmit the grand and solemn music of its oracles through so foul an organ pipe" (217), believing that he has quite possibly made a pact with the devil, the conflict is resolved when he realizes that he can make a public demonstration of his sinfulness, and receive approval, even forgiveness. It is also more honest as well as easier for him to obey the "generally received" laws which people of his own sex and his own temperament have created.

But nearly every aspect of Hester's experience as Callisto is affected and qualified, if not condemned, by society's disapproval. Disapproval governs the way in which she experiences the transformation symbolized by the scarlet letter, it governs the extent of her apotheosis. Consequently, at the end of the novel, we do not feel that she has acquired unmitigated psychological virginity, but has come as close as possible under the circumstances. If there is a real, free forest nymph in the novel, it is Pearl, and as Person has pointed out, it is the child's "outcast status," her "very uprootedness [which] differentiates her from Hester,"[14] and which makes one feel that she has the strength to transcend the limitations society would try to enforce. Through contrast, then, Hawthorne suggests that Hester has failed, whatever her strengths and beauties, to achieve the wholeness, the self-confidence required for psychological virginity, and he is willing to lay the blame for that failure on the Puritan society which precludes the achievement. Harding suggests that either rape or a sacred union with the god is enough to enable a woman to become one-in-herself; Hawthorne, perhaps more wisely, suggests that society, with its overwhelming power to meddle in the deeper recesses of the human soul, may sanction or deny the woman's experience.

CHAPTER SEVEN

Adam Bede:
Woman Empowered

Nine years after Nathaniel Hawthorne wrote *The Scarlet Letter* George Eliot re-read the book; in the same year she wrote *Adam Bede*. Although Robert K. Wallace has argued that Hawthorne's novel, which Eliot greatly admired, is a source for *Middlemarch*,[1] the names of her characters in her earlier novel – Hetty Sorrel and Arthur Donnithorne – are quite likely derived from Hawthorne's Hester Prynne and Arthur Dimmesdale. Both Hesters bring forth a child out of wedlock, and consequently suffer from public ostracism. If both women find their mythic ancestor in Callisto, however, Hetty Sorrel's character differs quite drastically from that of Hester Prynne.

Hetty Sorrel is a pretty young woman whose beauty is strikingly compared to that of animals – kittens, young ducks, a bright-eyed spaniel – prefiguring her Callisto fate as an animal which lives outside society. She is seduced by Arthur Donnithorne, a young country squire and militia captain whose reputation among his tenants is like that of a god, for "in those days the keenest bucolic minds felt a whispering awe at the sight of the gentry, such as of old men felt when they stood on tip-toe to watch the gods passing by in tall human shape."[2] The god to whom he is specifically compared by the narrator is Jupiter (105). Owner of a valuable forest of oaks, beeches, and limes, he uses their cover to meet the lovely Hetty, and during their courtship his affection for her is frequently described in terms of sunbeams (141,144,176). Hetty, "to whom a gentleman with a white hand was dazzling as an Olympian God" (145), is seduced as much by his god-like wealth and position as by passion, and conceives his child. When, in her desperation and shame, she goes to seek him at Windsor, she becomes, as did the Callisto-bear, "completely shut against her fellow-creatures" (467), and wanders the countryside "clinging to life as only the hunted, wounded brute clings to it" (435).

For Hetty, as for Hester Prynne, there is no single condemning Hera figure: once again Hera is replaced in part by society, Hera's judgment by

Hetty's trial. Although the jury, like Hera, would like to have the girl killed, Arthur, the Jupiter figure, arrives at the last minute with a stay of execution which orders that Hetty – like Callisto – be transported, but only to a colony, not to the skies. Eliot's text follows the configuration of the myth's iconography so closely that the significant aspect of her narrative, for a study of the Callisto myth, is her characterization of the various figures.

Eliot's approach is distinguished from Hawthorne's in that she seems to trivialize the two main actors in the Callisto myth. While her novel does not present us with the ambiguous point of view that is inherent in Hawthorne's narrator and is expressed largely in his attitudes toward Hester, Eliot's treatment of Hetty Sorrel nevertheless evinces an equivocal attitude. She attempts, in the opening three books of the work, to have us see Hetty as vain, shallow, and unfeeling. Her seemingly unsympathetic handling of Hetty is so at odds with the girl's tragic fate that we are made to question the purported inexorability of her destruction, and, more specifically, to ask if it is really necessary. Only in the last two books, which deal with Hetty's exile and trial, does Eliot allow her narrator to show any sympathy, and by this time the events themselves seem even more "unfair" than the earlier narrative tone. Hawthorne created a tension between his polarized attitudes toward Hester Prynne, and left that tension unresolved, making it essentially one of the dramatic forces in the novel, certainly one of the forces that has fascinated readers and critics. Eliot, on the other hand – possibly because she is a woman who is concerned with the status of her sisters – resolves the tension in such a way that the very unsatisfactoriness of the resolution echoes the unsatisfactoriness of woman's status in the nineteenth century.

Arthur Donnithorne resembles Rochester in that his Olympian powers are a direct result of his social position. Eliot's Jupiter, unlike Hawthorne's, derives his godliness from earthly, not spiritual wealth; in fact, he is depicted as a good-natured but spiritually trivial man. One might argue that Eliot presents a woman's version of the lusty, irresponsible thunder god. Certainly there is a moral casualness about him that one feels would be precisely that of a god's. Although he recognizes that he has shortcomings, he manages to think of his moral failings as part of his good nature: "He had an agreeable confidence that his faults were all of a generous kind – impetuous, warm-blooded, leonine; never crawling, crafty, reptilian. It was not possible for Arthur Donnithorne to do anything mean, dastardly, or cruel" (169). His social position, especially once his grandfather has died, allows him to believe that he has the omnipotence to make all well. In fact, his essential fault lies in believing that he can always "make up" for the "hobbles" he gets himself into, that his social and economic power confers on him the ability always to correct his wrong actions.

He is, like the lusty Jupiter of myth, most casual when it comes to his romantic affairs, certain that he can later make up for the damage that he wreaks. At one point, Arthur thinks to himself that "if he should happen to spoil a woman's existence for her, [he would] make it up to her with expensive bon-bons, packed up and directed by his own hand" (170). Yet the very good-naturedness of his intentions emphasizes his ignorance about what it means for a woman to have her existence spoiled.

It is precisely this attitude, which is good-natured, yet irresponsible, insensitive, and lacking in respect for a woman's integrity, that makes him the raping god in his relationship with Hetty. Although he seduces rather than rapes her, his unrealistic attitude about fixing up whatever happens to her once she has lost her virginity is a violation in itself. He simply is so caught up in himself that he cannot entertain the thought that there is no "fixing" a woman's lost virginity. After he has taken Hetty's virtue but refused to marry her, he comforts himself with these thoughts: "But – but Hetty might have had the trouble in some other way if not in this. And perhaps hereafter he might be able to do a great deal for her, and make up to her for all the tears she would shed about him. She would owe the advantage of his care for her in future years to the sorrow she had incurred now. So good comes out of evil. Such is the beautiful arrangement of things!" (358).

He thinks of getting Hetty pregnant in terms of going "a little too far in flirtation," and when the notion of her pregnancy crosses his mind, he dismisses it by remarking that *he* is too good a fellow for providence to allow this to happen to *him*: "Arthur told himself, he did not deserve that things should turn out badly – he had never meant beforehand to do anything his conscience disapproved – he had been led on by circumstances. There was a sort of implicit confidence in him that he was really such a good fellow at bottom, Providence would not treat him harshly" (361). In considering the outcome only so far as it affects him, he is like the medieval Jupiters who worry about Hera's anger and who intend to mend matters with a conjugal kiss. Eliot's portrait of the mortal Jupiter is harshly judgmental, uncanny because we realize that this is precisely the attitude that we have always suspected lay behind Jupiter's sexual escapades, here perfectly embodied in an English gentleman.

R.T. Jones has remarked that Arthur's ill-treatment of Hetty is caused by a failure of imagination, an inability to imagine marrying her.[3] Donnithorne tells himself, "No gentleman, out of a ballad, could marry a farmer's niece" (183), and when he writes to Hetty, he asserts "I know you can never be happy except by marrying a man in your own station" (378). He is so bound by class conventions that, on his return to Hayslope on the occasion of his father's death, he laments in one moment that he has not yet met the perfect wife for the perfect country squire and in the next realizes that he loves Hetty so much he "had not cared much to look at any other woman since he parted from her" (484–5). We sense that she is *superbly* fitted to be his wife, and, in fact, the narrator notes that there are similarities between Hetty and the typical society coquette who Arthur would think an appropriate wife: "For if a country beauty in clumsy shoes be only shallow-hearted enough, it is astonishing how closely her mental processes may resemble those of a lady in society and crinoline, who applies her refined intellect to the problem of committing indiscretions without compromising herself" (365). Yet because of class conventions, he cannot think of marrying her.

This failure of imagination, this taking of social barriers too seriously, constitutes another aspect of Arthur's rape of Hetty. Had he been able to think of her as a future wife, he certainly would not have seduced her, since her virginity would have been valuable to him. His inherent inability to respect her virginity, then, is a direct result of his emphasis on their different classes. Indeed, his willingness to make it up to Hetty by giving Adam more control and a better income is suggestive, as Mason Harris has noted, of *droit du signeur*.[4]

His frequent references to her as a little animal – a spaniel, a bird, a pet of some kind – or a "little thing" illustrate not only her animal beauty,[5] but his attitude toward her: as a "farmer's niece," she is not quite fully human, or at least not as human as a squire's son. In Arthur's world, some people are more human than others, as in the myth some are gods and some are mere mortals. In Apollodorus' version of the myth, Jupiter is credited with Callisto's transformation into a bear; in a sense, Arthur's seduction of Hetty accomplishes the same thing: he thinks of her as an animal and consequently treats her like one.

His love for Hetty comes to look very much like Olympian lust, and Eliot does little to dispel our sense of this – in fact, she uses several means to reinforce this impression. In order to escape his passion for Hetty at the beginning of the affair, he goes for a ride on his mare, thinking that there's "nothing like 'taking' a few bushes and ditches for exorcising a demon; and it is really astonishing that the Centaurs, with their immense advantages in this way, have left so bad a reputation in history" (173). That bad reputation is for rape,[6] and more than once in the novel Arthur resorts to "taking" a bush or two in order to avoid "taking" Hetty.

But take Hetty he inevitably does, and the disguise which allows him to do so is a subtle one. He knows that her dreams include marriage, and while he does not make any promises, neither does he attempt to contradict her hopes. Yet it is not a disguise that he purposefully assumes. He continually resolves to approach her in a manner appropriate to a young squire disinterestedly admiring her beauty, but continually fails to keep his promise to himself. In short, he intends to present himself for what he is: a young gentleman who has no intention of marrying beneath him. Yet he can never bring himself to behave like anything other than a lover. In the face of the honest passion that he feels, he becomes a dishonest moral quibbler who refuses to acknowledge the inevitable effects of his actions, because to do so would violate social convention. He prefers to violate Hetty instead.

It is difficult to conceive of a character less like Arthur Dimmesdale than Arthur Donnithorne. Eliot's conception of the god-figure is a trite, self-centred being, one who is singularly skilful at making the least of his moral failings. Hawthorne, on the other hand, has every intention of endowing his character with human dignity, and his Arthur judges himself perhaps too harshly. But Hawthorne's concern was with the spiritual health of his characters (though not necessarily in the Christian sense), while Eliot is far more concerned with the social forces which give her characters both their motives and their identities. Certainly she has implicitly compared Donnithorne, whatever sympathies she has with his strong, undeniable feelings for Hetty, with the irresponsible, lustful squire of literature (if not of life) that seduces the young women who are under his power.

Hetty Sorrel is also given an extraordinarily trite character. As Jones has noted, "in these early chapters, the novelist sometimes seems intent on imposing a moral structure on the world; she seems to need Hetty to be, if not positively wicked, at least in some perceptible degree blameworthy, so that the consequences of her relationship with Arthur can be regarded as having been brought on by her."[7] Preoccupied as she is by earthly matters – how she looks, what she wears, the social position of the man who is courting her – she has, in a sense, already violated her own integrity; at the very least, she invites that violation from others. And although Beth Burch suggests that Hetty's experience in the forest with Arthur is an initiation,[8] it becomes obvious that Hetty cannot be initiated, that "rape" is the inevitable outcome of her connection to any man who will merely reinforce the values which she holds. She is not concerned with any kind of autonomy; rather she is preoccupied with other people's images of her. Her exile and transformation into an animal come about for the same reason: overly concerned with what others think, she gives no thought to humane or moral values. She does not think of her child as a person, she is concerned only with her own reputation.

What is interesting is that Hetty begins to transcend her petty mortality about the time that her seduction is within imagining distance. As the narrator observes: "It is too painful to think that she is a woman, with a woman's destiny before her – a woman spinning in young ignorance a light web of folly and vain hopes which may one day close round her and press upon her, a rancorous poisoned garment, changing all at once her fluttering, trivial butterfly sensations into a life of deep human anguish" (295).

In this passage she ceases to be mortal, and becomes mythic, the representative of women who have been used by their god-like betters and who, in the interest of attracting those superior beings, have given up all claim to a personal validity.[9] At this point in the novel her shortcomings are perceived as results, not causes; they are presented as symptoms of the time, not of her character. As Adam observes, other "poor helpless things have suffered like her" (472).

Beginning with the following narrative passage in which the narrator muses aloud about Hetty's unfortunate, inevitable future, Hetty is consistently described in ways that suggest the mythic or archetypal, and suggest that Hetty's significance transcends her own limited reality: the narrator remarks, at one point, that "there are faces which nature charges with a meaning and pathos not belonging to the single human soul that flutters beneath them, but speaking the joys and sorrows of foregone generations" (330). Later, she comments:

Beauty has an expression beyond and far above the one woman's soul that it clothes, as the words of genius have a wider meaning than the thought that promoted them: it is more than a woman's love that moves us in a woman's eyes – it seems to be a far-off mighty love that has come near to us, and made speech for itself there; the rounded neck, the dimpled arm, move us by something more than their prettiness – by their close kinship with all we have known of tenderness and peace. The noblest nature sees the most of this *impersonal* expression in beauty (it is needless to say that there are gentlemen with whiskers dyed and undyed who see none of it whatever), and for this reason, the noblest nature is often the most blinded to the character of the one woman's soul that the beauty clothes. (400)

The passage itself not only suggests the way in which personal beauty transcends itself, but also the way in which the individual becomes mythic. Hetty, as Callisto, expresses, as Adam himself later acknowledges, the fate of many girls, and hence transcends her own small reality, just as her beauty transcends its vain limitations.

Such mythic stature belongs, it must be admitted, more obviously to Dinah, who plays Diana to Hetty's Callisto. If we miss the directive provided by the name itself, it nevertheless becomes difficult to ignore the way in which she is worshipped, the way in which love for her is continually suffused with religious awe, the extent to which she is continually associated with moonlight and trees, or the way in which her union with Adam, "a better harvest from a painful seed-time" (578) rejuvenates all of Hayslope, suggesting the cosmic dimension of the sacred marriage.

Dinah's divine qualities are most frequently expressed through her religious vocation. Yet Eliot is careful to keep her religious virtues grounded firmly in Dinah's femininity, not in the Judaeo-Christian tradition. Dinah's frequent resort to "Divine Inspiration," the narrator tells us, is little more than "rapid thought and noble impulse" (158): "Her reliance, in her smallest words and deeds, on a divine guidance, always issued in that finest woman's tact which proceeds from acute and ready sympathy" (156). In fact, by the end of the novel, the preaching which has been Dinah's main public religious activity has been forbidden, and Eliot shows that her effectiveness as a person who brings peace and comfort to others goes on without the approval of a synod.

Another aspect of Dinah's character which differentiates her from other women and makes her, in comparison, seem to have divine qualities, is her sense of purpose. Because she possesses her own inner-directed mission, she escapes the frustrating anonymity and powerlessness of the unmarried or widowed women. Unlike the Misses Irwine with their "obscure and monotonous suffering" (111) through beastly headaches, weak nerves and delicate constitutions, or Aunt Lydia who mourns "for the father who made her life important" (488), Dinah's life is justified by the good that she spreads in the world around her. This is a major component of her autonomy. All those around her respond to her quiet self-sufficiency, an "absorption in thoughts that had no connection in the present moment or with her own personality" (177), an ability to focus on others in a way that precludes a personal need for binding relationships to husband and children. Her sense of purpose, and the quiet, womanly tact which demands and gets attention, illustrate the extent to which she is free from the need to be defined by man, by fathers, husbands, brothers – a freedom which renders her a woman who is, in a very practical way, one-in-herself. Even her lovers, Seth and Adam, recognize in her a self-sufficiency with which they will not interfere.

The evidence of Pausanias, Guthrie, and Fox suggests that Diana and Callisto are two sides of the same figure, Diana the physically virgin goddess of the patriarchy, Callisto the repository of the qualities that the patriarchy found displeasing in the more ancient descriptions of the goddess. Diana, consequently, becomes pure, chaste, good – the very embodiment of virginity; Callisto comes to take on the less desirable qualities, specifically, the "sexual looseness" by which the earlier goddess might have been characterized. Eliot has established precisely this relationship between Diana and Hetty through a series of structural parallels which make comparison of the two women inevitable.[10] When Adam awakes the day after his father's death, he hears a woman downstairs and imagines that it is Hetty, only to find Dinah quietly cleaning the house: "It was like dreaming of the sunshine, and awakening in the moonlight" he thinks to himself when he finds out whose domestic noises he has been hearing (161). Later Adam comments upon Hetty's placement of a rose in her hair, and reminds her that real beauty like Dinah's needs nothing to adorn it. Hetty responds by disguising herself in a black stuff gown and one of Dinah's hats, momentarily fooling and shocking Mrs Poyser. Dinah leaves Snowfield for Leeds the same day Hetty leaves Hayslope. When Hetty is caught after her child's death, she has two names in her red packet, "Dinah Morris, Snowfield" and "Hetty Sorrel, Hayslope" and refuses to say which name is hers.

This series of structural parallels works in two opposite directions. It invites us to consider Hetty Sorrel and Dinah Morris as two sides of the same coin of womanhood, even while it emphasizes their differences. The chapter entitled "The Two Bedchambers" presents us with the most extended parallel. While Hetty, for example, performs "religious rites" which celebrate her beauty by gazing vainly in her mirror, Dinah looks out her window, praying and meditating on the fates of others. Eliot finally labels them "lower nature" and "higher nature" (206).

The essential differences in their natures have come about because Dinah has been taught to follow her own moral directives, and those directives have been, fortunately, legitimized by her Methodist brethren. In Hetty, triviality has been just as thoroughly inculcated. The result is two characters who fit the simplistic stereotypes of second-rate Victorian literature: the "good girl" who gets what she deserves, and the seduced "bad girl" who also gets what she deserves. But Eliot's use of this convention strikes us as contrived and unsatisfactory, largely because she has evoked in us just enough sympathy for Hetty that we feel, when Dinah gets all the rewards that Hetty might have had, that Eliot has been playing with us.

Eliot has deviated, however, from the typical depiction of the Victorian "bad girl," as Susan Staves points out in her article on "British Seduced Maidens." A typical quality of the maiden of seduction literature was her refinement: even if she did belong to the lower class, her exquisite sensibility differentiated her from her peers.[11] It is possible, therefore, to conclude that Eliot's characterization of Hetty as a shallow, trivial, vain kitten rises out of her judgment of maidens who go to the woods and get themselves seduced, as the moral interpretation of the novel would suggest. On the other hand, Eliot includes among her descriptions of Hetty her real justification for making her the way she is. Interestingly enough, Hetty is as often seen through the eyes of others as she is seen acting or thinking herself. In one such passage, Eliot's narrator muses about the way in which others inevitably interpret her beauty:

The dear young, round, soft flexible thing! Her heart must be just as soft, her temper just as free from angles, her character just as pliant. If anything ever goes wrong, it must be the husband's fault there: *he can make her what he likes, that is plain*. And the lover himself thinks so too: the little darling is so fond of him, *her little vanities are so bewitching, he wouldn't consent to her being a bit wiser*; those kitten-like glances and movements are just what one wants to make one's hearth a paradise.

Every man under such circumstances is conscious of being a great physiognomist. Nature, he knows, has a language of her own, which she uses with strict veracity, and he considers himself an adept in the language. Nature has written out his bride's character for him in those exquisite lines of cheek and lip and chin, in those eyelids delicate as petals, in those long lashes curled like the stamen of a flower, in the dark liquid depths of those wonderful eyes. How she will dote on her children! (197–8, emphasis mine)

The implication of this passage is that Hetty is vain, shallow, and trivial because this is what men expect of her. No one has any desire to see her as anything more. Men clearly prefer her apparent pliability and her trivial vanities to self-sufficient virtue and wisdom. She does not have, like Emily St Aubert, for example, someone interested in her moral education. Even her Aunt Poyser, a woman renowned for her sharp tongue, is so taken in by her beauty that she does little to correct her. But the "joke" is on the men who depend upon her beauty to reflect her nature. In passages which follow hard upon that quoted above, the narrator comments that this "was very much ... the way that our friend Adam Bede thought about Hetty," and that "Arthur Donnithorne, too, had the same sort of notion about Hetty, so far as he had thought of her nature at all" (198). Certainly it is a condemnation of both men that they prefer Hetty to Dinah: they do not have enough sense to care about her character. The men are presented as fools for reading her beauty and not her behaviour, and Mrs Poyser, who had "formed a tolerably fair estimate of what might be expected from Hetty in the way of feeling" (200) is negligent for not doing something about Hetty's great lapses.

Consequently, we begin to see that Eliot has split womanhood into two components, Dinah representing one, Hetty the other, for the purpose of subtly criticizing Victorian preferences. By adhering to the patriarchy's conception of woman, Eliot implicitly suggests the problems inherent in the way men think about and mold their women. Eliot, fan as she was of Hawthorne, must have been aware of the difficulties people had reading his two-sided, ambiguous Hester. In her own novel, accordingly, she tries another approach, simplifying Hawthorne's model along the lines of Victorian attitudes, giving Hester's strengths to one woman, her "faults" to another. By following this convention, she creates a work which is problematical because of its moral simplifications. This implies that the social attitudes which these simplifications echo are also problematical.

Eliot seems, moreover, to be aware that creating sympathy for a strong, independent woman who had committed adultery (one, perhaps, like Hester Prynne) was nearly impossible, and that the men of her age were far more likely to sympathize with the trivial creatures whom they themselves preferred.[12] In gaining sympathy for Hetty, Eliot at least gains sympathy for the "fallen woman." But because she must sacrifice the Callisto figure's quest for integrity, she makes an inadvertent comment upon the process that once created the distinction between Diana and Callisto, and that continues to classify women according to their virginity. Thus Eliot acknowledges that, in the context of the Victorian patriarchy, a single woman cannot be both "fallen" and "one in herself."

The happily-ever-after ending which involves the two "pure" souls of the novel also seems to fall into the category of moral simplicity. It is an ending which has prompted many critics to dismiss the novel as a wonderful pastoral with an unfortunate moral twist – and a very bad ending.[13] But the very unsatisfactoriness of the ending emphasizes the unsatisfactoriness of the attitudes toward women which the novel is designed to explore. At the same time, however, a series of structural parallels which emphasize not only the similarities between Hetty and Dinah but also between Arthur and Adam suggest ways in which the tragic, misdirected relationship of Hetty and Arthur can be redeemed.

Specifically, the relationship of Arthur to Adam lies not only in the different moral fabric of which they are made, but in Arthur's superior social position and the power which he derives from it. Adam often seems like a mere shadow of Arthur. The young squire owns the woods; Adam manages them. Arthur's affection toward Hetty is like sunshine; Adam's is a "mere picture of the sun" (144). Arthur courts Hetty in the forest, Adam in the Hall Farm kitchen garden. While the Chase is, for Arthur, a "sacred grove" which is "not to come by the hatchet" (343), for Adam it merely marks the end of his youth (341). Adam is the least mythic but most humanly satisfying character of the novel. One reason Dinah marries Adam, then, is that he realizes his own mortality and Dinah's divinity; he does not "put his soul above" hers (554).

The imagery in the Sixth Book suggests that the marriage of Dinah and Adam is the hierogamy that will rejuvenate Hayslope after the loss of Hetty and Arthur and the death of old Martin Poyser, Hayslope's oldest farmer.[14] At the beginning of the book that deals with the romance of Adam and Dinah, the cows ooze milk and the haywagon carries a golden load. Their marriage concludes the "painful seed-time" of the last few years with a bountiful "harvest" (578).

Through the contrast of the relationships between Arthur and Hetty and Adam and Dinah, Eliot makes a powerful comment. When the man occupies a superior and hence powerful social position that he uses to earn the favours of women, the result is rape. But should the woman's power be recognized, as Adam recognizes that of Dinah, the outcome is one which rejuvenates the microcosm they inhabit.

Eliot makes more than one comment on the beneficent effect of women who have power; specifically she deviates from Ovid's version of the myth with respect to the ways in which Dinah and Mrs Poyser play the roles of Diana and Hera, respectively. She places Dinah in the position of Hetty's comforter, not her condemner. In the scenes in the prison or on the way to the execution, Dinah not only offers Hetty the only human comfort and love the girl can feel, but Eliot frequently mingles their faces so that they seem, once again, one and the same figure. Although Dinah, in keeping with her religious vocation, utters words which are appropriately addressed to an unrepentant sinner, the real nature of her comfort is human, indeed feminine. It is Dinah's physical closeness, the tact, the understanding, the unwillingness to judge another that finally softens Hetty's heart.

Another deviation from the myth is expressed in Mrs Poyser's sympathy with Hetty. Mrs Poyser is a Hera figure who embodies only the kind, sympathetic qualities of the Goddess. She is querulous, to be sure, just as Hera seems to have been, and she rules the Hall Farm hearth with a domestic vengeance. Yet we can also see her as a patron of marriage, for she is careful not to criticize Hetty in Adam's presence and is quite obviously aware of the developing relations between Dinah and Adam. She is also quite ready to balk at the inferior position of women, much the way Hera was said to haggle with Zeus. Donnithorne lets her know he expects her to take more cows into the dairy and he wants to trade for farm land; she lets him know she won't be put upon, despite her sex: "For all I'm a woman, and there's folks as thinks a woman's fool enough to stan' by and look on while the men sign her soul away" (393). She also rebells against the kind of weak wife she perceives most men to want: "A poor soft, as 'ud simper at 'em like the picture o' the sun, whether they did right or wrong, an' say thank you for a kick, an' pretend she didna know which end she stood uppermost, till her husband told her. That's what a man wants in a wife mostly: he wants to make sure o' one fool as 'll tell him he's wise" (569).

Mrs Poyser's relationship to Hetty is unusual: she is aware of Hetty's failures, aware of the hardness which lies at the core of her personality, describing her heart as a "pibble" (200), or a "cherry w' a stone in it" (385). Yet her judgments are made without malice or vindictiveness: they are simply stated as fact and seem to have nothing to do with her feelings about the girl or her admiration of Hetty's beauty. She also has a surprising sympathy with Hetty at the last, condemning her not at all, as if she can understand Hetty's being driven to cast off her own child in order to avoid shame.

There is a great difference between the way Dinah and Mrs Poyser treat Hetty and the way the Puritan women treat Hester Prynne. The difference comes largely from the power which the women in *Adam Bede* wield, perhaps because they inhabit an agricultural world where their skills are valued and necessary for survival. Mrs Poyser rules Hall Farm kitchen and does not really need to repress another woman in order to maintain her own power. Likewise, Dinah has such wide respect from the community that she need not disassociate herself from a "sinner."

The primary value of Eliot's novel lies in its suggestion of the way in which society's trivialization of women, one which makes them into Hetty Sorrels, is destructive of the whole community, for her tragedy widens like the ripples from a pebble dropped into a pool, touching not only the Poysers, the Donnithornes, and the Bede family, but even Rev. Irwin and Bartle Massey. Yet the novel also suggests the beneficent effects of women who have been empowered. While Hetty is inevitably the victim of one kind of rape or another, Dinah has the power to renew the damages done. Moreover, we must consider the deceptions involved in the misleading title and the author's name: written by a woman who uses a male pseudonym, surely it is as much about Dinah and Hetty as about Adam Bede. The event that sparked the novel – George Eliot's aunt comforting an unwed mother condemned to die for the neglectful murder of her child – indicates the extent to which Hetty's situation is central both to Eliot's inspiration and to the finished work.[15] The need to misdirect readers' attentions may be a tribute to its subversive message.

CHAPTER EIGHT

Tess of the D'Urbervilles: *The Maid Who Went to the Merry Green Wood*

Noting the popularity of *Tess of the D'Urbervilles,* Arnold Kettle observes that "in Great Britain at least, thousands of people who have never opened the book 'know about' Tess." Irving Howe similarly draws attention to the almost inexplicable power of her character, while Virginia Hyman concludes: "No amount of explanation regarding Hardy's intellectual or artistic development can fully account for the creative energy and mastery that has created Tess."[1] When one recognizes the mythic dimensions of her character, however, the extraordinary response that she commands is not surprising, for one quality of mythic literature is its ability to evoke a response out of proportion to its ostensible cause.

The importance of myth in *Tess* has not gone unnoticed, but interpretations generally fall into one of two categories: those that focus upon Hardy's allusion to a variety of biblical and mythological figures in his characterization of Tess and therefore see her as a composite Great Mother figure,[2] and those that focus upon Hardy's use of sun imagery and reference to heliolatries and see the novel in terms of fertility myths[3] or myths of redemption.[4] The problem with the former type of criticism is that it fails to recognize the way in which Tess's experience is profoundly that of a mortal woman; the problem with the latter is that it ignores the presence of the moon at crucial stages in Tess's career. The real mythic dimensions of *Tess of the D'Urbervilles* are expressed through Hardy's exploration of the Callisto fate of his protagonist.

Tess is, after all, a young woman who, while resting in the forest after a hard day's work and a long journey, is raped by a man who has disguised himself as her benefactor and cousin. Subsequent aspects of her career also suggest this myth: her exile at Flintcomb-Ash, the animal imagery which is used to describe her wanderings, the return of Alec to "save" her from the killing labour at Flintcomb-Ash, and the final separation of her body from her soul, something which she tells us earlier that she can accomplish by looking at a star. What becomes immediately obvious from this summary, however, is that while the rape is attributed to Alec d'Urberville, the exile and the animal imagery are part of her relationship with Angel Clare. There are, then, two relationships to explore in the context of the Callisto myth. This is not a new technique: in *The Scarlet Letter* we find Hester involved with two very powerful men whose effects upon her are also very different.

But unlike Hawthorne's narrator, Hardy has no compunctions about giving all of his sympathy to Tess, his "pure woman." The tragic arc of her career makes it clear that, like Callisto, she experiences the difficulties of womanhood and feminine sexuality during a time when the patriarchy rules. Yet he has created a character who seems to be lifted from a pre-patriarchal time, one in which her seduction would have been "a liberal education."[5] That time is most often suggested in the novel's natural scenes: in the harvests, on the fields bordering the Froom, at Talbothays, and most obviously in the Cerealia which gives us our first glimpse of her.

The name of the ritual indicates that it is a celebration in the name of Ceres, the goddess of corn – and by extension, of all agriculture – whose marriage to Zeus was celebrated on May Day.[6] Tess's full name, Theresa, which means "the reaper" or "the carrier of the corn," identifies her as a votive of Ceres, and her exceptional face and demeanour further strengthen her association with Ceres, for, as Frazer tells us, the prettiest girl was often used to personify the May spirit.[7]

But Cerealias are not the only May Day rituals; the ancients once decked out a moon tree on May Day and danced to the moon goddess.[8] Moreover, the "moon owns" the willow wand which Tess holds in her hand. The willow is sacred to the moon for many reasons, and as "the fifth tree of the year," its month "extends from April 15th to May 12th, and May Day, famous for its orgiastic revels and its magic dew, falls in the middle."[9] In an earlier version of the novel, Hardy had called this celebration a Vestal Rite[10] and Frazer, by reminding us that at Nemi Diana was called Vesta,[11] further helps us to establish Tess's connection with Diana as well as with Ceres.

One of the ways in which Hardy conveys that Tess belongs to a matriarchal time is this connection between her and both the moon goddess and the earth goddess. They were both part of one goddess, the Great Goddess, before the patriarchy "departmentalized" her powers, spreading them among a variety of weaker deities in a "divide and conquer" manoeuvre.[12] The common denominator between Ceres and Artemis is, of course, that they both functioned as fertility goddesses. Long before man noticed the seasons which he believed Ceres' grief and joy controlled, he believed that the moon, bringer of a cool and undestructive light, fertilized the earth and women. He viewed the moon as "the cause of all growth and increase ... literally the *power* of growth."[13]

Consequently, Tess's most obvious connection with the Great Goddess is her tie with the agricultural world. Her first job as "supervisor, purveyor, nurse, surgeon and friend" to a "community of fowls" (99), associates her with the Lady of the Beasts, an ancient aspect of the Great Goddess who was "entrusted with the care of captive young animals; she was the tamer of domestic beasts and the founder of cattle breeding."[14] Tess's duties at Talbothays are also redolent with associations with the Lady of the Beasts. There, as in the scene of the Cerealia, Hardy distinguishes her with the same kind of slight emphasis: she is able to handle even the difficult milchers, and Dairyman Dick calls her "the prettiest milker I've got in my dairy" (174).

Similarly, Hardy singles out Tess as a fieldworker. But first he differentiates between the women and the men, again as if harkening back to an ancient, matriarchal time when it was believed that "only women [could] make things grow."[15] "Charm" he tells us, "is acquired by woman when she becomes part and parcel of outdoor nature and is not merely an object set down therein as at ordinary times. A field-man is a personality afield; a field-woman is a portion of the field; she has somehow lost her own margin, imbibed the essence of her surrounding, and assimilated herself with it" (137–8). Tess is, of course, the quintessential field-woman, "she being the most flexuous and finely-drawn figure of them all" who holds "the corn as in an embrace like that of a lover" (138). Tess is, like Callisto, the favoured follower of Diana, as is shown not only by the way in which Hardy depicts her as the "fairest" (Kalliste, Pausanius points out, means the fairest) in the Cerealia, in the fields, and at Talbothays, but also by the hair ribbon which distinguishes both Hardy's character and the nymph of Ovid's version.

The fecund Mrs Durbeyfield functions as Diana's surrogate here, and like the pre-patriarchal goddess who demands that the initiate give up her virginity to strengthen her, Tess's mother sends her to Trantridge with hopes that she can procure the aid which the family needs now that Prince has been killed. Taking advantage of Tess's passivity, Mrs Durbeyfield washes her daughter's hair and puts Tess's best dress on her in hopes of furthering Alec's obvious attraction. Finally, we see that Tess's mother has sent her to Trantridge in full knowledge of the likely outcome. As Tess climbs into Alec's trap, Mrs Durbeyfield says to herself: "And if he don't marry her afore he will after. For that he's all afire wi' love for her any eye can see" (93). Mrs Durbeyfield is aware of the inevitable outcome of Tess's sojourn at Trantridge, just as the goddess knows the outcome of her priestess' initiation. Like Emily, Jane Eyre, Hester, and to some degree, Hetty, Tess approaches her initiation alone, without guidance from another woman. In the myth, Callisto goes hunting and becomes separated from Diana's band, and the vulnerability which allows Zeus to rape her is primarily a result of her being alone, without Diana's protection or guidance. Mrs Durbeyfield has purposefully withheld her knowledge of the dangers of men for fear that her daughter will be reluctant to leave home.

Alec parallels Zeus in a number of ways, the most obvious of which is his disguise. Tess approaches him believing that he is a member of her family, but he has "grafted" the d'Urberville name onto his own. Hence, although she believes him to be kin – to be cousin, aristocrat, and a true d'Urberville – he is not. He is quite amused at her claim of kinship, by her theory that her family's name has fallen to Durbeyfield, by her assumptions that they are equals, much as Zeus was amused when Callisto praised the goddess above the god himself.

Like Zeus, Alec has a great deal of power. Not only does he own the forest, but he also has an ability to force plants – strawberries and roses – into abundance out of season, as if he has control over the natural world. His godliness is expressed largely through his wealth, however, and through the power he has over Tess as representative of her destitute family. It is a godliness that he exercises by forcing her to do things that she does not want to do – to take strawberries from his hand or to accept the kiss of mastery after the terrifying buggy ride. d'Urberville's power also lies in the fact that, although his name has been grafted, it has been sanctioned by society, and continues to be sanctioned because of his financial status.

Pretending to be both cousin and benefactor, Alec puts Tess further and further into his debt. Throughout the novel, Alec's love-making is invariably accompanied by some favour: she has a job; the family now has a new horse, some toys, or a home to live in. His ability to give Tess a job and to send the family whatever they need constitutes his godliness, but his combination of charity with love-making shows his true colours. That is to say, Alec abandons his disguise as benefactor when he continually asks Tess for sexual favours on the strength of what he has done for her family. Tess's helplessness in the face of Alec's generous godliness is expressed by her awareness that if she does not satisfy him in some way, her family will once again be destitute. She cannot protest or express her anger because she "cannot help [her]self here" (114).

Thus blinded by her own innocence, by her habits of passivity and tractability, and by her sense of his generosity, poor Tess, like her mythic prototype, Callisto, fails to "understand Alec's meaning till it was too late" (125). She does not penetrate the disguise soon enough. What we observe here is what we have already observed in three of the four novels: a woman's financial dependence upon men constitutes her vulnerability to rape, in a literal and a metaphorical sense. Men are gods because they have control over both wealth and social standing; women are mere mortals because they have no control.

Like the characters involved, the seduction scene itself contains strong echoes of the Callisto myth. On the night of her seduction she joins women who, when dancing earlier, had been described as "nymphs" (107), who have failed to elude the satyrs who chase them, women who are large, strong, and independent – the very image of the ancient matriarchal band of Diana. The Ovidian echoes in this passage are strong;[16] Hardy compares the dancers not only to a variety of mythological personages, but also talks of how they are "metamorphosed" (107) in their dance, much like the creatures of Comus' "wavering morrice." By the light of the moon Tess walks home with them, but she is only with them, not of them: she is one of the band, but she is also one of the uninitiated. It is her naïveté, more specifically her criticism of them, which arises out of her own moral innocence, that causes her rift with them and results in her forest ride with d'Urberville.

That forest scene also contains strong echoes of the Callisto myth. The sacred forest of the *Metamorphoses*, "whose trees had never felt the axe," is represented here by the "oldest wood in England" (116), "wherein Druidical mistletoe was still found on aged oaks" (77). D'Urberville reveals the true nature of his disguised benevolence when he makes it very clear that his favours to her and her family are meant to be repaid by sexual favours from her. And, like Zeus, who must have thought that no mortal woman could resist his desires, d'Urberville remarks, "What am I, to be repulsed so by a mere chit like you? For near three mortal months have you trifled with my feelings, eluded me, and snubbed me; and I won't stand it!" (115). The Jupiter in *The Barley-Breake* asks the same question when he complains that he has no power unless he can have the woman he desires.

The Great Mother is emblematically present in the seduction scene, where fog holds "the moonlight in suspension, rendering it more pervasive than in clear air" (114). While the celestial body seems to set just before Tess's seduction, it is in reality reincarnated in Tess's form: as Alec returns to her after reconnoitering, he finds "the obscurity was now so great that he could see absolutely nothing but a *pale nebulousness* at his feet, which *represented* the white muslin figure he had left upon the dead leaves. Everything else was blackness alike" (118–19, emphasis mine). On the one hand, Hardy's imagery suggests the way in which the goddess deserts her votive just before her seduction; on the other hand, that "pale nebulousness" evokes the moon itself, which the initiate becomes at the moment of her initiation.

Upon her return from the forest seduction, Callisto is perceived by her fellow nymphs to have changed irretrievably, and so is Tess. When the news of her homecoming spreads through the neighborhood, "former schoolfellows and acquaintances of Tess called to see ... a person who had made a *transcendent* conquest" (132, emphasis mine). When the community discovers that Tess is pregnant, but has not wed d'Urberville, they limit their ostracization to a few stares at church. One suspects, especially from the evidence in the harvest chapter (chapter 14), that their attitude is pretty much that of Mrs Durbeyfield: "Well ... Tis nater, after all, and what do please God!" (131). Not only do they tend to believe that d'Urberville over-powered her, but they think lightly enough of the situation to sing "a few verses of the ballad about the maid who went to the merry green wood and came back a changed state" (142), even in her presence. The very ballad itself suggests that these circumstances are not uncommon among them. In short, they accept her experience for what it is – an initiation, something so ritualized that they even have a song about it. The whole tendency of the field-folk not to condemn her bespeaks of a pre-patriarchal attitude which coincides with Hardy's pre-patriarchal descriptions of their existences.

Hardy makes it very clear that Tess's "exile," her feelings of tremendous guilt, are entirely self-imposed; they are a product of Tess's perception of the morality of her experience:

This encompassment of her own characterization, based on shreds of convention, peopled by phantoms and voices antipathetic to her, was a sorry and mistaken cre-ation of Tess's fancy – a cloud of moral hobgoblins by which she was terrified without reason. It was they that were out of harmony with the actual world, not she. Walking among the sleeping birds in the hedges, watching the skipping rab-bits on a moonlit warren, or standing under a pheasant-laden bough, she looked upon herself as a figure of Guilt intruding into the haunts of Innocence. But all the while she was making a distinction where there was no difference. Feeling herself in antagonism she was quite in accord. She had been made to break an accepted social law, but no law known to the environment in which she fancied herself such an anomaly. (135)

Such descriptions suggest that the natural world, the world controlled by the Great Mother, perceives her experience in an entirely different way than she. Hardy's later comment, that Tess's "corporeal blight had been her mental harvest" again reminds us, because of the nature imagery used, that in the context of the natural, and hence the feminine, Tess's experience would be looked on in an entirely salutary way.

Consonant with this observation about the real meaning of Tess's ex-perience is our sense that as a result of her seduction she has achieved psychological virginity. Her departure from Trantridge, in spite of the fact that she is fairly sure she is pregnant with Alec's child; her search for work in the fields, "to taste anew the sweet independence at any price" (141); and her move to Talbothays in search of "a means of independent living" (158) show her desire for independence and freedom. At the same time, we perceive an unmistakable growth in her emotional stature: "Almost at a leap Tess thus changed from simple girl to complex woman. Symbols of reflec-tiveness passed into her face and a note of tragedy at times into her voice. Her eyes grew larger and more eloquent. She became what would have been called a fine creature; her aspect was fair and arresting; her soul that of a woman whom the turbulent experiences of the last year or two had quite failed to demoralize. But for the world's opinion those experiences would have been simply a liberal education" (150). We sense that she has been initiated into her own sexuality (irrespective of Alec's crude intentions) in the best sense. The entire context of Tess's seduction evokes pre-patriarchal times. The agricultural setting where a field-woman is perceived as part of the landscape, the fecund, Diana-like Mrs Durbeyfield who purposefully sends her daughter off to her seduction, the community's accepting attitude, all suggest a time when chthonic womanhood and its rituals are an accepted part of life. Moreover, in spite of Tess's self-condemnation, she gains independence and womanhood through her encounter with Alec – gains, in short, psychological virginity. It is as if Alec has tried to rape her but cannot – which may account for Hardy's maddening reticence about what actually did happen on that evening in the Chase. What Alec intended to do to Tess and what she experienced seem to be two different things, partly because the community refuses to abandon and condemn her, as did Diana's band in the myth, and partly because her own independence (of which we had seen distinct signs earlier) is so strong that it cannot be violated.

The iconography of the Callisto myth is also part of Hardy's treatment of the relationship between Tess and Angel Clare. Clare's godliness in Tess's eyes is clearly evoked by Hardy's description of her adoration for this "divine being" (268), this "something immortal" (257) who has miraculously fallen in love with her. Hardy uses sun imagery to connect Clare with Zeus in much the same way that Charlotte Brontë used it to compare Rochester with the god: Tess "sun[s] herself in his eyes" (194), and when, on "sun's day" he carries her across the flooded road, he compares her to an "undulating billow warmed by the sun" (202). When he has left for a visit to Emminster, the "sunshine of the morning went out at a stroke (215). As Lewis B. Horne points out, "Tess's love for Angel and his love for her are expressed again and again in images associated with the sun."[17] At the same time, however, Hardy indicates through this same group of images that Clare, as Zeus, is able to destroy her. While she basks in his light, she also feels its capacity to scorch, and the "ardour of his affection [is] so palpable that she seemed to flinch under it like a plant under too burning a sun" (232), just as the ardour of Ovid's Zeus frightens Callisto.

At Talbothays, where Diana's nymphs are dairymaids (219), Clare is a gentleman pretending to be a farmer who is attracted by the particularly fresh, virginal beauty of Tess. Once he has convinced her to marry him, she utters a cry that echoes Callisto's own sense of having, by being raped, broken vows of eternal chastity: "I have broken down in my vow. I said I would die unmarried" (254). Callisto's struggle with the god has here been translated, as it was in *Jane Eyre* and *Mysteries of Udolpho*, into a struggle with her own conscience. Tess's unwillingness to saddle Clare with a woman who is not what he perceives her to be results in her continual rejections of his suits.

Hardy seems to imbue this love of theirs with all the magic of a sacred marriage. In his descriptions, the natural world seems to follow the increasing intensity of their love for one another: "July passed over their heads, and the Thermidorean weather which came in its wake seemed an effort on the part of nature to match the state of hearts at Talbothays Dairy" (207). Indeed, the natural world seems part of the conspiracy to force Tess to acquiescence: "Every see-saw of her breath, every wave of her blood, every pulse singing in her ears, was a voice that joined with nature in revolt against her scrupulousness" (241).

The rituals of the world of kine keep throwing them together in the magic light of dawn, in the languorous heat of the day, at sensuous moments after afternoon naps. And at every possible occasion, Clare "persistently wooed her in undertones like that of the purling milk – at the cow's side, at skimmings, at butter-makings, at cheese-makings, among broody poultry, and among farrowing pigs – as no milkmaid was ever wooed before by such a man" (245).

Just as the nymphs of Diana's band recognize the change in Callisto long before her pregnancy becomes visible, so do the milkmaids come quickly to acknowledge Tess's special place in Angel Clare's affections. When once her "seduction" is confirmed, and they know she is to marry him, they perform a ceremony the whole purpose of which is to examine her changed state. Yet it is totally unlike any we might have imagined as part of Ovid's myth. Their ceremony recognizes not a "fallen woman," but one whose special qualities deserve tribute. Her privileges seem to validate their own existence, their own feelings:

And by a sort of fascination the three girls, one after another, crept out of their beds, and came and stood barefooted round Tess. Retty put her hands upon Tess's shoulders, as if to realize her friend's corporeality after such a miracle, and the other two laid their arms round her waist, all looking into her face.

"How it do seem! Almost more than I can think of!" said Izz Huett.

Marian kissed Tess. "Yes," she murmured as she withdrew her lips.

"Was that because of love for her, or because other lips have touched there by now?" continued Izz drily to Marian.

"I wasn't thinking o' that," said Marian simply. "I was on'y feeling all the strangeness o't – that she is to be his wife, and nobody else. I don't say nay to it, nor either of us, because we did not think of it – only loved him. Still, nobody else is to marry'n in the world – no fine lady, nobody in silks and satins; but she who do live like we." (263–6)

This is not the rejection that occurs in Ovid's patriarchalized version of the myth; it is, instead, an intense recognition that Tess has achieved womanhood; it strikes us more as a ceremony which would form the prelude to an initiation than a casting out.

Their marriage is also coloured by imagery appropriate both to an initiation and to the Callisto myth. At the wedding, Tess seems to become the goddess to which woman gives her virginity, and her frame of mind fits that of the initiate, for whom the sexual encounter she thinks she is about to experience has nothing to do with sex in its ordinary, secular forms. At the church, Tess is "a sort of celestial person, who owed her being to poetry – one of those classical divinities Clare was accustomed to talk to her about when they took their walks together" (279); Tess's preoccupations are at "stellar distances" from those in the crowd who might think with the "ordinary sensibilities of sex" (279). It would seem that Tess, in her legal marriage to Angel, is experiencing the goddess within herself, which is part of the initiation.

But the imagery of their first night suggests a mock hierogamy. He intends to consummate the marriage not in a forest, but under a "roof-tree" (283). A bough of mistletoe, symbolic of both Zeus and phallic fertility, is present, but it is cut from the plant, suggesting the emasculation of the oak god with which it is connected.[18] Up to this point, the iconography of the myth is dominated by positive connotations, and one's tendency is to expect that Tess will, in her marriage to Clare, undergo initiation rather than rape. These expectations, however uneasily we hold them, are due in large part to prevailing opinions about marriage, which is always thought preferable to seduction, and to our perception of Angel's straightforward, disinterested character. Yet there is a whole group of situations and images, of which these are the first, that are more appropriate to the Callisto who is a victim of rape than to the woman who achieves her own apotheosis.

For Tess *is* cast out and exiled – not by her fellow nymphs, but by the god himself, who ironically condemns her for partaking of his own faults. As a result, she wanders toward Flintcomb-Ash like a "wild animal" (349). The death of her father puts her (and the family) in the same anomalous position as the death of Lycaon placed the Callisto of the medieval tradition and the whole process starts again, with Alec returning to take advantage of her helplessness. But the completion of this third cycle is interrupted by the arrival of Angel Clare, who is going to save her. In another ironic variation, however, Angel's desire to aid Tess results instead in her demise. When she, like the Callisto of Hesiod, trespasses upon the sacred precinct of the sun god, symbolically by breaking the law and killing Alec, physically by going to Stonehenge, he is unable to prevent her destruction; the "president of the immortals" thus ends his sport with Tess. Her transport to the skies comes only through her execution.

A question invariably arises out of this bare summary: if Hardy's treatment of the Tess-Angel relationship is so positive at the outset, what makes it so destructive in the long run? And in turn, one wonders why her unconsummated marriage to Clare is so much more destructive than her physical rape by Alec.

The disguise motif offers some insight into this problem. Not only does Clare pretend to be a farmer rather than a gentleman, but he also pretends to elevate "Helenic Paganism at the expense of Christianity; yet in that civilization an illegal surrender was not certain disesteem" (422). It could be said that it is ostensibly as a "pagan" that he approaches Tess. As a pagan he recognizes her true virginity, for what really attracts him to her are the qualities which she has achieved through her relationship with Alec. The first time he notices her she tells of her past as Callisto and her achievement of psychological virginity by describing how one can lose one's body and become a star: "'I do know that our souls can be made to go outside our bodies when we are alive ... A very easy way to feel 'em go,' continued Tess, 'is to lie on the grass at night and look straight up at some big bright star; and, by fixing your mind upon it, you will soon find that you are hundreds and hundreds o' miles away from your body, which you don't seem to want at all'" (175).

When he comments to himself "What a fresh and virginal daughter of nature that milkmaid is!" he speaks a truth which he himself does not understand, and acknowledges the way in which her virgin qualities attract him. She is a virgin in the sense in which she is *parthenos*, a woman who has come to Talbothays to seek independence. As their relationship develops it becomes very clear that it is not simply her prettiness which attracts him: her appearance is only the initial magnetism. What he comes to love is her soul. He is enchanted by the things that she knows about life and its trials; he is unaware that "Tess's passing corporeal blight had been her mental harvest." The pagan in him admires the mental harvest; the Christian is soon to condemn her for the corporeal blight.

Indeed, one of the very reasons why her attitudes and observations are so moving and attractive is that they reflect Clare's own professed rejection of Christian doctrine. Unable to believe Article Four, he keeps close acquaintance with the "seasons in their moods, morning and evening, night and noon, winds in their differing tempers, trees, waters and mists, shades and silences, and the voices of inanimate things"; as a result he is "wonderfully free from the chronic melancholy which is taking hold of the civilized races with the decline of belief in a beneficent power" (174). The result is not only that Clare seems to have pagan attitudes even while his moral sense is decidedly Christian, but that, in need of something to worship, he chooses Tess.

Consequently, Clare tends to distort Tess's character in a reversal of the disguise motif in the myth. His habit is to see her as a goddess: "She was no longer the milkmaid, but a visionary essence of woman – a whole sex condensed into one typical form. He called her Artemis, Demeter, and other fanciful names half-teasingly, which she did not like because she did not understand them. "'Call me Tess,' she would say, askance, and he did" (187). It is his tendency to misinterpret her, to envision her a goddess, a "soul at large" that brings him to accuse her of the "grotesque prestidigitation," a condemnation which, since it leads to her eventual exile, can be thought of as a form of rape. What Hardy suggests is that the tendency to disguise women, to force upon them the role of goddess, or immortal perfection, is a destructive tendency, one which, in essence, rapes them of their mortal sexuality. Clare, in envisioning in Tess a goddess, denies her right to be mortal.

In some ways, Clare's ability to get close enough to Tess to rape her is a result of a third disguise. According to Apollodorus, Zeus gained Callisto's trust by disguising himself as Apollo, and it has been suggested earlier in this study that the Apollonian disguise refers to the intellectual aspect of man which arouses no sexual fears in women. On the one hand, Clare's love has a decent, disinterested, responsible quality which, since it is so at variance with d'Urberville's behaviour, makes Tess feel safe. He is "an intelligence rather than a man (181); a "palpitating and contemplative being" (213) who "loved her dearly, though perhaps rather ideally and fancifully" (255). On the other hand, it is precisely Clare's rigid rationalism which is a moving force behind his rejection of Tess: "Within the remote depths of his constitution, so gentle and affectionate as he was in general, there lay hidden a hard logical deposit, like a vein of metal in soft loam, which turned the edge of everything that attempted to traverse it. It had blocked his acceptance of the Church; it blocked his acceptance of Tess" (311).

Andrew Enstice defines Clare's logical turn of mind as "a type of the Victorian rationalism, scholarship and philosophical exploration which, while purporting to free the human mind from the shackles of human superstition and darkness, only served to mask and distort true feeling and the inexpressible wonder of the human mind."[19] Yet this description does not take into account the enormity of the damage done by Clare's logical attitudes. Hardy suggests obliquely that "more animalism" would have made Clare "the nobler man", and that his "love was doubtless ethereal to a fault" (315). As in *Mysteries of Udolpho*, where Emily's fate is nearly ruined by men who are "superior" by virtue of their logical orientations, as in *Jane Eyre*, where Jane nearly experiences spiritual rape at the hand of the logical Rivers, Tess is abused by Clare's rigid logic. Yet the enormity of this violation is not realized in the two earlier novels: Jane barely escapes the demands of St John Rivers, and Emily more or less waits for everything to turn out satisfactorily. Only Hardy fully demonstrates the ways in which logic precludes the acceptance of any experiences that do not precisely fit man's logical labels.

Clare's rejection of Tess, then, is as much logical as it is Christian. Logic does not allow him to comprehend the true significance of Tess's seduction by Alec, and Christianity provides the rules by which a seduced woman is automatically labelled an adulteress. There is, in addition, a powerful irony in the fact that Clare loved Tess because as part of the natural world she relieved him of his melancholic lack of faith, a lack of faith which is caused by his inability to believe what is illogical – the bodily resurrection of Christ. He can imagine neither of them transcending the experience of their bodies. Consequently the very "logical" disbelief which she cures is the same as the logical disbelief that destroys her.

Tess is aware that reason is the source of Angel's power and his condemnation. She is also curiously aware that she can either acquiesce passively to Angel's rejection, or fight against it through her continuing corporeal presence. She tells Clare: "You once said that I was apt to win men against their better judgement; and if I am constantly before your eyes I may cause you to change your plans in opposition to your reason and wish ..." (315). Yet because she understands Angel's unearthly, spiritual love and his active intelligence as his godliness, she drifts into that "passive responsiveness to all things her lover suggested" (269), a passive responsiveness that is the very basis of her acceptance of his judgments and edicts.

Tess's passivity is evoked in some versions of the myth by the image of the sleeping nymph which attracts Zeus, and is echoed in the novels by Emily's deference to the reasonable, knowledgeable Count de Villefort, and Jane Eyre's paralysis at the hands of the rational St John Rivers. Milton's Lady evades Comus' literal rape because she exercises the masculine power of logic; women who do not do so find themselves vulnerable. In *Tess of the D'Urbervilles* we see the emotional dynamic of such passivity. Tess's acquiescence to Clare comes out of a complete devotion and adoration. She must not contravene his wishes in any way because he is, after all, the god, and she a mere mortal – and a faulty one at that. Hardy suggests, then, that the inability of Callisto to fight off the god who is going to rape her is less a function of her physical helplessness than of her tendency to perceive him as right because he is powerful. In accepting Clare's judgment Tess accepts the patriarchy's logical, Christian definition of a "pure woman" – a definition that Hardy clearly meant to contravene in this novel. The field-folk at Marlott do not condemn her, nor would the women with whom she works at Flintcomb-Ash. But she does not accept the more beneficent judgment which is characteristic of people who live in a world with pre-patriarchal attitudes; instead, she internalizes the judgments of her "god," and acquiesces passively to her own exile. In this way, Hardy again emphasizes the extent to which Tess's self-condemnation is responsible for her downfall. The extent to which she accepts and carries out the patriarchy's judgments of her is a measure of her complete victimization.

As in *Jane Eyre*, the Moon Mother is emblematically present in the scene of Tess's ultimate passivity, the one in which Clare sleep-walks with his beloved in his arms. But in Brontë's novel, the moon effectively shocks Jane out of her passivity and guides her once more to an active role in her own future. Hardy's vision is quite different; it shows his awareness of the moon goddess' helplessness in this issue, for her image is split (319), as if her character, like Tess's, is fragmented. The young girl who once walked away from the security that Alec d'Urberville offered, despite the fact that she carried his child and doubtless would face social ostracization as a result, now lies passively in her sleep-walking lover's arms: "So easefully had she delivered her whole being up to him that it pleased her to think he was regarding her as his absolute possession to dispose of as he should choose" (318). Hardy continually emphasizes the extent to which Tess's passivity is at least a partial agent of her destruction. When Clare leaves her, she does not in any way try to persuade him to stay: "Her mood of long-suffering made his way easy for him, and she herself was his best advocate" (324). While Hardy agrees with Brontë and Radcliffe in showing passivity to be a dysfunctional behaviour, he is less sure that the matriarchal spirit is strong enough to guide its followers out of the morass of acquiescence.

Tess's exile is made all the more difficult by a very practical problem: her inability to get work except in circumstances that are hostile and miserable. The way in which Tess's fate in this part of the novel is echoed by the industrialization of agriculture has been noted by Douglas Brown and Arnold Kettle,[20] but it has not yet been linked to the destruction of a whole matriarchal way of life. By drawing upon the Callisto myth's oldest implications, Hardy elevates Tess's tragedy from the merely personal level to the universal. Callisto's rape is the rape of womanhood; it echoes the patriarchy's destruction of the matriarchate and the matriarchal ways. Such destruction is expressed not only through man's suppression of woman as an independent person and as a sexual being, but also through the disenfranchisement of women that resulted from industrialization. The agricultural world, in the early sections of the novel, was replete with descriptions which conjured up a matriarchal way of life. Moreover, in Hardy's creation of Tess, he has paid special attention to her peculiarly feminine relationship to nature and he draws upon this to describe her final destruction as victim of the industrialization of agriculture.

We know that part of Hardy's intention in writing *Tess of the D'Urbervilles* was to illustrate these destructive and disintegrating changes in agricultural ways. Mrs Hardy writes that for two years before the composition of *Tess*, her husband observed "in greater detail than ever before the scenes of the story and was powerfully impressed by the massing evidence of the decay in agricultural life."[21] Hardy had, in fact, been observing these changes for quite some time and had catalogued them in an article titled "The Dorsetshire Labourer," published in 1883, eight years before *Tess*. Many of the observations he made in his essay make their way into the novel. In his article, for example, he writes that the hacking of swedes was brutal work, but that sometimes it was the only winter job that could be found by a woman; he relates that there was a new tendency to evict "liviers" for ostensibly moral reasons, while the real purpose was greater efficiency and income for the farmer if he tilled these lands himself. He also suggests that a prayer should be said for good weather on Lady Day for the easier migrations of the hundreds of workers unable to find permanent employment that suits them. His description of the typical Lady Day evacuation is lifted verbatim from the article and placed in the novel to describe the removal of the Durbeyfield family from their country home: "The tendency of rural populations towards large towns ... is really the tendency of water to flow upstream when forced by machinery."[22]

Tess's third crisis and third rape is a direct result of her inability to get work in the agricultural community because she is a woman. Talbothays needed very little female help while the cows were calving; she could return to her old work harvesting only while the season lasted. Thus she comes to wander in exile both from Angel Clare and from her role as a field-woman, and like Callisto in her exile "there was something of the habitude of the wild animal in the unreflecting instinct with which [Tess] rambled on" (349).

Thus Tess's demise as a woman is echoed and reinforced by her demise as a field-woman. This is the role to which she returns once Clare's sovereigns are gone: "Thus Tess walks on: a figure which is part of the land-scape; a field-woman pure and simple" (355). But she is forced to leave the lands of her birth and her love, forced to leave the hills which resemble Cybele the Many-breasted (355) to wander towards Flintcomb-Ash where the trees of Diana's temples are the tenant farmer's enemies (356). Even Tess's last encounter with the forest is ominous: she shares her nest with dead and dying birds who have been hunted down – as she is soon to be. Her favourable comparison of her own situation to theirs is sadly ironic. It bespeaks both her determination to endure Clare's cruelty, and foreshadows her death.

The work at Flintcomb-Ash has about it none of the pleasure or joy of harvesting. Hacking swedes in the pouring rain, drawing reeds, all of this work is done with Farmer Groby at Tess's back. The work becomes so onerous that Tess contemplates going with Alec as an escape, yet these thoughts are always mere fantasy until the day of the threshing, when Tess is so driven by the *machinery* that she feels her body and soul becoming separated: her body works on constantly, while her soul endeavours to escape. The final demise comes when Tess's father dies, and the family's lease on their home is ended. The main reason why they have no employment arranged is that "they were only women; they were not regular labourers" (443).

When Alec finds the exiled Tess once more financially vulnerable, the whole rape process begins again. D'Urberville, closely associated with the sun which reveals him to Tess while he is preaching the word of God, is disguised as a lay minister, and Hardy's description of him emphasizes the extent to which he is not really himself, but "a transfiguration." (See chapter 45, where these images are frequent.) His disguise as a man for whom spiritual things are uppermost encourages Tess to believe momentarily that she is safe.

Alec's pursuit of Tess occurs in the context of his own religious wasteland. That which once seemed "a jolly new idea" (387) gets its first real questioning when it seems to contradict his overwhelming passion for Tess. When Tess repeats Clare's "merciless polemical syllogism" (400), malevolent logic completes the destruction which passion had begun. Alec tells Tess: "I thought I worshipped on the mountains, but I find I still serve in the groves" (402). The groves are, of course, those of the Great Goddess, and he finds that in returning to Tess, he must perforce abandon Christianity.

The problem lies in the fact that he is unable to appreciate or understand the qualities of the goddess or her devotee for whom he has traded his Christian beliefs. He seeks, once again, to possess her, to treat her as Eve or the wicked witch of Babylon – "Christian" images of womanhood which remain with him even when his faith is abandoned. He has no models for womanhood other than those which Christianity has provided, and Christianity's women are typically characterized by extreme looseness or absolute purity. These images provide no way of comprehending a mortal woman who nonetheless strives for a decent, respectable existence. Like Clare, he loses his faith but retains its attitude toward such an unusual woman as Tess. Since she cannot be worshipped in the context of the Christian values he has supposedly discarded, the appropriate response is to treat her like Christianity's whores.

This tendency to divide women into the two Christian categories is reminiscent of Lefevre's attitude toward his Callisto figure in *Recuyell of the Historyes of Troye*. In a very Lefevrian way Alec shifts the blame for his passion to her beauty and its seductiveness. Echoing Lefevre's clerical attitude toward his medieval Callisto, Alec thinks of the impure woman as another Eve. Consequently he asks if there has ever been "such a maddening mouth since Eve's!" (402), or "such eyes … before Christianity or since!" (396). When he cannot leave her alone, he comments: "What a grand revenge you have taken! I saw you innocent, and I deceived you. Four years after, you find me a Christian enthusiast; you then work upon me, perhaps to my completed perdition!" (409). Alec's accusations regarding her seductiveness are voiced frequently enough that Tess comes to think of herself as responsible, much as did Lefevre's Callisto figure: "There was revived in her the wretched sentiment which had often come to her before, that in inhabiting the fleshly tabernacle with which nature has endowed her she was somehow doing wrong" (388).

Yet Alec comes to her initially with an appreciation for what she once was and for the psychological virginity she gained at his hands. Thinking himself a "scamp ... to foul that innocent life" (393), he comments, "I never despised you; if I had I should not love you now! Why I did not despise you was on account of your being unsmirched in spite of all; you withdrew yourself from me so quickly and resolutely when you saw the situation; you did not remain at my pleasure; so there was one petticoat in the world for whom I had no contempt, and you are she" (402). This attitude, however, changes when her independence is no longer merely a basic part of what is attractive about her, but a major part of her defense against his continued attentions.

His anger at Tess for refusing first his advances and then his protection against Farmer Groby's unfair treatment and the family's loss of home – for refusing, in short, to be anything less than the independent person she has made herself – combines with his estimate of her as a seductress and results in an attitude much like Zeus' when Callisto hails him as Diana and praises the goddess above all the other gods. At first d'Urberville is amused, and even attracted. But finally, it becomes a question of power. Her independent manner so rankles d'Urberville that, regardless of the amiability of their first few encounters and the honest anger he feels at her family's dispossession, he remarks: "I will be your master again!" (412), and "Mind this; you'll be civil yet!" (449).

When she is forced into acquiescence by her family's need, she gives only her body – the only part he really wants or can appreciate – causing Angel Clare to note, in their brief encounter at the lodging house, "that his original Tess has spiritually ceased to recognize the body before him as hers – allowing it to drift, like a corpse upon the current, in a direction dissociated from its living will" (467). It is an ironic apotheosis which Hardy describes here: Tess's soul has transcended her body after the "rescue" of the god, but that transcendence is forced upon her by Alec's demand that she become his mistress.

When Clare, another manifestation of the god, comes to rescue her and reinstate her in her proper place as his wife, some complex inversions result. First, Clare cannot "save" her; her murder of Alec is beyond his power to undo. But because of this very lack of power, they can, during their stay in the *New* Forest, regenerate the love they once had. As long as the sun, symbol of Zeus, of the godly power Clare once had, and of the patriarchy, does not shine, they are safe. When forced, however, by the threat of discovery on a sunny day, to leave the forest and seek another asylum, they come to Stonehenge – and this is where Tess is captured.

The symbolism of this final scene is the ultimate proof that Tess's fate is not merely physical rape by a young dandy and unfair desertion by her husband, but a whole series of rapes by men who represent the values of the patriarchy. Stonehenge is identified in the novel as a place where sacrifices to the sun were once conducted; Tess herself has been sacrificed to and raped by the patriarchal values of both Alec and Angel.

The progression of the rapes and their effect upon Tess provides Hardy's final comment. Alec d'Urberville rapes her physically, yet the result is not Tess's destruction, but her initiation. Although he has power over her, she does not see him as godly, and consequently does not accept the implicit judgment of his casual use of her body. Moreover, the community's refusal to condemn her, their acceptance of her fate as part of life, aids in her self-renewal.

In contrast, Clare's spiritual rape is so devastating because Tess perceives him as godly, and she is therefore ready to accept his judgment of her. In spite of the fact that the women around her are supportive, she is ready to accept the contrary word of a single man because she worships him. Any psychological virginity that she gained through her survival of the affair with Alec is now destroyed by Angel's treatment. Rather than being independent, she is passive. Moreover, the fact that Angel sees her as something of a whore, and that she accepts that judgment, contributes to her giving in to Alec's desires at the end of the novel.

Yet what must be emphasized about the third rape is that not only are Tess's personal resources of independence and pride devastated, but so are the external supports she might have drawn on. A whole way of life, a way that connects woman with the earth in a manner that supports her and gives her a place in the world, has been destroyed, and Tess has been destroyed with it. We see here the culmination of a theme that appeared tangentially in *Mysteries of Udolpho, Jane Eyre, The Scarlet Letter,* and *Adam Bede*: the conflict between woman's essential tie to the earth and society's urbanization and industrialization. Jane Eyre and Rochester, Emily and Valancourt avoid life at London or Paris, preferring their quiet, secluded country estates. Essentially they are attempting to avoid society's inevitable condemnation of their unusual and equal relationships. Hester Prynne's rosebush seems to be out of place near both the prison door with its iron spikes and the "penal machine" on which she is forced to stand. Moreover, attributing the planting of that rosebush to Anne Hutchinson, a woman who attempted to place women in control of their religious lives, further identifies nature with the feminine in that novel. Hester's comfort at the edge of civilization and in the forests and Pearl's wildflower and seaweed toys all contrast with Bellingham's attitudes toward a natural world which he feels he must compel to grow what he wishes. Finally, Hetty's satisfying life at Hayslope contrasts with her imprisonment and trial in the industrialized town of Stoniton. Hardy, by paying special attention to Tess's tie to the earth and to agriculture, illustrates that part of her tragedy is precipitated by the fact that she cannot find work in the changing agricultural system. Thus her tragedy seems to transcend the personal and to involve the destruction of a way of life in which women had some power.

Tess is also overwhelmed by the power men have to define her experience and her womanhood. In the matriarchal or initiatory aspect of the myth, the nymph knows herself to be, for a moment at the very least, the goddess herself. Women defined what happened to them in their rituals, and by defining, made it so. Moreover, that definition suggested that every woman represented, in some way or another, the goddess herself. But Alec d'Urberville and Angel Clare perceive only a single facet of Tess's womanhood. In one sense their rape of her is their limited perception of her as a woman. Essentially, they redefine her to meet their own needs and expectations: Alec perceives her as nothing but a sexual being; Angel refuses to acknowledge her sexuality and conceives of her as a replacement for the divine being in whom he can no longer believe. What we come to see, as we watch her tragedy unfold, is that either approach is one-sided, and either limits Tess too much or asks too much of her. In essence, they repeat a process that occurred long before Ovid ever wrote the *Metamorphoses*: by fragmenting Tess into woman-flesh and goddess they repeat the patriarchy's fragmentation of the Great Mother herself. Such fragmentation accounts for the polarity of Mary and Eve, of the whore and the saint, of the way in which woman has been defined for eons.

CHAPTER NINE

Lady Chatterley's Lover: *Liberating the Myth*

D.H. Lawrence's *Study of Thomas Hardy*, like so much of his literary criticism, is as much about his own predilections and his own work as it is about his predecessor. As such, it forges a link between Hardy's fiction, especially the Wessex novels, and Lawrence's own passionate observations on modern life and love. The heat of his prose in the *Study* betrays, in particular, the great love he had for *Tess of the D'Urbervilles*: "The whole book is true, in its conception" he remarks.[1] Yet while he loved Tess herself, he was almost indignant about Hardy's treatment of her.

The first image Lawrence employs in the *Study* is that of the blooming poppy, which, by achieving "its complete poppy-self" (403), realizes a kind of psychological virginity. Lawrence begins his study of Hardy with this image because he feels so strongly that Hardy's novels are about Wessex poppies, people "struggling hard to come into being ... through love and love alone." This coming to oneself requires of the poppy or the character the willingness and ability to shoot "suddenly out of a tight convention" (410). The poppy is, then, very like the Callisto figures of all of the works that have been examined, with the exception, perhaps, of Milton's *Mask*, wherein the Lady chooses to abide by the conventions of her age.

Lawrence's admiration for Tess Durbeyfield is partly accounted for by what he calls her "aristocracy":

She is of an old line, and has the aristocratic quality of respect for the other being. She does not see the other person as an extension of herself, existing in a universe of which she is the centre and pivot. She knows that other people are outside her. Therein she is an aristocrat. And out of this attitude to the other person came her passivity ... Tess is passive out of self-acceptance, a true aristocratic quality, amounting almost to self-indifference. She knows she is herself incontrovertibly, and she knows that other people are not herself. This is a very rare quality, even in a woman. (483)

"Knowing herself incontrovertibly" is Tess's strength, yet Lawrence is also aware that her psychological virginity involves a weakness – a naïveté, perhaps – about the cruelty of others who do not know themselves. He also maintains that her self-knowledge constitutes a vulnerability particular to the time in which Hardy writes: "The female was strong in her. She was herself. But she was out of place, utterly out of her element and her times. Hence her utter bewilderment. This is the reason why she was so overcome. ... Tess was herself, female, intrinsically a woman" (486). Thus, as Lawrence sees it, in spite of her self-knowledge, and in spite of the way in which her aristocratic respect for others results in her tolerance toward them, the tolerance which Tess ought to have for herself is granted instead to the systems which other people have formulated, and which eventually destroy her because they misunderstand her.

Lawrence accurately observes that rebellion does not go unpunished in Hardy's microcosm of Wessex, but he is unable to separate Hardy's vision of the way the world is from his own vision of the way the world ought to be. He finds it disturbing that Hardy's characters tragically fail because they "subscribe to the system" (411). More specifically, he says of Tess and other Hardy characters like her that they "were not at war with God, only with Society. Yet they were all cowed by the mere judgment of man upon them, not the judgment of their own souls or the judgment of Eternal God. Which is the weakness of modern tragedy, where transgression against the social code is made to bring destruction, as though the social code worked our irrevocable fate" (420).

What Lawrence fails to see is that, in allowing social convention to control fate, Hardy is making a comment upon Victorian society. But at the same time, his *Study* does give us a sense of the kinds of errors he attempts to avoid in his own works. When he comes to write *Lady Chatterley's Lover*, his own Callisto narrative, he tries to correct many of the defects that he sees in Hardy's novel. Unlike Tess Durbeyfield, Connie is allowed control over her fate and she can, with the aid of 500 pounds a year, safely transcend the limited vision of her culture. She chooses her exile: it is not imposed upon her. By giving Connie the courage to leave Wragby, Lawrence avoids what he saw in Hardy: "the tragedy of those who, more or less pioneers, have died in the wilderness, whither they had escaped for free action, after having left the walled security, and the comparative imprisonment, of the established convention" (411).

Lawrence and Hardy reveal similar concerns in their respective conceptions of the wasteland which Zeus is overseeing when he finds Callisto. Wastelands in the previous works have ranged in character from Milton's moral wilderness, Emily St Aubert's sense of personal loss, Rochester's ill-lived life, to the poverty of the Durbeyfield family. What these wastelands have in common is that they are largely limited to their effect upon the protagonists. Hardy begins to widen the sphere when he implies that the fiery machine of the engineer at Flintcomb Ash threatens the livelihood of the entire farming community, much as the fire of Phaeton's ride scorched the earth. Lawrence's creation of the wasteland at Wragby picks up precisely where Hardy left off. First, the setting of *Lady Chatterley's Lover* is one in which industrialization is somewhat more prevalent than it was in Hardy's work. As Julian Moynihan describes it, Wragby and it's surroundings are "a portion of English soil in transition from a semi-rural, semi-industrial condition to one of total industrialization."² The fiery machinery of the engineer at Flintcomb Ash is expanded into the industrial fire at Tevershall pit and Stacks Gate: "bright rows of lights at Stacks Gate, smaller lights at Tevershall pit, the yellow lights of Tevershall and lights everywhere, here and there, on the dark country, with the distant blush of furnaces, faint and rosy, since the night was clear, the rosiness of the outpouring of white-hot metal. Sharp, wicked electric lights at Stacks Gate! An undefinable quick of evil in them! And all the unease, the ever-shifting dread of the industrial night in the Midlands."³

Lawrence's depiction of the wasteland which surrounds Wragby has been noticed in the context of the Fisher King myth; Scott Sanders argues that the relationship of Connie and Mellors is a kind of grail, the purpose of which is to renew the symbolic wasteland Wragby and its environs represent.⁴ Mandel refers to Tevershall and Stacks Gate as the "symbol of all that is moribund and mechanical in England, and destructive of the human values Lawrence affirmed."⁵ They dehumanize the workers, making them little more than physical and emotional cripples: men with "one shoulder higher than t'other, legs twisted, feet all lumps!" (228), "men [who] aren't men [so] that th' women have to be" (229). Yet the industrial desolation which Lawrence describes, with its descriptive emphasis upon the fires and the lights, bears a far more direct relation to the havoc wrecked by Phaeton's uncontrolled ride than to the wasteland of the Fisher King. The colliery fires impinge upon the forest: the fine old park of oak trees is overshadowed by the "chimney of Tevershall pit with its clouds of steam and smoke" (13). While the critics have noticed the wasteland element of the novel, they have incorrectly identified the myth to which it belongs.

For the coal pits do not comprise the only wasteland in the novel. At the outset of the novel an emotional barrenness is described in terms which evoke the wreckage which Phaeton caused when his father's chariot fell from the skies: "We've got to live, no matter how many skies have fallen" (5). The fallen skies of the novel are the destructions of World War 1, whereby the forest is decimated to make trenches and a man is deprived not only of the feeling in his legs but of feeling altogether. This loss of physical feeling is compensated for by what Clifford and his cronies call the life of the mind, which is in fact another wasteland. Tommy Dukes describes it in terms of a separation from or destruction of nature, just as the wasteland in the myth is indicated by the destruction of the forest: "But, mind you, it's like this; while you *live* your life, you are in some way an organic whole with all life. But once you start the mental life you pluck the apple. You've severed the connection between the apple and the tree: the organic connection. And if you've got nothing in your life *but* the mental life, then you yourself are a plucked apple ... you've fallen off the tree" (39).

These two wastelands, the industrial one represented by Tevershall Pit, the emotional one precipitated by the war and manifested in the life of the mind, have in common not only their tendency to cripple people and deface the forest, but their demonstration of the inability to discern the sacred. People crippled by industry have lost their sense of what is holy; the factories which destroy their humanity are elevated to a religious status; the "works" are "the modern Olympia with temples to all the gods" and they send up "a whole array of smoke and steam to whatever gods there be" (160-1). The workers' new temples include the "Primitive Chapel," movie houses that play films like "A Woman's Love" which are substitutes not only for religion but also for real love (158). The grail quests which are frequently seen to inform this novel usually entail a hero's recovery of some ignored religious dimension. In this passage, however, the wasteland and religion are one; clearly any renewal will not come in the "typical" way.

The mental lifers have also lost a sense of what is sacred in sex. For them a relationship with a woman is no different than "talking to her about the weather. It's just an interchange of sensations instead of ideas" (34). The relationship between the sexual and industrial has been noted by Peter Balbert: "These men limit, or pervert, or deny the sexual love of women, and this failure merges with and exacerbates their inability to respond confidently, with a proud and existential urging of the whole self, to the postwar issues of the growing power of the machine, the entrenchment of industry, and the social and psychic devastation occasioned by the slaughter of a generation of English men."[6] They have missed the way in which sex links us with all that is sacred and magical in the universe. In "A Propos of *Lady Chatterley's Lover*" Lawrence writes of this powerful connection:

Sex is the balance of male and female in the universe, the attraction, the repulsion the transit of neutrality, the new attraction, the new repulsion, always different, always new. The long neuter spell of Lent, when the blood is low, and the delight of the Easter kiss, the sexual revel of spring, the passion of mid-summer, the slow recoil, revolt, and grief of autumn, greyness again, then the sharp stimulus of winter of the long nights. Sex goes through the rhythm of the year, in man and woman, ceaselessly changing: the rhythm of the sun in his relation to the earth. Oh, what a catastrophe for man when he cut himself off from the rhythm of the year, from his unison with the sun and the earth. Oh, what a catastrophe, what a maiming of love when it was made a personal, merely a personal feeling, taken away from the rising and the setting of the sun, and cut off from the magic connection of the solstice and the equinox! This is what is the matter with us. We are bleeding at the roots, because we are cut off from the earth and sun and stars, and love is a grinning mockery, because, poor blossom, we plucked it from its stem on the tree of Life, and expected it to keep on blooming in our civilized vase on the table.[7]

In the context of the matriarchal aspect of the Callisto myth, the forest traditionally provides a place for the discovery of these sacred dimensions of love and life; it is typically a place of initiation, the realm where the mortal woman meets the god in a ritual which re-enacts "the sun in his relation to the earth." It is also the chapel where she dedicates herself to the goddess.

The sacred quality of the experiences of Callisto figures has been expressed in a variety of ways – through the woodland convent of *The Mysteries of Udolpho*, the "consecration" of Hester's experience, or Hetty's meeting with a godly young man. Similarly, Connie's retreat to the forest is described in ways that suggest a search for the sacred and a rejection of Wragby's denial of that aspect of life; she would "rush off across the park, and abandon Clifford, and lie prone in the bracken. To get away from the house ... she must get away from the house and everybody. The wood was her one refuge, her *sanctuary*" (21, emphasis mine). Moreover, her need for this particular flight is created by her father's concern with her "demi-vierge" status (18). (Connie is a "demi-vierge" in spite of her affair with Michaelis because their sex is so mechanical, so lacking in the mystical dimension.) We might say, without being thoroughly inaccurate, that Connie goes to the forest precisely to get rid of her semi-virginity, as girls once went to sacred forest temples (or sanctuaries, to use Lawrence's word) to be initiated into their sexuality and to understand the sacredness of the experience. With respect to this aspect of *Lady Chatterley's Lover*, Ian Gregor writes that Lawrence was

intent on restoring a sacred character to sex – he would not have it vulgarized and degraded in what he considered the "modern way" – he would reveal it again as a holy mystery. Mircea Eliade, in *Patterns of Comparative Religion* writes: "For the modern man, sex is a physiological act, whereas for the primitive it was a sacrament, a ceremony by means of which he communicated with the force which stood for life itself." It is in the light of this primitive vision that Lawrence writes. Hence his sexual descriptions are charged with the language of religion, and language which is rich in biblical association and power.[8]

Connie instinctively, but unconsciously, perceives that the forest is what Eliade calls "sacred space," and that only the natural world has the potential to reintroduce her to the sacredness of sex and of life.

Clifford is what might be called the "false god": while he has the most obvious sources of power in the novel – owning the woods and being, after all *Sir* Clifford – he has no sacred or religious qualities. Like so many of the Zeus-figures – St John Rivers and Villeroi, for example – he is also characterized by his faithfulness to what Lawrence calls the life of the mind. His attitude toward his relationship with Connie embodies the Logos-Eros struggle exactly: the Eros principle of relatedness has been reduced to intellectual sympathy. His *theories* about brief sexual encounters excuse his emotional and physical paralysis. He fully believes that because they have this sympathy of minds, her relationships with other men will not affect the "integrated life," the "harmonious thing" that they have created together (47). Like St John Rivers, he believes that what he thinks about love is far more important than what he feels. And like Jane Eyre at Moor House, Connie must flee from his emotional impotence. The life of the mind, with its control of a woman's sexuality, is what Connie must fight against, as Callisto fought the god about to rape her; the conflict with the false god is translated once again into woman's struggle with male attitudes.

The way in which this masculinized life of the mind has been the agent of her rape becomes clear to Connie as she and Clifford take a walk in the park and forest to see what the new spring has brought. Clifford's reaction to the natural beauty is to quote Keats. "Thou still unravished bride of quietness" in his response to the flowers that they find. Connie feels Clifford's language "ravishing" to the natural world and hence to herself. Moreover, she feels that Clifford's appreciation of beauty via literary allusion is too intellectual: "Suddenly, with all the force of her female instinct, she was shoving him off. She wanted to be clear of him, and especially of his consciousness, his words, his obsession with himself, his endless treadmill obsession with himself, and his own words" (93). Playing on this word "ravished," Connie observes that she, like Callisto, has been sexually abused, even though it is not a physical ravishment, but rather a rape by "dead words become obscene, and dead ideas become obsessions" (97). Clifford's excessively mental reaction to everything from flowers to sex comes very close to destroying Connie's perception of the magic, wonder, and sacredness of life. Lawrence's translation of Connie's mental exertion into physical terms emphasizes the connection to the myth, for what she must "shove off" is not Clifford's body, but the intellectual attitude he wants her to adopt.

Connie's sense that she is being raped by Clifford's language and ideas is strengthened when she comes back from seeing Mellors' vibrant and beautiful nakedness to examine her own body and to realize that she has been cheated, her body has been "disappointed of its real womanhood" (72). In this scene she becomes aware of the way in which her situation with Clifford has "defrauded" her, "even of her own body" (73). More specifically, she is aware of the extent to which the "life of the mind" has been the agent of her rape. Angel Clare exerts a purely mental control over Tess's sexuality by refusing to acknowledge her sexual power and her lost innocence; similarly, Clifford rationalizes away Connie's sexuality and belittles it drastically by suggesting that sexual encounters are essentially so unimportant that they cannot damage their relationship. Certainly a vehicle of this cheat is language, the ease and nonchalance with which the impotent talk about sex and reason about its proper place in their lives.

When a woman is raped in the conventional way, we think of it as an act of violence to her integrity; the attack on her sexuality is the means of eroding that integrity. The rape in this novel is not essentially different. Connie, because she is defrauded of her true physical feelings, loses her female integrity, and while the means used to effect this deprivation is language, the end is nevertheless control of her sexuality. What Lawrence emphasizes, as did Hardy, is that physical rape has its more subtle, non-physical counterparts.

Connie's retreat to the forest is, in one respect, like that of the Callistos of the medieval versions who want to escape the attentions of the amorous Jupiter, and who try to preserve their virginity by joining Diana's virgin band. Connie seeks sanctuary in the forest, sanctuary from the ravishment of words. But at the same time she is like the Callisto of the matriarchal configuration of the myth who goes to the forest to be initiated into her sexuality as a means of getting in touch with the feminine.

Although Connie does not join any literal virgin band, Lawrence's novel provides us with two surrogates. Like Tess and Hetty, Lady Chatterley finds that the women around her are sympathetic. In their supportive sympathy, they replace the band of Diana and even Diana herself. Both Mrs Bolton and Hilda, for example, are women without men, neither virgins any longer, like the matriarchal Diana, but both a little contemptuous of men and their helplessness. Hilda, we are told, "was a woman, soft and still as she seemed, of the old amazon sort, not made to fit with men" (79). Mrs Bolton, although she has respect in the extreme for Clifford as a member of the gentry, thinks that as a man he is a little bit like all men – a bit of a baby who adores the Magna Mater in her. And while she does not withdraw from this role, she fails to respect Clifford because of his dependence upon her willingness to play her part. She also resents the kind of power that he exercises capriciously and she "shares with [Connie] a great grudge against Sir Clifford and all he stood for" (146).

Both Mrs Bolton and Hilda are quite concerned about Connie's health. Mrs Bolton, rather like the matriarchal Diana, continually suggests that Connie go for a walk in the forest or the surrounding park. Connie needs *sunshine*, Mrs Bolton tells her. In a sense, Mrs Bolton covertly, and perhaps naively, suggests that Connie is in need of "renewal," but the problem is not her health, rather it is her sexuality which only the god can arouse. Later, when Connie and Mellors have had their mutual orgasm in the woods, Mrs Bolton, like the nymphs of the myth, immediately recognizes the change in Connie, and realizes that she has a lover, just as she later knows intuitively who that lover is.

Connie is aware of Mrs Bolton's knowledge, and vaguely aware of the nurse's complicity, although it is a complicity that she cannot quite understand. Connie herself feels that society is likely to condemn her for her affair, and she expects Mrs Bolton, in society's place, to be highly critical. Yet the nurse frequently protects Connie's interests, going to the forest to find her instead of letting Clifford send the servants, for instance. On this occasion, Connie expects the kind of casting-out which Callisto experiences, but is surprised to find that Mrs Bolton, although knowing, is thoroughly sympathetic, and has followed Connie not to condemn, but to protect her. She is never guilty of casting Connie out, yet she warns her of the likelihood of such an event when she talks of what happens to men and women when they are really together. As she and Connie work in the garden, she talks about her relationship with her Ted and about his death in the mines, warning Connie that men "*want* to separate a woman and a man, if they're together" (171). In her knowing, approving sympathy, she resembles the goddess of a matriarchal time, not the vengeful virgin Diana of a patriarchal era.

If Mrs Bolton provides an interesting version of Diana, the brooding hens represent an even more curious variation on the virgin band. Jane Eyre joins the girls at Lowood to gain a sense of who she is as a woman; those brooding hens also tell Connie something about her femininity: "One day when she came, she found two brown hens sitting alert and fierce in the coops, sitting on pheasants' eggs, and fluffed out so proud and deep in all the heat of the pondering female blood. This almost broke Connie's heart. She, herself, was so forlorn and un-used, not a female at all, just a mere thing of terrors" (117). As she watches the hens with their "hot, brooding female bodies," she becomes acutely aware "of the agony of her own female forlornness" (118).

Mellors approaches Connie, then, at a time when she is tremendously aware of her thwarted femininity. He approaches her, as did Zeus in the myth, in a kind of feminine disguise indicated by a vague femininity in his manner, his slenderness, and his lack of obvious machismo. This gentle, sympathetic nature of Mellors' approach contrasts with the trickery we usually associate with the disguised god. But in this instance his camouflage seems to indicate that he knows something about the female that she does not – he is, after all, overseer of all these brooding hens. His reasons for taking her into the hut and making love to her evolve out of his tremendous sympathy with her "female forlornness," which he understands intuitively without words or explanations, as if he had perhaps once known it himself.

Zeus' success while disguised as Diana is an indication of his ability to approach the woman through her femininity. How he uses that ability differentiates rape from initiation, and because Mellors uses his power caringly, we immediately sense that his disguise is beneficent.

The scene of their first love-making certainly resembles that of Callisto's seduction. Mellors drops his feminine disguise and surprises Connie when he makes love to her in the hut that is "illuminated by a very brilliant little moon shining above the afterglow over the oaks" (121). Yet many aspects of their love-making suggest that what occurs is an initiation, not a rape. First, the hut itself, which Connie later calls "a sort of little sanctuary" (91), suggests the temple where virgins are initiated. Second, her motives for allowing Mellors to make love to her suggest the initiate's awareness that this episode is necessary to her growth as a woman, that her own feminine nature is at stake because she can no longer cope with her thwarted femininity.

Third, the language describing their encounter carries sacred connotations. Michael Black notes, for example, that Mellors "ministers to her"; Mark Spilka suggests that their touch is a "mode of communion"; Mark Schorer describes these passages as "a great hymn to true marriage."[9] Rapes never possess religious dimensions. When a woman is raped, her feminine nature is violated; when she is initiated, it is enhanced. The rapes of *The Mysteries of Udolpho*, for example, are all efforts – whether conscious or not – to undermine Emily's sense of herself as a woman. Similarly, St John Rivers' assertion that Jane was "formed for labour, not for love" and Hester Prynne's confinement of her hair – a gesture meant to help her gain the approval of the elders – both illustrate the ways in which a raped woman is forced to repress her femininity as part of the rape or as punishment for "allowing" the violation.

Finally, the encounter which results in initiation usually has an impersonal character. As Harding observes: "At first it was the priest, who was not considered to be a man like other men, but was believed to be an incarnation of the god; he was recognized as functioning only in his office. In other cases the image of the phallus of the god was used. This rite was entirely without personal connotation. When the 'stranger' enacted the part of the priest or god, too, the impersonality of the situation was evident. ... In this way the nonpersonal, or divine aspect of the rite was impressed upon the participants."[10]

This impersonal quality is precisely described by Connie as she muses about her experience with Mellors:

And he was a passionate man, wholesome and passionate. But perhaps he wasn't quite individual enough; he might be the same with any woman as he had been with her. It really wasn't personal. She was only really a female to him.

But perhaps that was better. And after all, he was kind to the female in her, which no man had ever been. Men were very kind to the *person* she was, but rather cruel to the female, despising her or ignoring her altogether. Men were awfully kind to Constance Reid or to Lady Chatterley; but not to her womb they weren't kind. And he took no notice of Constance or of Lady Chatterley; he just softly stroked her loins or her breasts. (126)

There is a consistent pattern within all the love-making scenes that continually reiterates the Callisto myth in its initiatory aspects. Like Callisto, Connie is frequently unwilling to make love to Mellors. Although there is never any physical struggle, she must consistently cope with her own uncertainty about what their love-making means. Her metaphorical struggle with the god is represented by her continual striving to overcome Clifford's and Wragby's Logos orientation which she has internalized in spite of her hatred of it. Her criticism of the "life of the mind" of Clifford and his Wragby cronies is continually abandoned when "her spirit seemed to look on from the top of her head" (179) to watch Mellors' intercourse with her. Only slowly does Connie learn to reject in her actions the attitude she has long rejected mentally. She has to learn not to resist what her very instinct says she needs to escape the life of the mind and its wasteland: a vital connection with this man of the forest. When she does give up this resistance in their fourth encounter, she becomes a "sacrifice, and a new-born thing" (182), a woman who has been reborn through the giving up of herself in the sacred encounter.

Connie experiences not only the initiate's uncertainty of what her experience means, but also the woman's fear of losing herself, of being "encompassed," of becoming "slave to the male," just as Jane feared her servitude to St John Rivers. When she comes from Flint's farm and Mellors expresses his urgent desires, she is hesitant: "Her old instinct was to fight for freedom" (138). But like a woman initiated into her sexuality, Connie loses herself in this encounter: the achievement of psychological virginity means that one must be willing to lose in order to gain. At first, "they lay and knew nothing, not even of each other, both lost" (139). But as Connie begins to consider their love-making, she realizes that this "loss of herself to herself ... made her feel she was very different from her old self, and as if she was sinking deep, deep to the centre of all womanhood and the sleep of creation" (140–1). Although she remains afraid of his godliness, "lest if she adored him too much, then she would lose herself, become effaced" (141), her primary reaction is one of surrender, of relief at having been able, like a true initiate, to give herself up and gain, in return, a truer sense of herself, and most importantly of her womanhood.

This pattern of losing and regaining herself is consistent throughout the love-making scenes. When Connie is willing to lose herself, she is reborn.

In one such scene Lawrence writes of her experience: "She was gone, she was not, she was born: a woman" (181). This pattern illustrates the way in which Lawrence perceives Connie's growth in terms of a death of the individual, non-sexual self and a rebirth into the sacredness of sexuality.

Harding's descriptions of initiations suggest that a woman need give herself to the god only once to be a changed person, to have all the effects – religious and sexual – firmly entrenched in her personality. But there are seven love-making scenes in *Lady Chatterley's Lover*. Lawrence obviously felt that the change is not effected so easily, that our modern sense of the sacred is too weak. Each time that Connie and Mellors make love, Connie seems more acquiescent, more comfortable with the situation: her resistance is not so strong. Yet Lawrence feels that it is no easy process to escape the Logos-attitudes which British society in general, and Wragby in particular, have inculcated in Lady Chatterley.

One of the outcomes of Callisto's meeting with the god – in this case Connie's meetings with Mellors – is the encounter with Hera which results in Callisto's transformation into a bear. Bertha Coutts is the obvious Hera figure of this novel; as Mellors' wife she rants and raves about her "husband's" unfaithfulness, resembling in her fury both the other shrewish Juno from Caxton's *Metamorphoses* and Bertha Mason from *Jane Eyre*. A more interesting Hera figure is Clifford, whose physical impotence parallels Hera's inability to control Zeus' sexual escapades. Hera's treatment of Callisto results in the latter's transformation into a bear, a manifestation of the bestial in her character and behaviour. Clifford effects this same change by condemning the animal within the human, by preferring "self-important mentalities" to "self-important animalities" (203).

Connie learns, through her relationship with Mellors, to trade the mentalities, which she perceives as confining, for the positive aspects of the animal that are evoked by Callisto's transformation into the goddess' totem beast. Once she has come to terms with her relationship with Mellors and finally abandoned the Logos attitude completely, she and Mellors work on their "animalities."

Specifically, the scene in which they make love in the rain contains playful echoes of the Callisto myth. As prelude to their love-making, Connie and Mellors sit inside during a thunderstorm – which of course evokes Zeus – and Mellors, mixing his angry voice with the voice of the thunder god, denounces the industrial wasteland and the spiritual wasteland that goes with it. Connie, threatened by his godly pontifications, turns nymph, takes off her clothes, and goes running in the forest. Mellors, like Zeus of the myth, runs after her, chasing her through the trees until he captures her and takes her "short and sharp and finished, like an animal" (231). In one of the variations it is Zeus, not Hera, who transforms Callisto into a bear, as if giving a physical form to the sexuality he has evoked in her; this is precisely what Mellors does here. The final element of the myth reenacted in this scene is Connie's offer of a child, for hope, to Mellors. Like Callisto, who gives birth to Arcas, the ruler of the pastoral Arcadia, Connie believes that her child may likewise offer a contemporary Arcadia, a bastion of some kind, perhaps simply a bastion of hope, against the industrial wasteland which Mellors has condemned.

Once before Mellors had taken Connie like an animal, on the occasion when she is discovered coming from Flint's farm. But then she resisted the animal implications of their love-making outdoors. Now she comes to embrace them. And on the evening of the "phallic hunting-out" when Mellors makes her come to the "bed-rock of her nature," he fully exposes her to the animal side of her sexuality. Like the initiatory encounters described by Harding, which are not interested in love so much as in the giving up of oneself to one's own sexual nature, this meeting of Connie and Mellors has nothing to do with personal love but with "sensuality sharp and searing as fire, burning the soul to tinder" (258). Connie's frame of mind is like that of the initiate, who is both awed and terrified by the experience.

While the ingredients of the novel conform with fair straightforwardness to the myth, and while the quality and nature of Connie's and Mellors' love-making seem to echo that of the myth's matriarchal, initiatory variation, there are inevitably some deviations from the pattern of the myth. We might note for example that the imagery which indicates Mellors' godliness is not as prevalent as it is in some of the other works, and seems to develop very gradually. Only after they have made love three times does Connie note the holiness of his touch and decline to bathe because she does not want to erase it from her body (142).

And it is a long time before the central image which links Mellors to Zeus unfolds. The morning after their night in the cottage together, Connie observes that his "love-hair" is "like a little bush of bright red-gold mistletoe" (229), and mistletoe, as J.G. Frazer so laboriously points out in *The Golden Bough*, is a symbol of the sun god. That it is lit up by the morning sun reinforces our impression that the purpose of this image is to align Mellors with the sun-god of the myth.

The question that arises is why Lawrence, who certainly knew his mythology, waited so long to reinforce our sense that Mellors is functioning as the sun-god with concrete imagery. A number of critics have observed that he is a kind of Green Knight, a fertility figure, a man "whose task it is to repair the damage to natural habitat and life,"[11] but Lawrence does not immediately make his similarity to the god explicit for two reasons. The first is that Mellors is not, *de facto*, a representative of Zeus, but *earns* that role through his initiation of Connie. More important, this deviation may be traced back to another, for Mellors is not characterized by the obvious machismo of a sun-god; rather he retains his feminine disguise longer than the heroes of the other novels. There is something inherently feminine in him.

Connie's apocalyptic vision of Mellors comes when she is seeking him to relay a message from Clifford. Like *Zeus*, Connie has just left a wasteland, has fled from Wragby, where "all the great words ... were cancelled for her generation" and from where she can hear the collieries: "The air was soft and dead, as if all the world were slowly dying. Grey and clammy and silent, even from the shuffling of the collieries, for the pits were working short time, and today they were stopped altogether. The end of all things!" At first she feels that the forest is as full of "silence, nothingness" as the rest of the world. When she listens more carefully, however, she notices "the inwardness of the remnant of forest, the unspeaking reticence of the old trees" (67). Having escaped from the wasteland, then, Connie, like Zeus, comes upon a bathing nymph, but here the nymph is, somewhat paradoxically, Mellors.[12] Yet Lawrence does not end the turned-about situation here. For Connie, seeing Mellors, is attracted to him in precisely the way Zeus was attracted to Callisto. What strikes her is his *virginity*: "the sense of aloneness, of a creature purely alone, overwhelmed her. Perfect, white, solitary nudity of a creature that lives alone, and inwardly alone. And beyond that, a certain beauty of a pure creature. Not the stuff of beauty, not even the body of beauty, but a lambency, the warm, white flame of a single life, revealing itself in contours that one might touch: a body!" (68–9).

There are other things that indicate that Connie is, on some occasions, the Zeus figure of this novel and that Mellors plays Callisto. There is, for example, the scene in which Connie finds Mellors building the pheasant coops in the oak forest. As Connie approaches, Mellors is startled and perceives her as a threat, much as Callisto must have felt the presence of Zeus in the forest to be a threat. Moreover, we must note that Callisto was the hunter in the myth and one of Diana's nymphs – both at home in and part of the forest as well as someone who gains her sustenance there. Mellors, the keeper in *Lady Chatterley's Lover*, is, like Callisto, at home in the forest, and the continual presence of the gun slung across his shoulder evokes Callisto, the hunter.

Just as the Callisto of the medieval redactions of the myth has retired to the forest to escape from a world which has become too pressing, more specifically because the Jupiter's attentions have been too forceful, so Mellors has retired to the forest to escape his life with the willful, and, in a sense, pressing and masculine Bertha Coutts. Mellors' descriptions of their intercourse bear, in fact, a close resemblance to rape; he tells Connie how Bertha would "sort of tear at me down there, as if it was a beak tearing at me" (210). The result of her "rape" of him – her destruction of his male sexuality – is that he chooses, like Callisto, to exile himself from society, to live alone in the forest. "Especially he did not want to come into contact with a woman again. He feared it, for he had a big wound from old contacts. He felt if he could not be alone, and if he could not be left alone, he would die. His recoil away from the outer world was complete; his last refuge was this wood; to hide himself there!" (91). He feels betrayed in much the same way as does the Callisto of *The Golden Age*, and is unable to face society any longer because he has lost faith.

In the scene in which Mellors and Connie struggle over jurisdiction over the hut, Connie, not Mellors, wins the fight, much as Zeus won the struggle with Callisto, and was able physically to overcome her. Mellors' reaction to her presence and her power over him as *Lady* Chatterley reflects a fear of experiencing a kind of rape, a rape of his privacy: "He dreaded with a repulsion almost of death, any further close human contact. He wished above all things she would go away, and leave him to his own privacy. He dreaded her will, her female will, and her modern family insistency. And above all he dreaded her cool, upper-class impudence of having her own way. For after all he was only a hired man" (92). He recognizes the power of her class, just as Callisto recognized the power of Zeus' godliness. And what he fears most is contact, just as Callisto fears the physical contact of rape. When they finally do make love, it is Connie's body which is described as feeling like "little flamey oak leaves" (126), an image associating her with the sun god, even though it was Mellors who made the advances. The final parallel comes with Mellors' exile from Wragby which comes about because Bertha, the Hera figure of the novel, raises such a fuss about his having had an affair with Lady Chatterley, just as Callisto is exiled because she has consorted with the god.

Is Lawrence confused here? Possibly not. As in Connie's metaphorical rape by Clifford, Lawrence's deviation from the myth could be quite purposeful, and engages us in a "liberated" discussion of the myth. First, we realize that he sees that the needs of men and women are not as radically different as might be supposed. Other authors, by limiting Callisto's fate to the female characters, suggest that only women are vulnerable to rape, that only women achieve psychological virginity, and that only women are subject to the kind of growth which the heroines achieve, as well as that only women are threatened by the Callisto-like fate of societal disapproval. By making Mellors a Callisto figure, Lawrence makes us realize the vulnerability of men, and suggests that society has come farther than it had come in Hardy's time in terms of its acceptance of women who are like Callisto.

In a sense, Lawrence is also pointing out that it is his femininity that makes Mellors so masculine. Mellors himself admits his femininity when he tells Connie: "They used to say I had too much of the woman in me. But it's not that. I'm not a woman because I don't want to shoot birds, neither because I don't want to make money, or get on" (289). Mellors's speech here points out something that other writers have not acknowledged: that definitions of masculinity and femininity are often largely cultural. The community does not acknowledge that Mellors is a man because he does not do those things that men typically do: kill birds and earn a large income. Lawrence's honesty and vision strike us here, for in a sense he is observing and admitting that *pure* masculinity and *pure* femininity are, in the twentieth century at least, anachronisms, if they were not always lies. He reinforces our sense of a new kind of masculinity by characterizing Mellors with the "courage of his own tenderness." Lawrence's comment in *The Study of Thomas Hardy* upon this is especially pertinent here:

The greatest and deepest human desire, for consummation, for Self-Knowledge, has sought a different satisfaction. In Love, in the act of love, that which is mixed in me becomes pure, that which is female in me is given to the female, that which is male in her draws into me, I am complete, I am pure male, she is pure female; we rejoice in contact perfect and naked and clear, singled out unto ourselves, and given the surpassing freedom. No longer we see through a glass darkly. For she is she, and I am I, and, clasped together with her, I know how perfectly she is not me, how perfectly I am not her, how utterly we are two, the light and the darkness, and how infinitely and eternally not-to-be-comprehended by either of us is the surpassing One we make. Yet of this One, this incomprehensible, we have an inkling that satisfies us. (468)

This "surpassing freedom" is psychological virginity – the very kind which Harding discusses in *Woman's Mysteries* and which is the object of the matriarchal, initiatory version of the Callisto myth. The preoccupation with psychological virginity is an old one for Lawrence. It is reflected in the "star-equilibrium" of *Women in Love* and in what Balbert calls "the phallic imagination, the 'pure singling out' of Lawrence's 'Pollyanalytical' essays."[13] Charles Rossman points out the frequency with which Lawrence reiterated this idea:

One idea remained with Lawrence throughout his life: the need for relationship as the means of individual fulfillment. The most concise expression of his attitude appears in the essay on Poe, where Lawrence asserts two basic laws of life. "The central law of all organic life," he declares, "is that each organism is intrinsically isolate and single in itself" (SCAL, 62). He then adds an apparently conflicting principle: "The second law of all organic life is that each organism only lives through contact with ... other life." Lawrence elsewhere included both ideas in a succinct paradox: "We have our very individuality in relationship" (190). Of course, the most important relationship for Lawrence, through most of his career, was between man and woman."The *via media* to being, for man or woman, is love, and love alone," as Lawrence put it in the *Study of Thomas Hardy* (410).[14]

We recognize in both Connie and Mellors the desire for the personal integrity and independence which says "I am I." Such a need is not limited to the woman, and in Lawrence's version of the myth, Connie plays the role of restorer for Mellors just as he plays it for her. But the ancient mysteries of woman affirm what Lawrence in the twentieth century reaffirms: that the ability to say "I am I" depends entirely upon the ability likewise to affirm "You are you." Or, as Lawrence expresses it in the *Study of Thomas Hardy*: "But what is Love? What is the deepest desire Man has yet known? It is always for this consummation, this momentary contact or union of male with female, of spirit with spirit and flesh with flesh, when each is complete in itself and rejoices in its own being, when each is in himself or in herself complete and single and essential" (465–6).

Both Connie and Mellors, like the Callisto of the matriarchal versions of the myth, are seekers after psychological virginity, but neither quite know how to go about it. Connie's desire, in her early experiences with sex is to remain "free" (8–9); her sense that the "pure beautiful freedom of a woman was infinitely more wonderful than any sexual love" (7) is but an adolescent yearning for psychological virginity, an adolescent yearning with no adult sense of how to obtain the real virginity of love. She comes to realize the cheat only after several years of "pure" talk with Clifford, after several empty years of "inner freedom" begin to defraud her of her body altogether. Similarly, Mellors' misanthropic isolation in the keeper's hut is an effort to regain his integrity after Bertha's willful destructiveness of his sexuality. Both have, in a sense, undergone the rape of Callisto, and what they now seek is the psychological virginity which either undoes the rape or makes it a salutary experience.

Consequently, we see the configuration of the Callisto myth being arranged in a somewhat unusual way. The elements of Ovid's story about Callisto's rape by Zeus are re-arranged so that both Connie and Mellors suffer spiritual rape, and that both become candidates for psychological virginity. Both are exiled from Wragby, Mellors after Bertha's accusations, and Connie because she chooses to escape from Clifford and the Wragby way of life. Both became animals during their more tempestuous love-making: bear-like creatures of Ovid's myth. Moreover, we see that both of them, in trying to change the wasteland of Wragby and Tevershall, function as Zeus characters.

Their love-making is continually associated with rebirth,[15] both of themselves and of the natural world they inhabit. The very time of year in which the novel is cast – early spring through late summer – echoes, in the growth of the natural world, the growth of their love. Moreover, when they make love for the first time, Mellors is painfully aware that he has begun "Life!" again, and Connie is able to perceive the mystery of the forest, which is the "mystery of eggs and half-open buds, half unsheathed flowers" (127). The process of natural rebirth is continued when Connie feels "like a forest soughing with the dim, glad moan of spring, moving into bud. She could feel in the same world with her the man, the nameless man, moving on beautiful feet, beautiful in the phallic mystery ... She was like a forest, like the dark interlacing of the oak-wood, humming inaudibly with myriad unfolding buds. Meanwhile the birds of desire were asleep in the vast interlaced intricacy of her body" (143–4). In becoming one with the forest, Connie recovers what Sanders terms "that state of primal oneness between man, woman and nature which had been dissolved by consciousness, and by mind's chilling instrument – language."[16]

These images of rebirth are cited by critics who read *Lady Chatterley's Lover* as a kind of grail quest. Yet the impracticality of Mellors' cures for a better world – short jackets and tight trousers – suggests that although Mellors has achieved a personal regeneration, he has not effected a cosmic one. The Knight of the Burning Pestle has hardly brought a grail to the industrial wasteland. Any hope for the world resides in Connie's womb, not Mellors' imaginative cant (which contains the right spirit but which proposes impractical methods). The significant part of their relationship is what they have made between them – the love and the child – not what Mellors has done. He describes their achievement in terms which evoke the sacred marriage, which is the prototype of the Callisto myth, when he writes to Connie: "We fucked a flame into being. Even the flowers are fucked into being between the sun and the earth" (316). The point to be emphasized is that Lawrence, by invoking the Callisto myth, exchanges the cup and lance of the grail that the hero has achieved for a thoroughly different Icon – that of a virgin holding her child. Mellors may have "saved" Connie, but she is the one who now holds the potential saviour.

Seeing *Lady Chatterley's Lover* through the Callisto myth also gives us insight into that problematical area of Lawrentian criticism, Lawrence's attitude toward the feminine.[17] Lawrence was admittedly often hard on women, and in his fiction frequently worked out the rage and the feelings of powerlessness involved in his own difficult relations with Frieda. At the same time, however, he was – like Mellors – kind to the feminine, and his sensitivity ought not be rejected with his anger and frustration. The very employment of the Callisto myth bespeaks his desire to address issues important to women.

In addition, a brief comparison between Tess, as he so sympathetically treats her in the *Study*, and his own Lady Chatterley, reveals his awareness of the problems inherent in womanhood. Tess's economic powerlessness which made her so vulnerable is countered by Connie's independent income.

Tess is tied to conventions by her natural aristocracy; Connie is beyond them by virtue of her social class. Lawrence is also aware of the way in which "the female ... has become inert" (*Study*, 482) in Tess, leaving her vulnerable to d'Urberville. Alec, by reaching the "deepest sources of the female in a woman" as the disguised god does in the Callisto myth, betrays Tess because he lacks what Lawrence calls, not uncoincidentally, aristocracy. Mellors is, on the other hand, a "natural aristocrat" (483): someone who knows that other people are outside him, and respects their differences. The kinds of changes that Lawrence has made in *Lady Chatterley's Lover* are meant to counteract these destructive tendencies in *Tess of the D'Urbervilles*. We note, for example, that while Connie's femaleness is rendered inert by Clifford's treatment of her, she nevertheless actively seeks its renewal. Finally, the whole male-female power play which Lawrence characterizes as a struggle between Law and Love in his *Study*, and which consistently puts women at a disadvantage, is symbolically mitigated in *Lady Chatterley's Lover* through representation of Mellors as a Callisto-figure, someone who is likewise in search of psychological virginity.

Lawrence's emphasis upon the wasteland element of the myth also suggests that the union of male and female in a sacred spirit has become increasingly important in a world where the ability to feel has been threatened and machines have come to transplant our humanity. That such a message is embodied in a myth about a woman, and that most of Lawrence's deviations from the myth are present in his feminization of Mellors, suggests Lawrence's vision of a world which needs more of the feminine principle to mitigate the wasteland created by intellectuals and industrializers.

CHAPTER TEN

Surfacing: *The Matriarchal Myth Re-surfaces*

Critics concerned with the mythic dimensions of Margaret Atwood's *Surfacing* have often observed that the patterns of male-oriented myth are inadequate as a basis for coming to terms with this novel. In "Nature as Nunnery," her *New York Times Book Review* commentary, Francine du Plessex Gray points to this problem when she identifies the narrator of Atwood's novel as a "heroine of a thousand faces."[1] Although studies of *Surfacing* based on the patterns formulated in Northrop Frye's *Anatomy of Criticism* and Joseph Campbell's *Hero of a Thousand Faces* have provided perceptive observations on Atwood's novel,[2] many critics object to their method on the grounds that such

categories, like myths of old, simply do not allow for women heroes. In the standard romances, female characters play secondary roles. Polarized into the virtuous maiden or the evil temptress, they mostly help or hinder the male protagonist ... But mostly maidens service as prizes. As Frye dryly observes, "the reward of the quest usually is or includes a bride." To be just a bride, of course, is to be defined by someone else. It is to exist *for* the hero, not *as* the hero. In both the old myths and the modern society, there is therefore a definite place for an Anna, but not for a female mythic hero.[3]

A second response has been to seek distinctly feminine mythic patterns which inform the novel. Consequently, Evelyn J. Hinz and John J. Teunissen, in exploring the mythic reverberations of *Surfacing*, identify the narrator as the *Mater Dolorosa* and point out that she and the nymph of Andrew Marvell's poem, "A Nymph Complaining for the Death of her Fawn," are signatures of the same archetype. Such conclusions lead them to assert that the narrator's quest is one which allows her to "regain her virginity through nymphhood" and that integral to this achievement is her transformation into "The Lady of the Beasts."[4] Annis Pratt, in her study,

Archetypal Patterns in Women's Fiction, likewise comments upon the narrator's achievement of psychological virginity: "In Atwood's narration, as in Harding's definition of 'Virgin,' we can perceive a woman who is fully 'feminine' but in a forceful and autonomous way, a giver of birth independent of patriarchal institutions."[5] Pratt maintains that this achievement comes to the narrator through her union with Joe, her "Green World Lover."

Each of these studies, accordingly, points in the direction of a recognition that the Callisto myth is the informing archetype of *Surfacing*, just as preceding Callisto narratives may be said to find their culmination in Atwood's novel. For even looking briefly at the work we can see once again the two-encounter form illustrated in *Jane Eyre, The Scarlet Letter*, and *Lady Chatterley's Lover*. Like Jane, Hester, and Connie, the narrator of *Surfacing* has two relationships, one which violates her integrity and one which is renewing. As the novel opens, we find her occupying natural and emotional wastelands – a scarred environment and a scarred psyche. The destructive relationship with her former lover and the ensuing abortion have left her feeling emotionally violated and fragmented. Desiring to renew the wasteland she has created of her own life, she is convinced that acting out the vision she sees in a pictograph of her childhood – one which depicts the pregnant Great Mother – holds the key to making everything come alive again. So she takes Joe out into the forest, in the presence of the moon, to make love. The narrator, like Callisto, is exiled from society, although hers is a self-chosen separation from people with whom she has no sympathy; like Callisto, she becomes a kind of animal during the exile; unlike Callisto she actively seeks that condition.

Like Radcliffe, Atwood begins her novel by establishing the narrator's relationship to her father, who, she fears, lingers on the edge of the forest as a yellow-eyed wolf.[6] This image inevitably recalls the transformation of Callisto's father, Lycaon, into a wolf as punishment for having tested Zeus' godliness by trying to feed him human flesh. Although the narrator's father is not a wolf, his death can nevertheless be seen as a punishment for questioning the sacred. His impiety, which the narrator comes to believe he has been attempting to rectify, is the same as that of Lycaon: a refusal throughout his life to acknowledge the gods. His tendency to argue logically that "resurrection is like plants ... people are not onions ... they stay under" (104) gives us the impression of a man who, like Lycaon, refuses to accept or admit that there is a sacred dimension to life. He considers the beliefs of the Judaeo-Christian tradition to be pure deception: the narrator remarks that "Christianity was something he'd escaped from, he wished to protect us from its distortions. But after a couple of years he decided I was old enough. I could see for myself, reason would defend me" (55). The final, scientific, rational approach to the gods he seeks through the photographs inevitably causes his doom: it is the camera, a machine with which he hopes to capture the sacred images, that keeps his body under water, and may even be the reason for his drowning.

Like Lycaon, the narrator's father has built a fortress, the home in northern Quebec. But the cottage becomes synonymous with the father's vague misanthropy, a result of his feeling that people are not logical. His home, then, is a bastion of logic and eighteenth-century rationalism, and one which, because the gods are not logical, excludes them also.

When the narrator is outside her father's fortress, she finds, like the Callistos of tradition, that she is unsure about her status in society and about her womanhood. The social retardation which has left her prey to the silly but powerful conventions of the schoolyard is simply an earlier, less potent version of a very real emotional retardation: she does not know how to relate, and the problem that she has on a small scale in the schoolyard becomes a larger problem when she falls in love. Like Emily St Aubert, she has been given the wrong knowledge for coping in a world which is not at all like the one her father created especially for her safety: "Always carry matches and you will not starve, your hands and feet are the most important, if they freeze you're finished. Worthless knowledge; the pulp magazines with their cautionary tales, *maidens who give in* and get punished with mongoloid infants, fractured spines, dead mothers or men stolen by their best friends would have been more practical" (48, emphasis mine). Moreover, when the narrator in her youth contemplated her feminine identity, she saw herself becoming, not a woman, but what she thought of as a "lady": that acceptable, refined, truncated version of womanhood which seemed defined entirely in terms of husband and children. She is distinctly in need of some practical feminine knowledge, more information about why and how maidens give in.

Most importantly, however, her father's refusal to recognize the gods leaves her with a very real weakness: she cannot recognize them either. The narrator's problem is, in a sense, the opposite of that of Callisto: the latter cannot recognize a real god when he is before her, whereas the narrator does not see the false one in her teacher and lover, whom she "worshipped" (148-9). Consequently, she is fooled by the social expectations that accompany his role. Teachers typically guide, initiate; they are, by and large, benevolent, helpful beings. But here the lover's benevolence is as much a disguise as was Alec d'Urberville's or Count Villefort's.

Her teacher's apparent godliness also constitutes part of his disguise. Teachers derive their godly power from their superior knowledge and from the academic system which sometimes gives them a god-like right to judge their students, a prerogative which often makes their students idolize as well as fear them. The narrator is so awed by the power attributed to her lover by the academic system that she is unable to see that "he was only a normal man, middle-aged, second-rate, selfish and kind in the average proportions; but I was not prepared for the average, its needless cruelties and lies" (189).

His rape of her is not, of course, literal, but is a subtle attack on her femininity which culminates in his insistence that she have an abortion. First he erodes her sense of herself by telling her there are no fine women painters, by being her lover only when his schedule allows, by viewing his relation with her as unimportant in comparison with other things – his family, his children's birthday parties, his scholarly objectivity. Her sense that as a woman she is second-rate increases when he denies one certain female power that she has – the power to give birth – by insisting that she have an abortion.

The extent to which his insistence upon an abortion is very much like rape has been noted obliquely by Arnold and Cathy Davidson, who liken the demand to an "adulteration of her body that corresponds to the adulteration of the native woods in which she was born and raised."[7] Carol P. Christ notes a similar connection when she observes that the narrator's inability "to come to terms with his violation of herself and her body [makes her focus] her attention on the violation of the Canadian wilderness."[8] She is "raped" not merely because she has intercourse with a married man who has power over her, but because the whole experience with him deprives her of emotional and sexual wholeness.

The point of the initiatory encounter is just such an achievement of wholeness. The god of the matriarchal myth introduces a woman to her sexuality and leaves her pregnant, offering her an introduction to the maternal aspect of the feminine, to one of the few relatively powerful aspects of womanhood.[9] As M. Esther Harding points out, it is the child that symbolizes her achievement. In Ovid's patriarchal version of the myth, however, Callisto's problem is not so much the psychological effects of rape, which are given insignificant consideration, but the pregnancy. Her visible shame comes from the fact that she has conceived. Although the narrator, because she does get an abortion, has none of the visible signs of pregnancy, and although she does not bear a child out of wedlock, the effect of her encounter is as destructive as it was for Callisto. Ironically, it is the fact that her lover does not allow her to have the child that makes this so. So while her lover does get her pregnant, the demand that she have an abortion deprives her of the motherhood that she wants, destroying her femininity to such an extent that she becomes unfeeling altogether.

The narrator's inability to acknowledge feelings of grief is expressed through the emotional disguises which she uses to re-focus the pain she feels about the unwanted abortion. At first she maintains that her real worry is over her father, and performs her melodramatic, dishonest ice-cream-cone anaesthetization: "I bite down hard on the cone and I can't feel anything for a minute but the knife-hard pain up the side of my face. Anaesthesia, that's one technique: if it hurts invent a different pain. I'm all right" (13). Her feelings about her former lover and the discrepancy between her story and reality reveal the emotional repression she typically exercises. The story which she invents essentially blames her teacher for forcing upon her responsibilities which she cannot accept. She has left her child because he "imposed" it upon her; this is a more palatable version of the abortion, which is what he did impose.

The narrator's whole response to the abortion epitomizes the female passivity that is often characteristic of Callisto figures just before they are raped. She allows her feelings and her actions to be completely governed by the male; she does only what she is supposed to do and feels only what she is supposed to feel, and then only in painless and powerless doses. Unable to admit that she aborted a child she might have wanted, she instead maintains that she left the child whom she did not want with a husband who did want it. The invented version may indicate that she is a "bad mother," but the truth makes her feel tremendously destructive because she did not want to abort. There is, however, a common denominator between the truth and the falsehood: in both cases, she has let her lover make decisions which she ought to have made for herself. This complete abnegation of responsibility, which allows him to make the decisions which so intimately effect her, amounts to encouraging, and even allowing, herself to be raped.

As usual, the struggle with the god is represented as a struggle within the narrator herself, but that struggle is essentially an attempt to maintain emotional equilibrium via the masculine habit of logic. She uses the rules of logic to transform her experience into something emotionally acceptable. Hinz observes that "faced with the trauma that such an incident [the abortion] occasioned, finally, she is unable to give expression to her feminine feelings of outrage, because by virtue of her father's values such behavior would be irrational."[10] The various versions of the abortion – the image of her drowned brother, or of the child in the bottle, or of her "husband" who has kept a child she did not want – are "logical, pure logic ... secreted by my head, enclosure, something to keep the death away from me ... Ring on my finger. It was real enough, it was enough reality for ever, I couldn't accept it, that mutilation, ruin I'd made, I needed a different version. I pieced it together the best way I could, flattening it, scrapbook, collage, pasting over the wrong parts" (143–44). Logic is a two-edged sword for the Callisto figure, as we have seen in *Comus*, *Jane Eyre*, *The Scarlet Letter* and *Lady Chatterley's Lover*; it both protects her from (further) rape and cuts her off from the possibility of the initiatory encounter which might renew her own personal wasteland. With her logic, the Lady refuses Comus' overtures; Jane

Eyre uses reason to rationalize her departure from Thornfield. But if both women, at those particular points in their careers, escape rape, they also forestall initiation.

Reason operates in precisely this way for the narrator of *Surfacing*, by making her wary of Joe's overtures. Logic has told her that since one man said he loved her and obviously did not mean it, love is a dangerous, unbelievable word. Consequently, her habit of being logical, of using logic to protect her from the deceitful, male world, makes her unable to accept Joe's love. Her inability to make emotional commitments, to trust the word "love," is shown by her first love-making with him, where she tries to be so uninvolved: "What impressed him that time, he even mentioned it later, cool he called it, was the way I took off my clothes and put them on again later very smoothly as if I were feeling no emotion. But I really wasn't" (28). Almost anticipating the moment when he will finally speak to her about love, she begins to examine her own feelings:

I'm trying to decide whether or not I love him. It shouldn't matter, but there's always a moment when curiosity becomes more important to them than peace and they need to ask; though he hasn't yet. It's best to have the answer worked out in advance; whether you evade or do it the hard way and tell the truth, at least you aren't caught off guard. I sum him up, dividing him into categories: he's good in bed, better than the one before; he's moody but he's not much bother, we split the rent and he doesn't talk much, that's an advantage. When he suggested we should live together I didn't hesitate. It wasn't even a real decision, it was more like buying a goldfish or a potted cactus plant, not because you want one in advance, but because you happen to be in the store and you see them lined up on the counter. I'm fond of him, I'd rather have him around than not; though it would be nice if he meant something more to me. The fact that he doesn't makes me sad. (42)

The cold-bloodedness with which she weighs Joe's worth, and the clumsiness with which she explores her own emotions, betray her discomfort with, and even fear of, the territory of love, as do her wooden and inadequate responses to his questions about love and marriage. She does, however, become increasingly aware of the abnormality of her emotionlessness; when she talks to Anna about Joe's proposal, she finally admits to herself that she had not felt for a long time (105). This leads her to begin to focus not on her father's death, the one that she has ostensibly come to investigate, but on her own metaphorical death (107), and to become aware of her own need for renewal and redemption. Like Connie and Mellors, she believes, or at least hopes, that she can find that renewal in love-making:

In the night I had wanted rescue, if my body could be made to sense, respond, move strongly enough, some of the red lightbulb synapses, blue neurons, incandescent molecules might seep into my head through the closed throat, neck membrane. Pleasure and pain are side by side they said but most of the brain is neutral: nerveless, like fat. I rehearsed emotions, naming them: joy, peace, guilt, release, love and hate, react, relate; what to feel was like what to wear, you watched the others and memorized it. But the only thing there was the fear that I wasn't alive. (111)

She becomes aware, in short, that *she* is the wasteland that needs renewal.

Like Lawrence, Atwood gives us a version of the Callisto myth in which the rape of the protagonist is a direct cause of the emotional wasteland that needs renewal. The narrator arrives in the north to find a natural wasteland of dead elms and dying birches, of moose that are killed, stuffed, costumed, displayed, of crucified herons, onto which she tries to project her inability to feel grief over her father's death, to face the emotional complexities of Joe's proposal, and, most important, to acknowledge the grief and guilt she feels over her abortion. Her focus upon the waste of the natural world is another of the emotional disguises which takes her mind off the more frightening personal problem.

Yet, as is typical of the two-encounter structure, the sexual act does have the potential to initiate her into living sexuality, as it does with Connie, for example. Consequently, echoes of the sacred marriage, prototype of the initiation ritual, are also contained in the narrator's (perhaps mistaken) hope that their sexual union has the potential to renew the natural wasteland of which she and Joe are a part. But she is also painfully aware that neither of them are capable of being redeemers (112), certainly not on a cosmic scale.

For the narrator's Joe is not only *not* a god, but vaguely subhuman as well, a buffalo man who grunts rather than talks. He is not powerful, but a failure; and the narrator finds comfort in that failure, in that resistance to the cultural and masculine norms which might have governed his work. He is not the renewer of worlds, which is truly a "man's" job, but the maker of squashed, mutilated clay pots – feminine vessels. Ironically, it is his very ungodliness that makes him a fit partner for the narrator. Like so many of the heroines of this study, the narrator finds that the godly are more apt to rape than to renew the women with whom they couple, because their godliness is but a reflection of their power and their willingness to exercise that power.

Arthur Donnithorne, Alex d'Urberville, and Sir Clifford, for example, derive their power from economic advantage which they use to inveigle the Callisto figure into a compromising relationship; likewise the teacher's power blinds the narrator to the extent to which their liaison is one-sided and damaging. The implication is that power which is exercised in an association that ought to be equal perverts the very quality of the intimacy. The exercise of power does not belong to the realm of love, but rather to the pale of rape. Consequently, Joe's failure and his refusal to play power games have two effects: he does not have enough control, either social or emotional, to rape her, nor does he have the manna to bestow renewal and redemption. Renewal may, in Atwood's version, come through the child. It cannot come through the lover. His power is limited to his ability to impregnate her.

Since the narrator must be her own redeemer, a major part of her quest involves a search for the feminine knowledge which Callisto sought in Diana's band, and the masculine god-knowledge of the drawings, knowledge which Callisto must make her own in order to gain power and attain the balance of masculine and feminine which is an integral part of psychological virginity.

The narrator's own emotional wasteland is but a microcosm, however, of a general malaise that also affects the ability of Anna, David, and Joe to be good friends, and even more, Anna's and David's ability to love one another. We see it first in the quality of friendship which these people share. Anna is the narrator's "best friend," yet they've known each other only for two months – not long enough apparently to warrant "personal questions" about being on the pill, or to give Anna a sense of the best ways of comforting a friend who may be silently grieving over the disappearance and probable death of her father. None of her companions is comfortable with the emotionally-charged situation, but neither are they uncomfortable enough to indicate that they feel its emotional potential. They have discarded their parents, and quite possibly cannot comprehend her state of mind. In any case, the narrator's comments about their probable inability to cope if she begins to cry or becomes hysterical are almost as much a comment on her preoccupation with control as they are a comment on their lack of emotional understanding and sympathy. She seems more worried about embarrassing them than about coping with her own feelings of grief and loss, submerged as they are. Such odd priorities suggest that their friendships are very fragile things.

This inability to feel sympathy for a friend is symptomatic of the general emotional disability. David, Anna claims, cannot feel at all: "There's something missing in him, you know what I mean? He likes to make me cry because he can't do it himself" (122). Moreover, David and Anna are victims of a sexual wasteland as well; for them, sex is not something neutral, as it was for the mental lifers at Wragby; it is a weapon, a source of power and powerlessness. Even Anna, who presumably can feel, seems to ignore David's presence when they are making love. What feeling she does have is channelled into not losing what little power she has.

Like Lawrence, and to some extent Hardy before him, Atwood is aware that there is an industrial wasteland which exists side by side with the sexual one. Her novel is riddled with negative references to machinery and electronic gadgetry, but more pertinent to the focus of this study is her use of mechanical imagery to indicate a mechanized approach to sex, thus expressing concretely the relationship between industrialization and dehumanization which Mellors tried to express.

Each of the characters, with the exception, perhaps, of Joe, is guilty of the mechanical approach to love. The narrator's response to Joe's lovemaking is "crisp as a typewriter" (68), and she attributes to Joe a desire for sex that is "intricate as a computer" (161). But Anna and David seem mostly guilty of unloving and sometimes even hateful mechanical sex. Anna, once "a chemical slot-machine," (80) is essentially a lobotomized woman, female without any spiritual femininity, someone who "copulates under strobe lights with the man's torso while his brain watches on from its glassed-in control cubicle at the other end of the room" (165). David is a proponent of "geometrical sex." The scene where he propositions the narrator, suggesting that they need to "get even" for Joe's and Anna's defection, is a parody of the impersonal initiatory encounter: "He needed me for an abstract principle; it would be enough for him if our genitals could be detached like two kitchen appliances and copulate mid-air, that would complete his equation" (152).

The relationship between Anna and David contains the negative elements of the Callisto myth with occasional ironic touches. David, although he has tremendous, almost god-like power over Anna, power which he uses partly to be as promiscuous as Zeus, is emphatically not a superior being, but merely an ex-theology student. Flabby and balding, he predominates in spite of his human faults because society approves his prerogative. Just as the god fooled Callisto with his disguise, David has convinced Anna that this is how marriage is supposed to be; just as the narrator mistook her lover for a god, so does Anna. By giving David some of the qualities of the god and then undercutting his superiority with implicit criticism of the misuse of authority, Atwood comments critically on the way power damages intimacy.

Anna may look lovely in her urban costume, but without her make-up and clothes she is anything but nymph-like. Their love-making has the impersonality of the initiation to it as Anna "prays" to herself; "it was as if David wasn't there at all." But what ensues is not rebirth, but death: "Then something different, not a word but pure pain, clear as water, an animal's at the moment the trap closes" (82). That closing of the trap indicates the death of animal passions which are the achievement of the woman in the Callisto myth. A later reference to Anna's metaphorical inability to "eat or shit or cry or give birth" (165) also suggests repression of the basic human animal.

When David criticizes Anna's tendency toward possessiveness, claiming that jealously is bourgeois, he echoes some of the dialogues in *Lady Chatterley's Lover* where Logos is praised over passional, even animal, relatedness. Like Clifford, who justifies Connie's affairs for her, David tries to justify his own and encourage Anna in the same habits. Anna is painfully aware that David, like Clifford and other Zeus figures who embody Logos, rationalizes: "all that theorizing about it is coverup bullshit garbage" (99); he continually uses logic to formulate power games which hide his inability to feel, just as Clifford's theories about brief sexual encounters excuse his emotional and physical paralysis. Anna, on the other hand, claims to be committed to feeling and to speaking those feelings out, committed, as it were, to the feminine principle of Eros: "'But I say there are these basic emotions, if you feel something you should let it out, right?' It was an article of faith, she glared at me, challenging me to affirm or deny (99). In spite of the suggestion that this is almost an "article of faith" we sense that it is one which Anna cannot live by for want of the strength and emotional resources it requires.

David's unreasonable criticism of Anna's appearance constitutes another kind of rape. His demands about her makeup – that he never see her without it – his constant references to her spreading hips, his demand for "a naked lady with big tits and a big ass" in his film are destructive of Anna's femininity. He continually demands that she meet his expectations – whatever they are at the time. He may want her to behave stupidly to boost his ego, or he may criticize her for being so stupid. He may demand that she learn, like other women, to switch off her head, but he also may hold her in contempt for doing so. It is this constant destruction of her identity, the assumption that she forges an identity out of his demands and needs, which constitutes David's "rape" of Anna, just as it partly characterizes the "lover's" rape of the narrator.

The essential difference between Anna and the narrator is that the latter chooses to act upon her awareness. But the awareness must come first: like Jane Eyre or Lady Chatterley, it becomes important for her to know what is happening. If Callisto had known that the female form which approached her was not Diana but Zeus in disguise, she might have escaped rape. Knowledge was the Lady's armour against Comus, a way of coping with a Logos-oriented world; it was Jane Eyre's protection from the attractiveness of Rochester. Similarly, the narrator's first task is to come to terms with the real cause of her emotional paralysis – the unwanted abortion – and to face her guilt and her grief. She must destroy all those emotional disguises which have helped her to focus her pain elsewhere.

Her dive into the water is shamanic in its origins,[11] and as a symbolic descent into the unconscious indicates a shedding of the encumberments of

Logos. But the experience is also a lifting of disguises. Whereas the Callisto of the myth must cope with the disguise which her rapist assumes, the narrator finds that not only has her lover turned out to be someone other than she thought he was, but that the whole ugly experience has been shrouded by the lies she has tried to tell herself to justify what has happened. These are perhaps disguises the narrator imposed upon the events of her life rather than something taken on by the god to fool her, but they nevertheless function as agents of a metaphorical rape. As long as she disguises her abortion, she cannot come to terms either with it or with the emotional destruction the experience wrought. There is also, in Atwood's novel, an unusual kind of shame the narrator feels at having been "raped," one which contributes to her desire to hide the situation. On one hand, she is a "liberated woman," sixties-style: she is free to do what she pleases with whom she pleases. On the other hand, her experience with her teacher belies both her liberation and the accompanying mores. If she *allowed* herself to be "cut in two" – raped – then she is not liberated. And the devastating quality of the encounter suggests that her free mores are not sufficient to guide her through the maze of sexual experience. She has discovered, through the affair with a married man who fully controlled her womanhood, that she is not as free as she imagined.

She also needs to come to terms with her father's status, and as long as she believes him to be a kind of god, she cannot dismiss or escape the male orientation toward logic which is so multi-faceted: it provides an emotional armour even while it keeps her emotional wound from healing. What she discovers is that knowledge and logic, qualities of the Logos-oriented male world, are insufficient. "After the failure of logic," she needs to know "how to act."

Now disillusioned with the male approach to her problems, she seeks the guidance of her mother, much as Callisto sought the guidance of Diana when she found herself vulnerable after Lycaon's defeat. Callisto did not know what to do with herself once she had left her father's fortress; the narrator does not know what to do once she abandons the male bastion of logic. The dive into the lake is not only a descent into the unconscious, but a vivid realization of the failure of the logical, male-dominated world and its Logos oriented consciousness. Her father has failed her, her lover has failed her, the male-oriented world of David and the "Americans" is terrifying and destructive.

Coming up from the glimpse of her father's body, the narrator finds herself immediately faced with the same situation as Callisto. Just as Callisto was pressed by Jupiter immediately following her father's defeat, the narrator encounters Joe, who wants to make love on the spot. Just as the Callisto of the medieval versions finds the god's friendliness a bit too much, so the narrator finds herself fending him off, telling Joe that she does not love him, and that if they do make love she will get pregnant. Neither of them, obviously, are ready for the sacred marriage.

She encounters yet another rape attempt in another ironic inversion of the myth when she refuses to make love to David. He cannot rape her because she knows what he is; she recognizes what he is trying to do, just as Callisto could perhaps have escaped rape had she been able to identify Zeus: "I could see into him, he was an imposter, a pastiche, layers of political handbills, pages from magazines, *affiches*, verbs and nouns glued on to him and shredding away, the original surface littered with fragments and tatters. In a black suit knocking on doors, young once, even that had been a costume, a uniform; now his hair was falling off and he didn't know what language to use, he'd forgotten his own, he had to copy" (152). Knowledge is going to get her this far, it will protect her against rape, but it will not bestow psychological virginity upon her: "the power from my father's intercession wasn't enough to protect me, it gave only knowledge and there were more gods than his, his were the gods of the head, antlers rooted in the brain" (153).

Her way of coping with the lack of the knowledge her mother should have provided is much like that of the nymph. Just as Callisto sought the female protection and knowledge of Diana's band, the narrator seeks the female knowledge of her mother, who is "the embodiment of nature, the body, the feminine" and is "identified with emotion."[12] Atwood has embodied the narrator's mother with many qualities of the Great Goddess. She is part of the natural world, part of its cycles, which she records and reflects; her illnesses are only "natural phases" (35); she disappears into the forest during the afternoons she spends alone. At the time of her death, she is concerned about rebirth, wondering if she got the bulbs in. The most evocative episode is the one in which she seems to have magical power over a hungry bear: "She yelled a word at it that sounded like 'Scat!' and waved her arms, and it turned around and thudded off into the forest ... She knew a foolproof magic formula: gesture and word" (79).

Yet if this woman embodies the Great Mother, her power is silent. She gives no answers, has given no answers. Part of her mystery is her powerful silence; it is her silence which makes the narrator feel sure that she has answers (74). The childhood picture that her mother has saved and purposefully misplaced provides the narrator with direction, yet she must be able to read the picture, to divine its meaning; in fact the picture itself comes from her: "It was mine; I had made it" (158). The drawing literally depicts the narrator's birth, but she perceives it to be a vision of her rebirth as well. Hinz and Teunissen observe that the drawing depicts the pregnant Mother, with her great "moon" stomach, beside whom stands the horned god-consort;[13] from this the narrator divines her own rebirth through a ritual union with Buffalo Joe. After having found the picture, the narrator experiences uncharacteristic elation: "But nothing has died, everything is alive, everything is waiting to become alive" (159).

The pictograph has given her the procedure for renewing the wasteland, everything that seems to her to have died. That process, of course, involves the initiatory aspect of the Callisto myth, ritual union with a god or god-substitute which the narrator institutes when she seduces Joe that evening. But while Joe can impregnate her and "undo" the most wasteful act of her past, only she can rescue and save herself. Consequently, it is she who takes the sexual initiative, not Joe. In *Lady Chatterley's Lover*, Lawrence breaks down the gender identities of the participants by allowing Connie to play the part of Zeus. Atwood echoes this by giving her narrator some of the god's power, his knowledge, his logic, as well as allowing her to lead Joe into the forest on the night of their union.

There is a second and equally significant change in the usual configuration of the myth. The moon is almost always present on occasions when Callisto figures are either raped or initiated. But in this scene, both the moon and the sun are evoked: "I lie down, keeping the moon on my left hand and the absent sun on my right" (161). As in the drawings from her childhood, which indicate a continual preoccupation with fertility and renewal, the moon is placed on the left, the side associated with the unconscious and the intuitive, and the sun on the right, the side associated with consciousness and reason. What the narrator is seeking, then, is a balance between the two principles of Logos and Eros, of sun and moon.

The rebirth of her wounded psyche is to come in the form of the child she believes she has conceived. As she and Joe make love, and her lost child surfaces, the emotional wounds inflicted by the abortion and the emotional wasteland attendant upon those wounds begin to heal. The birth of the child will be attended by the moon goddess, the finest of all midwives and patron of women giving birth, and will signal the beginning of a new world: "The baby will slip out as easily as an egg, a kitten, and I'll lick it off and bite the cord, the blood returning to the ground where it belongs; the moon will be full, pulling. In the morning I will be able to see it: it will be covered with shining fur, a god, I will never teach it any words" (162).

Like the Callisto of the myth, the narrator experiences an exile, but it is an exile she chooses. What she chooses to separate herself from is the image of woman which Anna represents. Anna is, once again, an ironic inversion of what the myth deals with. Not a nymph or a virgin, she is a member of a harem. Rather than possessing psychological virginity, she is the "captive princess in someone's head" (165). Unable to experience the true animal passions, her face merely "twists into poses of exaltation and total abandonment, that is all" (165). Like Helen Burns, who provides Jane Eyre with a vision of what she does not want to be, with a vision of all the traps of passive womanhood, Anna similarly gives the narrator a vision of modern womanhood, and it is a vision which she rejects. Trying to rebell against the image of what Anna represents and against the machine which she perceives has made Anna what she is, the narrator dumps the film out of the camera and heads for voluntary exile in the bush. Atwood directly invokes Ovid here by calling the narrator's rebellion a "metamorphosis" (167). The narrator intends to become the animal of the Callisto myth, a gesture which in this case signals her rejection of civilized and stultified images of womanhood: "I tried all those years to be civilized but I'm not, and I'm through pretending" (168).

One reason why Callisto heroines typically go to the forest is in search of the sacred. Hetty Sorrel goes to the Chase to find a man she thinks of as "godly," Emily wants religious comfort from the nuns at the convent and Connie seeks "sanctuary" from the empty world of Wragby. Having lost, or perhaps having never had a sacred tradition, the narrator of *Surfacing* finds it difficult to acknowledge sacred dimensions of the myth. Even Hester Prynne could feel that "what we did had a consecration of its own", Connie can acknowledge the holiness of Mellors' touch, but the narrator's sense of the mystical dimensions of her experience are limited to her perception that her child will be a god. Her exile helps her to achieve a sense of her own ties to the sacred, which comes to her through her identity with the natural world, and which has dimensions of religious experience as well as aspects that suggest the recovery of the basic animal identity of the myth.

The objective of her exile is a discovery of the balance and poise needed in the very threatening real world. She must achieve this sense through identity with the natural world and with its gods and goddesses. Wanting to grow fur, wanting to give birth like an animal, wanting most of all to discard and transcend human boundaries of house, garden, paths, is essentially her way of approaching the gods. Perception of the sacred comes through union with the natural. Like Connie, the narrator becomes part of the forests (181). This identity has its reward in a brief vision of the goddess, here her mother. Similarly, she has a vision of the god in the guise of her father: He is standing "near the fence with his back to me, looking in at the garden. The late afternoon sunlight falls obliquely between the treetrunks on the hill, down on him, clouding him in an orange haze, he wavers through water" (186). The sunlight with which he is irradiated, as well as the narrator's realization of the truths about logic, both suggest that here he plays the role of the sun god. Annis Pratt also recognizes these roles that parents play, and consequently remarks: "The parental figures thus transcend the personal and familial and become universal, or archetypal. The hero, having absorbed her personal history transforms it into a phase of her rebirth journey. ... She initiates herself into the mysteries of femininity through her mother and into those of the power of nature through both her mother and her father and induces Joe to impregnate her as part of a process of creative solitude."[14]

Writing of the religious experience which the narrator has during her exile, Roberta Rubenstein notes the narrator's efforts to balance the masculine and feminine within herself: "In establishing identification with both the feminine (maternal, generative) and masculine (knowledge, wisdom) principles, she generates her own creative potentiality through rejoining the severed halves of her being."[15] Both her mother and father, the sun and the moon, are part of what she seeks – a workable balance between the masculine and the feminine. Stepping into her father's footprints, feeding the jays as her mother did, she takes on their power.

Apotheosis, in Atwood's novel, is emphatically *not* becoming a star, not moving out of society, to Ferndean or to a small rural farm. It is a matter of taking back one's power and wisdom, little as that seems. What is offered is only perspective. The gods retreat and become mortal, one's powerful vision becomes only normal blindness. Nature, once the metamorphosis is over, is indifferent. The only thing she has left to take back is the child, her boon.

The return to society with a boon is not enthusiastically or overtly provided in the novel's ending. The *hero* returns to society with news or a gift which will change the world; the *heroine* knows better. But it is also true that she has gained a good deal of wisdom. She knows, for example, that being saved does not mean fitting oneself into the patriarchal structure, but finding a "mediator" like Joe who will allow her to move beyond those masculine circumscriptions. Joe does not return like Zeus to legitimize her; both he and the narrator know that this is something he cannot do. She has seen that men are not gods and accepts Joe as a mere mediator. He lacks the hubris to believe that he can save her, for he has no faith in the system which proclaims his powerfulness in this issue. But the fact that he does return suggests the extent to which he accepts her for what she is – accepts her rebellion, her rage, her conscious rejection of "the system."

Acceptance of herself is a large part of the narrator's own personal growth. The patriarchal aspect of the myth, with its sexual violence against the woman, shows that certain aspects of womanhood are typically rejected by the patriarchy: woman's sexuality, when it is autonomous, independent of the god's own desires, is seen as "bestial." As Sherry Ortner points out, the painful and yet energizing tie to nature and to one's passional self is rejected as chthonic and regressive in the modern world.[16] Motherhood, which men perceive as frighteningly powerful, is, as Rich has argued, systematically belittled.[17]

But the narrator's active choice of many aspects of the Callisto myth frees her from the constraints under which she has lived for so long. When she chooses to become pregnant, she asserts the power of motherhood. When

she chooses her temporary exile, she asserts that living within the patriarchal structure is not always ideal or desirable. When she chooses her animal
metamorphosis she asserts that woman's sexuality and her tie to nature are
not bestial or shameful but a source of vision, power, and independence.

The acceptance and even the active seeking-out of the experiences of
Callisto give the narrator psychological virginity. In coming to know her
own strengths, resources, and responsibilities, she becomes her own person. Atwood modifies Harding's notion that psychological virginity is
something which results *inevitably* from a pre-ordained ritual event. Since
those rituals are no longer part of our culture, such autonomy must be earned through their re-invention; it is not a fact, but a vision.

CHAPTER ELEVEN

Beyond Rape

The myth of Callisto does not belong entirely to the past. Although it has not been noticed as a controlling myth in literature written after 1972, the date of Atwood's *Surfacing*, and although significant changes have been made benefitting the status of women in Western society, the circumstances of modern women's lives continue to reflect the patterns of the ancient myth. Attitudes about rape, about women's right to independence and control of their own lives, attitudes that women have toward their fellow women, attitudes toward girls who "get themselves in trouble," still remain elements of the patriarchal aspect of the myth. At the same time, Atwood's novel evinces an attempt to rescue the more ancient, pre-patriarchal version; such recoveries need to be accompanied by analyses that provide artists and women with a grounding in a mythic tradition that validates their work and their vision. Myths will continue to evolve and metamorphose, necessitating new directions in mythic criticism once women's liberation is no longer a social issue, but a given.

A modern women's experience of rape is not at all unlike that of Ovid's Callisto.[1] First, women have been encouraged to be passive, as was Callisto, when threatened with rape; they are told that any attempt to repulse the male physically may result in severe injury or even death. Yet such passivity is in itself attractive to the rapist, especially in instances where the rape is meant as an expression of power. Such rapists want their powerfulness verified or demonstrated by the victim's passivity; moreover, the victim's lack of resistance convinces the rapist that his power is indisputably attractive.

If the rape victim was passive, if she was not severely bruised or injured, or if she was initially gullible, trusting, or friendly, society is not likely to believe that she was raped. In *The Ultimate Violation*, Judith Rowland writes of her attempts to get the California State Supreme Court to credit expert testimony on victim response to rape. In her work as a prosecutor she learned that jurors have preconceptions about how a rape victim *ought* to have reacted if she truly protested the sexual assault. In short, they expect her to run, scream, or try to escape, and fail to understand that victims often are literally frozen with fear. The Court's negative position on her use of expert testimony to describe the typical – not stereotypical[2] – response of rape victims amounted to proclaiming it "irrelevant whether the jury believed the victim resisted what she thought was a rape ... the issue was whether the defendant believed, as a result of her having resisted 'so little' that he had consent."[3] The male is still transcendent, godly; his interpretation of the victim's response defines her experience socially and legally.

Moreover, the effects of the rape do not end with the psychological trauma incurred during the attack. The victim finds that much of society persists in believing that she somehow "asked for it." Just as Callisto finds that she is defamed and censured by Diana, the being whom she has trusted to guide and protect her, so does a rape victim often find emergency room medical staff and police department personnel generally unsympathetic if she is not badly bruised or not of "impeccable" reputation. Because rape is still often seen as a violation of the chastity of a man's wife, some women cannot, by definition, be raped: specifically women who are, perhaps like nymphs, "unchaste." Women, Rowland writes, are the most inclined to be unsympathetic: "It was impossible for them to comprehend, sometimes, even in the face of overwhelming evidence ... that a woman could be made to have intercourse if she didn't want to."[4] The victim may also be outcast because she reminds other women (as Callisto reminded the judgmental, frustrated Hera) of their own potential vulnerability, their own helplessness, and their own acceptance of society's other violations. Understood only by people who have come to see rape as an expression of power and anger rather than of sexuality, the victim often finds herself, like Callisto, exiled and alone.

In a feminist context, then, a study of this myth inevitably provides a perspective on some of the dynamics of rape. Approaching the myth through literature, however, imposes certain restrictions. We assume, for example, that none of the writers was ever raped; none of them wrote from personal experience that would have given particular validity to their rendering of the event. In most cases, the issue of rape has been clouded by cultural and historical biases, so that the rape described in the myth is viewed in the literature as a seduction, as a matter of uncontrolled lust. In periods when social delicacy absolutely precluded any discussion of literal rape, the violation is expressed in a metaphorical gesture that deprives the female character of the right to determine her own fate, or as a gesture that emphasizes a woman's unfittedness to control her own life. In these cases, rape is seen as a psychological violation rather than both psychological and physical. Nevertheless, this study contributes to the body of knowledge about the phenomenon of rape, largely by supporting recent feminist theories and observations with material from four centuries, not necessarily written by people one would consider "feminist."

Only recently has rape been viewed by feminists as an expression of power and anger intended to humiliate and denigrate the victim. Brownmiller's seminal study of rape pays particular attention to the rapist's expression of a desire for power. Defining rape, she writes "all rape is an exercise in power, but some rapists have an edge that is more than physical. They operate within an institutionalized setting that works to their advantage and in which a victim has little chance to redress her grievance ... But rapists may also operate within an emotional setting or within a dependent relationship that provides a hierarchical, authoritarian structure of its own that weakens a victim's resistance, distorts her perspective and confounds her will."[5] Her study suggests that society's view of women, with its vaguely misogynistic bias encoded in male fantasies and jokes, directly influences its tendency to silently approve rape. By portraying women as weak and easily victimized, by treating them like personal property – even in a legal sense – the patriarchy emphasizes its belief in the value and magnetism of male power. The work of anthropologists Margaret Mead and Peggy Reeves Sanday also suggests that the desire to rape women is shaped by culture – not, as we tend to believe, kept in check by it.[6]

But not everyone has ascribed to the feminist view of rape, and hence a controversy still rages. The main issue in this controversy is whether rape constitutes an expression of physical desire, or whether physical rape is only the most extreme variety of a whole host of messages intended to communicate to women that they are powerless, and had better not forget that fact by stepping out of their place.[7] Literature's reconfiguration of the Callisto myth to express various kinds of violations strongly suggests the deep interdependence between rape and society's institutionalization of women's subjection. In these narratives, written by men as well as women, some written long before the women's liberation movement, rape is depicted as having many facets aside from the physical violation. In short, these narratives bear out Brownmiller's observations.

Although the authors examined in this study see uncontrollable lust as the major, motivating cause of rape, virtually all of them see the rapists' exercise of or desire for control as at least a secondary, if not a primary motive. That rape is an expression of power – thought to be a modern, feminist view – is a recurrent theme in the narratives studied here. In the medieval and Renaissance versions of the myth, the issue of power is never far from the act of rape. The Callisto figures are all too aware that the death of Lycaon leaves them powerless, and they avoid Jupiter's proposal precisely for that reason. Jupiter's subsequent rape is a response to their refusal to marry him willingly. First, each Callisto's denial of his proposal represents an insult to the attractiveness of his power, one he could vindicate only through rape. Second, he hopes that having gained physical possession he will be able to persuade them to allow him legal possession as well. The Jupiter of *The Barley-Breake* expresses this attitude when he proclaims that as father of the gods he should not have to beg for love from a mere mortal like Callisto. Montoni's threat of rape is also an expression of power: Emily can either obey him or risk being raped by one of his bandits. Alec d'Urberville repeatedly expresses his frustration with Tess's refusal of his overtures; "What am I, to be repulsed so by a mere chit like you," he exclaims to Tess just before their encounter in the forest; just before his final rape, he threatens "I will be your master yet." In *Surfacing*, the narrator's lover denigrates her by giving her mediocre grades, telling her that there are no fine women artists, and forcing her to have an abortion she does not want.

These narratives also illustrate the role of power in rape by suggesting that women are more prone to violation when they perceive men as beings who are more powerful than they are. Because Emily St Aubert believes that men have a distinct right to shape the affairs of her life, she endures threats to her physical, emotional, and financial security. Jane Eyre initially accepts St John's cruel notions about her purpose in life because she believes him to be a much nobler, wiser person than she is. Because Tess believes Angel Clare to be a godly young man, she defers to his judgment of her, whereas her disdain of Alec prevents her initial encounter with him from amounting to rape. The narrator of *Surfacing* is raped by her teacher because she accepts his professorial claim of superiority.

That rape is an aspect of social control is indicated by the ways in which the male characters' control of women's attitudes, opinions, behaviour, places of residence, choices of jobs, incomes, and marriages is expressed in terms of rape, through the use of the myth. Those metaphorical rapes in *Mysteries of Udolpho* and *Jane Eyre* all point to the writers' perhaps unconscious recognition that women are violated by a variety of common social practices that usurp their right to make their own decisions. If women should, like Emily, spurn the "protection" of the men who ought to make decisions for them, they are no longer "good girls" and hence no longer deserve to be guarded from the lusts of less scrupulous men.

The more socially powerless they are, the more the female characters are prone to victimization. Thus, a woman not protected by the social power of money or family is very vulnerable. Montoni knows that he has complete control over Emily's life as long as she is his economic dependent; Rochester feels safe in offering a bigamous marriage to Jane because she has no family to protest and no way to provide herself with a living. Arthur Donnithorne underestimates the importance of Hetty Sorrel's virginity because he thinks of her as a member of a lower economic class, for whom such virtues are not important. Tess is finally vulnerable to Alec's violation because she and her family need his financial support.

A rape victim often feels that some bestial aspect of herself brought on the rape, and feminists have argued that the system has blamed the victim by creating misconceptions about the motives for rape and by sympathizing with the "poor, sick rapist."[8] But once again, what is often thought to be a feminist twist in thinking about rape is underscored by the literature in which the myth of Callisto occurs. In *The Barley-Breake*, for example, Callisto knows that she will be condemned for her pregnancy and that Zeus' part in it will be "winked at." Hawthorne is quite explicit in illustrating that society chooses to treat this Zeus and Callisto, Dimmesdale and Hester, quite differently: while society has punished Hester for years, a large part of it refuses to acknowledge Dimmesdale's confession. In *Tess*, Hardy proposes that this habit is so deeply engrained that the victim learns to blame herself. These attitudes are by no means dead now; even in feminist crisis groups there can be a tendency for women who have claimed their power, proclaimed their powerfulness, to adopt attitudes toward victims that make them feel more victimized, attitudes that subtly abuse women who "allowed" themselves to be overpowered.

Yet these novels indicate that rape is not always inevitable, that it can be prevented, and that the effects of metaphorical violations can be undone. The myth takes on the quality of a hierogamy in *Surfacing, Jane Eyre*, and *Adam Bede* because the women do not perceive the man as innately superior, god-like. The narrator of *Surfacing* knows that Joe cannot save her, that in the society to which they return he is as much a failure, an outcast, as she is. But she believes enough in the sacredness of their child's conception to give her the hope she needs. Dinah Morris's spiritual strength and her integrity are such that her marriage to Adam constitutes the hierogamy which regenerates both the natural world and the spirit at Hayslope. Rochester's maiming and Jane's acquisition of family and fortune finally place them on an equal footing in the worldly sense, and they regenerate life at Ferndean. The spiritual equality which Rochester acknowledges in the garden has always been there, but Jane recognizes how tenuous it is when not supported by its practical counterpart. Similarly, Connie Chatterley can escape rape by Clifford because she has an independent income. It is perhaps no coincidence, then, that research done among rapists reveals that one successful method for fending off a rape is to refuse to cower, to refuse victimization, to send a clear message to the rapist that one is human, equal, and that such a violation is out of the question.[9] By doing this, women are refusing to be Callisto, nymph and victim, and instead asserting their association with the powerful goddess.

In approaching the rape of Callisto, I have proposed that the Ovidian version, in which Callisto is raped by Zeus, was the result of certain changes which patriarchalized the event. Along with other scholars, such as Walker and Gimbutas, I have suggested that an earlier version existed, one in which Callisto, as the goddess, joined with Zeus in a sacred marriage meant to rejuvenate Arcadia, and that Ovid's narrative is a somewhat skewed version of the initiation ritual that would have grown out of this earlier myth. In such a ritual, young women would have been introduced to their sexuality via a ritualized union with the god's representative, and that initiation would have marked their achievement of psychological virginity. The patriarchal transformation of the myth in itself represents an effort to undermine women's power and independence, to denigrate the power of their beliefs and their ceremonies. In making the myth about rape, the patriarchy effected another metaphorical rape, cheating women of the vision that the myth offers.

The texts analysed here reverse that loss by portraying women who have claimed, earned, found, or been granted worldly and spiritual equality: their experience transforms the myth of rape back into that of hierogamy. Jane's quest for independence; Dinah's unshakable spirituality and sense of purpose; the refusal of Atwood's narrator to take part in a society that rapes the land as well as women; and Connie's five hundred pounds a year and her rebellion against an exclusively masculine, logical way of life empower them – enable them – to achieve the sacred, equal marriage. These narratives represent the re-transformation of the myth, so that it once again celebrates the sacred marriage, the regenerative partnership of men and women.

One might well wonder why a myth with such a subversive message continued to appear in literature for over four centuries. But because myth is a structure to which the age and the individual can append meaning via a signature, it functions as a perfect vehicle for subversive or even unconscious messages. It is also very easy, in this particular myth, to ignore its pre-patriarchal overtones and see it as exclusively concerned with rape or lust. It belongs to a whole cluster of rape myths, like those describing Daphne, Persephone, Io, Europa, and Zeus's other conquests, which reflect a reality of women's lives. Ironically, this was a reality that did not make men particularly uncomfortable at the time. Yet that undercurrent of the myth which describes a woman's initiation, not her rape, can be said to lie quiescent until such time as an author *does* become uncomfortable with rapists' views on and violations of women. Should she or he begin to wonder if women deserve their victimization, or to consider ways for women to escape the boundaries and circumscriptions of their status, the author might conceivably stumble upon the initiatory aspect of the myth. To question the ways in which women accept their passivity, the inevitable powerfulness of men, men's ownership of women's sexuality, the belittling of motherhood, and the value placed on men's chivalric rescue, is to question the authority of the Ovidian version. An author who proposes that women not be passive, that they demand their equality and their own definition of their sexuality, that they refuse any attempts to undermine their motherhood, that they recognize the egotism and possessiveness of the chivalric rescue, has come a fair way toward recognizing the pre-patriarchal myth. But recognizing the full implications of the myth and allowing those implications full play are two very different things. Consequently we see that after the myth became part of the tradition, its expression in literature was frequently disguised by purposeful ambiguity, by narrative techniques that came at the myth's issues only indirectly, by predictable misreadings invited by the genre or tradition in which the writer was working, and by a readership whose interpretive habits did not include sensitivity to any point of view but its own.

The myth found its way into the tradition in the Middle Ages, partly because it was integral to the "matter of Rome" package and partly because men were inclined to think that it was about them – hence the tendency to retell it in the context of Jupiter's early military career and love life. The euhemerist tradition would also have made it a popular tale, serving, as it did in its patriarchal form, as a warning for girls who were not scrupulous enough about their behaviour.

The harsh judgments of Callisto were softened somewhat in those depictions that come out of the Renaissance, just as attitudes toward women underwent minor but significant changes for the better during that period, expressed, for example, by Castiglione. Thomas Heywood, who generally gives women sympathetic roles in his plays, poises himself precariously between the patriarchal view of women and history as presented by his narrator, and his own, more sympathetic view – largely by presenting Callisto as a woman of integrity and independence, and implicitly contrasting the playboy image of Jupiter. W.N., Gent. had more freedom in his/her depiction of Callisto, given that he/she chose to remain anonymous and to work within the form of a poem dedicated to a specific young woman. Indeed, I would argue that W.N. was herself, like anonymous, a woman: hence her use of the initialed dedication and her full and open sympathy with the young nymph. Yet both Heywood and W.N. were protected by the disguise of the euhemerist tradition; it is quite possible they recognized that anyone who chose not to attend to the very real misfortune of their respective Callistos could, by way of interpretation, quite easily envision their texts as another comment upon the fate of careless girls. Paradoxically, then, we see the myth both protected and stunted by cultural and literary traditions.

Milton's text is similarly camouflaged. The Lady's preoccupation with her chastity and the Earl's hope that the masque itself be a ritual celebrating the unshakable virtue of Lady Alice Egerton furnish a cover for Milton's more complex and subtle concern about the confrontation of two radically different world views and sets of values. Moreover, the tendency of audiences to focus on heroes or male characters further facilitates the disguise;

the very nick-name given the work, *Comus*, serves to indicate the character who has typically been the most interesting to critics concerned with the dramatic aspects of the masque. From that perspective, Lady Alice is a good girl who has done nothing particularly interesting – only what is expected of her. Comus's tempting, sybaritic values and his exuberant character are traditionally seen as the source of the masque's drama. Those who are interested in the Lady are concerned with her values, her virtues: she is for them an abstract embodiment of Milton's moral message, not a young woman whose sense of herself and integrity are boldly threatened.

Radcliffe's Gothic novels were composed during a period when women were beginning to consider their status. The French Revolution's slogan of liberty, equality, and brotherhood, and French women's response to the call to arms suggested the heretofore unthinkable: that women might be included in some notion of equality. In addition, the early romantic ethos celebrated the intuitive and the irrational – qualities previously associated only mockingly with women. This anti-rationalist spirit was manifested in part in the emotionally-charged form of the Gothic novel with its emphasis on sensibility. Two of Radcliffe's devices are a response to the Gothic spirit: the orphaned heroine and the nasty villain. These were important to the dramatic success of her novels: a helpless girl in the clutches of an unscrupulous man would arouse the requisite sympathy in the reader. Yet at the same time, these devices function as metaphors for the status of women: in the patriarchal society she inhabited, given the property and marriage laws that were prevalent, all women were as orphans, all equally helpless when faced with husbands or relatives who chose to exercise their will. Furthermore, Radcliffe's villains, as mentioned earlier, merely articulate attitudes about women that are slightly more extreme than those shared by their more benevolent counterparts. In a sense, Radcliffe's formula, which so closely follows the myth of Callisto in both *Mysteries of Udolpho* and *Romance of the Forest*, reflects with daring accuracy the status of women in the late eighteenth century. But like Heywood, she uses a genre and a tradition which deflects one's conscious interest away from the issues at hand. The cult of sensibility more or less dictated the reader's response: she was to be sympathetically involved with the heroine's fate; such involvement would have precluded a critical response to the injustices of the status of women portrayed in the fiction.

Like Milton and Radcliffe, Hawthorne disguises his interest and his viewpoint with a literary device: the obfuscating narrator who perhaps shares – or perhaps does not share – the attitudes of the author himself. The amount of literary criticism generated regarding the *moral* position of Hawthorne himself is an indication of the extent to which his attitudes have seemed obscure. As is appropriate for a work deeply concerned with myth, however, Hawthorne is not interested in dictating moral standards. Like Milton, he is more concerned with the clash between two sets of values: Hester's matriarchal orientation, which emphasizes emotion, connectedness, and intuition, and the patriarchal, legalistic, rationalistic bent of the Puritan fathers. The critics who find Hester fascinating, but conclude that she is morally at fault, reveal more of their own cultural predisposition than Hawthorne's, thus indicating how easily a patriarchal culture can impose its standards upon its reading of a work of literature – and consequently how easily a work can elude society's censors.

George Eliot had an opportunity to observe the effects of Hawthorne's narrator; thus when she came to write her Callisto narrative about her Arthur and Hester, she had already learned about the disguises necessary to such a vision. To call her novel *Adam Bede* is to deflect concern away from the Arthur-Hetty relationship. Her unsatisfactory simplification of woman into good girl and bad girl components and her comments on the way in which Hetty has been socialized to be thoughtless, empty-headed, and malleable, form a subversive criticism of Victorian attitudes about womanhood. At the same time, however, her pastoral and moral tone allow her to present this image without endangering her credibility or reputation, as Brontë endangered hers by openly discussing Jane Eyre's frustration.

Eliot's novel contains the last attempt to disguise its position: Hardy's subtitle for *Tess of the D'Urbervilles,* "A Pure Woman," indicates that he had no intention of being at all obscure about his sympathy for Tess Durbeyfield (which caused him no end of difficulty with the serialization of his novel). His vision of Tess's victimization is quite clearly stated throughout, and by no means flatters the Victorian Era's treatment of women. Yet his insistence upon Tess's purity suggests he must have believed that sympathy for her might be forthcoming – that his age was in some manner ready for his undisguised vision.

The number of Callisto narratives brought forth in the nineteenth century suggests that something about the age was conducive to the expression of this myth. Certainly Angel Clare's response to Tess reveals some very concrete reasons for the surfacing of myths about women. His loss of faith in the Judaeo-Christian deity has caused him to seek out another source of the divine in woman, as exemplified by the way in which he calls Tess by the names of the goddesses of Greece and Rome. As the fresh, virginal child of nature, she further invites worship as an intrinsic part of the natural world, since Clare, like many of his fellow Victorians, turned away from an "irrational" faith to embrace the more "rational" natural world. In exploring the image of women as it is expressed during the Victorian Era, Nina Auerbach concludes that the crisis of faith in a patriarchal deity gave rise to an "ethos of humanism" and a mythic imagination which fostered the expression of myths about women as well as about men.[10]

Another aspect of the age further contributes to attitudes about women which were conducive to the resurgence of the Callisto myth. The reign of Queen Victoria would have had an implicit influence upon the way in which women were viewed: the leadership of a powerful woman would have inevitably affected one's preconceptions about the amount of power women possessed and could wield. At the same time, however, Victoria's opposition to women's suffrage might conceivably have dictated that images of women's powerfulness be expressed in an underground manner. Thus it must be said that attitudes about women that deify and empower her image were implicit, rather than explicit. Woman was not consciously deified; it was more a matter of the "angel in the house" giving sublime comfort to her disillusioned husband. Likewise woman was not consciously seen as powerful, yet the image of the Queen's powerfulness dominated the history of the Victorian Age.

Indeed, it must also be admitted that in many ways the Victorian Period was repressive of any overt expression of women's powerfulness. The "delicacy, the purity, the refinement, and the elevation" of woman's nature[11] which made her the "angel in the house" was also the justification for keeping woman "innocent" of worldly ways, and hence powerless. Both the nineteenth-century's victimization of women and its motives for deifying her are summed up in Tess Durbeyfield and reflect the destructiveness of the split image of women contained in the two characters of Callisto herself – goddess and victim.

Yet this duality of the nineteenth century's view of women precisely reflects the duality of myth's function. On the one hand, mythic art shows life as it is: it is a reflection of society. The more tragic depictions of women, those of Hester Prynne, Hetty Sorrel, and Tess Durbeyfield, fulfill precisely this purpose: they are vivid demonstrations of the way in which women were disenfranchised. On the other hand, myth has a compensatory function: the visionary aspects of myth arise in art as a response to the weaknesses and shortcomings of society, as compensation for its tendency to be one-sided. Precisely because they spring from the deepest sources of the author's creativity and are an intrinsic part of the work – not a didactic overlay, but a nearly invisible spine – they do not usually incur the opprobrium heaped upon other expressions of unpopular opinion. Hence Jane Eyre, Dinah Morris, and to some degree Tess, reflect the plane to which women might aspire under different circumstances.

The false clues – misleading titles, obscuring narrators, the ways in which the writers have hidden behind euhemerist traditions and gothic devices – have made past criticism of many of those works difficult at best. The inability to define chastity in Milton's *Mask*, to discern adequately Hawthorne's "moral" position in *The Scarlet Letter*, to address satisfactorily the difficulties of narrative tone in *Adam Bede*, or to define precisely the power of Tess Durbeyfield, all point to the inadequacy of the masculine ethos of criticism. The interpretation of an open text is never complete, can never embrace within its system all the variables of a work of literature,[12] but some systems of interpretation have been ignored, not because of their failure to be complete or illuminating, but because they present a viewpoint that has not until recently been recognized in the masculine province of literary interpretation.

This study began by suggesting that the patterns of traditional male criticism were insufficient when it came to dealing with literature by and about women; perhaps it is appropriate to end by reiterating this need for altogether different approaches. Although feminist criticism has nearly come into its own and need no longer be defensive about its validity, there is still a tendency, and even in some cases a conscious attempt, to refuse to see that women's experiences are *not* like men's. In his recent study of *Antigones*, for example, George Steiner addresses the fact that feminist approaches to Antigone exist, but proceeds to ignore them. Throughout his study he continually finds himself unable to escape the fact that Antigone was a woman and that her womanhood would have shaped her response to the situation, but he is never willing to explore the implications of that fact. More interested in Antigone as a facet of nineteenth-century German philosophy than as a person who is female, tending to see her as the anima of Oedipus, and envisioning her actions as masculine when she asserts her power over the situation, Steiner has produced a study of astounding intellectual brilliance, but one that brings us no closer to comprehending Antigone's complex, rebellious, dangerous decisions regarding her fate, her life, and her values.[13]

Nevertheless, the recognition of the need for women's myths has produced a spate of new books: Annis Pratt's *Archetypal Patterns in Women's Fiction*, Lee Edwards' study of Psyche, Estella Lauter's *Women as Mythmakers*, all speak, through example, of the fascination with a new mythology. Edwards describes one practical application of such studies: "The most mundane societies sustain themselves by myth as well as logic; humanity will accept as revelations truths whose existence ordinary life obdurately refuses to demonstrate ... Against a myth, one must send another myth."[14]

One might wonder, then, what myths we are going to send. Yet it is neither the artist's nor the critic's job to send myths deliberately. The artist can only find them through a thoroughly un[self]conscious exploration of his or her own psyche. Lauter's examination of myth in twentieth-century poetry and visual art strongly suggests that this search is indeed going on, but that the process is in some respects problematic. On the one hand, artists are not finding a workable tradition in other Greco-Roman myths; the way in which Callisto's myth has been distorted would suggest that many of those myths have been too patriarchalized to resonate in the work of contemporary women artists. This consequent lack of a tradition leaves these people feeling that they work in unbearable isolation.

This in turn suggests that the critic's function is to examine the contemporary mythic work and link it to the archetypal forms precisely to provide women with a legitimate sense of a mythic tradition. Remembering that the mythology with which we are commonly familiar is only one manifestation of the archetype as such, we must be sensitive to new manifestations that do indeed differ from the Greco-Roman tradition and the signatures that we have come to expect. The tradition had once seen Callisto only as a careless nymph who got herself in trouble; Psyche was once a disobedient wife who had to be rescued by her husband. Yet new studies of Psyche envision her as the prototype of the female hero. Similarly, Callisto's rape can now be seen in terms of a sacred marriage or an initiation.

Just outside the Italian city of Paestum, University of Michigan archaeologists are now excavating a site that contained the sanctuary where Bona Dea, the good goddess, was worshipped by women from the sixth through the first centuries, BC. Several aspects of the site point to the great importance of the cult, especially its large size and evidence that both the Greeks and Romans worshipped Bona Dea there.[15] John Pedley's study of the goddess is only the most recent of a series of studies beginning perhaps with the work of Graves and Neuman, continued by Mary Daly, Merlin Stone, Barbara Walker, and Maria Gimbutas. Who is the White Goddess, the Triple Goddess, the Great Mother, the Lady of the Beasts? Where are her myths?

In the patriarchal tradition, the goddess has been fragmented and derogated, deprived of the aura of wholeness which was an implicit aspect of her power. We have images of the Great Goddess, the Lady of the Beasts, and we know something of her qualities and her character. But we do not have myths: the narrative structures that provide paradigms for literature. Recent critical studies have dealt with several clusters of myths that have traditionally informed literature, two of which are the rape myths concerning Callisto, Persephone, and Daphne, and the myth of Cupid and Psyche. Powerful as these are, as potently as they still speak to us, they by no means encompass the whole of woman's experience and can hardly be the only archetypes available to us. Consequently we must be sensitively alert, ready to recover the narrative structures that tell us more about the Great Mother. We must be ready to find myths in which woman is not merely victim but goddess, myths that illustrate a woman's ability to give birth to and mother herself, myths of women in bloom, myths that attest to the powerfulness of motherhood, myths that show woman as creatrix of her own world, myths that examine sisterly relationships with other women, and finally myths that will "express affiliation [between men and women] without simultaneously imposing a hierarchy, that will render life not as endless battle, but a celebration."[16]

One pattern that Estella Lauter observed most frequently in the work of poets and visual artists was a preoccupation with metamorphoses. She argues convincingly that this pattern arises out of a woman's realization, one which comes out of her own experience as a nurturer, that the boundaries between herself and others are quite fluid.[17] But it seems also possible to conclude that the metamorphoses she observes constitute, like Ovid's work, an attempt to begin the catalogue of new mythology. Just as Atwood metamorphosed the myth of Callisto in her novel, just as her heroine undertook her own metamorphosis by rediscovering an ancient ritual, so are women now in the process of metamorphosing their world and the mythology that gives it shape and meaning.

Appendices

APPENDIX A

The Callisto Story According to Hesiod.

The Great Bear ... Hesiod says she (Callisto) was the daughter of Lycaon and lived in Arcadia. She chose to occupy herself with wild-beasts in the mountains together with Artemis, and, when she was seduced by Zeus, continued some time undetected by the goddess, but afterwards, when she was already with child, was seen by her bathing and so discovered. Upon this, the goddess was enraged and changed her into a beast. Thus she became a bear and gave birth to a son called Arcas. But while she was in the mountain, she was hunted by some goat-herds and given up with her babe to Lycaon. Some while after, she thought fit to go into the forbidden precinct of Zeus, not knowing the law, and being pursued by her own son and the Arcadians, was about to be killed because of the said law; but Zeus delivered her because of her connection with him and put her among the stars, giving her the name Bear because of the misfortune which had befallen her.

APPENDIX B

The Callisto Story According to Apollodorus.

Callisto and Arcas. Eumelus and certain others maintain that Lycaon also had a daughter named Callisto, although Hesiod says she was one of the nymphs, while Asius identifies her father as Nycteus, and Pherecydes as Ceteus. She was a hunting companion of Artemis, imitating her dress and remaining under oath a virgin for the goddess. But Zeus fell in love with her and forced her into bed, taking the likeness, some say, of Artemis, others, of Apollo. Because he wanted to escape the attention of Hera, Zeus changed Callisto into a bear. But Hera persuaded Artemis to shoot the girl with an arrow like a wild animal. There are those who maintain, however, that Artemis shot her because she did not protect her virginity. As Callisto died, Zeus seized his baby and handed it to Maia to rear in Arcadia, giving it the name Arcas. Callisto he changed into a star, which he called Arctus.

APPENDIX C

The Callisto Story According to Hyginus.

We begin ... with the Great Bear. Hesiod says she is named Callisto, daughter of Lycaon, who ruled in Arcadia. Out of her zeal for hunting she joined Diana, and was greatly loved by the goddess because of their similar temperaments. Later, when made pregnant by Jove, she feared to tell the truth to Diana. But she couldn't conceal it long, for as her womb grew heavier near the time of her delivery, when she was refreshing her tired body in a stream, Diana realized she had not preserved her virginity. In keeping with her deep distrust, the goddess inflicted no light punishment. Taking away her maiden features, she changed her into the form of a bear, called apktos in Greek. In this form she bore Arcas.

But as Amphis, writer of comedies, says, Jupiter, assuming the form of Diana, followed the girl as if to aid her in hunting, and embraced her when out of sight of the rest. Questioned by Diana as to the reason for her swollen form, she replied that it was the goddess's fault, and because of this reply, Diana changed her into the shape we mentioned above. When wandering like a wild beast in the forest, she was caught by certain Aetolians and brought into Arcadia to King Lycaon along with her son as a gift, and there, in ignorance of the law, she is said to have rushed into the temple of Jove Lycaeus. Her son at once followed her, and the Arcadians in pursuit were trying to kill them, when Jupiter, mindful of his indiscretion, rescued her and placed her and her son among the constellations. He named her Arctos, and her son Arctophylax. About him we shall speak later.

Some, too, have said that when Callisto was embraced by Jove, Juno in anger turned her into a bear; then, when she met Diana hunting, she was killed by her, and later, on being recognized, was placed among the stars.

But others say that when Jupiter was pursuing Callisto in the woods, Juno, suspecting what had happened, hurried there so that she could say she had caught him openly. But Jove, the more easily to conceal his fault, left her changed to bear form. Juno, then, finding a bear instead of a girl in that place, pointed her out for Diana, who was hunting, to kill. Jove was distressed to see this, and put in the sky the likeness of a bear represented with stars.

APPENDIX D

The Callisto Story According to Ovid.

Meanwhile the omnipotent father of the gods made a tour of the great walls of heaven, inspecting them to see whether any damage had been done by the violence of the fire. When he saw that all was in good repair, and that their original strength was unshaken, he looked abroad over the earth and man's handiworks. Most of all he was anxious about his dear Arcadia. He restored its springs and the rivers which had not yet dared to flow; he clothed the earth with grass, the trees with leaves, and commanded the blasted forests to grow green again.

As he was hurrying busily to and fro, he stopped short at the sight of an Arcadian maiden. The fire of passion kindled the very marrow of his bones. This girl was not one who spent her time in spinning soft fibres of wool, or in arranging her hair in different styles. She was one of Diana's warriors, wearing her tunic pinned together with a brooch, her tresses carelessly caught back by a white ribbon, and carrying in her hand a light javelin or her bow. None of the nymphs who haunt Maenalus was dearer than she to the goddess of the Crossways: but a favourite is never a favourite for long.

The sun on high had passed its zenith, when she entered a grove whose trees had never felt the axe. Here she took her quiver from her shoulders, unstrung her pliant bow, and lay down on the turf, resting her head on her painted quiver. When Jupiter saw her thus, tired and unprotected, he said: "Here is a secret of which my wife will know nothing; or if she does get to know of it, it will be worth her reproaches!"

Without wasting time he assumed the appearance and the dress of Diana, and spoke to the girl. "Dearest of all my companions," he said, "where have you been hunting? On what mountain ridges?" She raised herself from the grass: "Greetings, divine mistress," she cried, "greater in my sight than Jove himself – I care not if he hears me!" Jove laughed to hear her words. Delighted to be preferred to himself, he kissed her – not with the restraint becoming to a maiden's kisses: and as she began to tell of her hunting exploits in the forest, he prevented her by his embrace, and betrayed his real self by a shameful action. So far from complying, she resisted him as far as a woman could – had Juno seen her she would have been less cruel – but how could a girl overcome a man, and who could defeat Jupiter? He had his way, and returned to the upper air.

The nymph was filled with loathing for the groves and woods that had witnessed her fall. As she left, she almost forgot to pick up the quiver that held her darts, and the bow she had hung up.

Now, as Diana with her attendant company was making her way along the lofty ridge of Maenalus, in high fettle after successful hunting, she caught sight of the nymph, and called to her. At the sound of her name the girl fled, afraid at first lest this was Jupiter in disguise: but when she saw the nymphs accompanying Diana she realized that there was no trickery here, and she joined them. Alas, how difficult it is not to betray guilt by one's looks! She scarcely raised her eyes from the ground, and did not stay close by the goddess as she usually did, nor did she take her place in the forefront of them all. Instead she remained silent, and by her blushes gave clear indication of the wrong she had suffered. If Diana herself had not been a virgin goddess, she could have perceived her guilt by a thousand signs; the nymphs perceived it, so men say.

Now the moon's horns were filling out to complete their ninth circle, when the goddess wearied with hunting in the fierce heat of the sun, came to a cool grove, from which there flowed a murmuring stream that rippled over its smooth sandy bed. Diana exclaimed with pleasure at the sight, and dipped her foot in the water: delighted with this too, she called to her companions: "There is no one here to see us – let us undress, and bathe in the brook." The Arcadian maiden blushed. All the rest took off their garments, while she alone sought excuses to delay. As she hesitated, the others pulled off her tunic and at one and the same time revealed her body and her crime. She stood dismayed, and with her hands vainly tried to cover up the evidence of her guilt. But Diana cried: "Off with you! Do not defile this sacred spring!" and ordered her to withdraw from her company.

The wife of the mighty Lord of Thunder had long since realized what had happened, and was resolved to inflict stern punishment, but had postponed doing so until a suitable opportunity should arise. There was now no reason for delay: already a child, Arcas, had been born to her rival, and that in itself enraged Juno. She regarded the boy, with anger in her heart and in her eyes. "This is the one insult that was lacking, you shameless woman," she cried, "that you should bear a son. Now the wrong done to me has been made public by the birth of your child, and there is proof of my husband's misdemeanour. But you will not escape unpunished! For I shall rob you of that beauty, in which both you and my husband take such delight, you minx!"

With these words she seized the hair above her rival's brow, and tugged till the girl fell forward on the ground. As she lay there, stretching out her arms to beg for mercy, these arms began to bristle with coarse black hairs, and her hands curved round, turning into crooked claws, which then served her as feet. Her face, which Jupiter had once praised, was disfigured by wide gaping jaws. Then, lest her prayers and imploring words should wake sympathy, the goddess deprived her of the power of speech. A harsh growling issued from her throat, angry and quarrelsome, frightening to hear; she had become a bear, but even so her mind remained unchanged, and she declared her grief with continual lamentations, raising to the stars in heaven such hands as she had, and feeling Jove's ingratitude, though she could not speak of it. Many a time, not daring to rest in the lonely wood, she wandered before the home and in the fields that once were hers. Many a time, barking hounds drove her through rocky places, and the huntress fled, terrified of the hunters. Often she forgot what she was, and hid when she saw wild beasts; though a bear herself, she shuddered at the sight of bears in their mountain haunts, and feared wolves too, though her father was one of them.

Meanwhile her son Arcas had reached the age of fifteen. He was quite unaware of what had happened to his mother, Lycaon's daughter. But one day, when he was engaged in tracking wild creatures in the woods, choosing suitable hunting grounds and encircling the copses of Erymanthus with his nets, he came face to face with her. She stopped when she saw Arcas, and seemed to recognize him: but he, not knowing the reason for such behaviour, shrank back, terrified of this beast, which gazed at him so fixedly, never taking her eyes off him. As she tried, in her eagerness, to approach him, he would have pierced her heart with his deadly spear; but almighty Jupiter stayed his hand, and prevented a crime being committed, by removing both mother and son. A whirlwind carried them up, together, through the void of heaven, and then he set them in the sky, as neighbouring constellations.

When her rival was shining among the stars, Juno's wrath knew no bounds. She went down to the side waters to visit hoary-headed Tethys and the aged Oceanus, for whom the gods have often shown reverence. When they inquired the reason for her coming, she replied: "You ask me why I, the queen of the gods, have left my heavenly abode to come here? It is because another, in my place, holds sway in the sky! Unless I am mistaken, when night darkens the world, you will see two constellations newly raised to the honour of a place in highest heaven, expressly to insult me! Look for them where the last and narrowest circle surrounds the tip of the pole. And do you suppose that anyone will hesitate to wrong Juno, or fear to offend her, when I alone actually do good to those I try to harm? Great indeed are my achievements, and mighty my strength; I denied her the rights of a human being, and she has become a goddess! So much for the punishment I inflict on the guilty! So much for my tremendous power! Let Jupiter now restore her former shape, and rid her of her bestial appearance, as he did before in the case of the Argive Io. Why does he not go so far as to divorce Juno, and marry this new love – set her in my wedding chamber, and take Lycaon as a father-in-law?

"I implore you, if this contemptuous treatment of one who was your nursling distresses you, prevent the Bear from entering your dark blue waters: repulse those stars which have been received into heaven as a reward for a shameless conduct, and do not let my rival bathe in your pure tide."

The gods of the sea nodded in consent. Then Saturn's daughter drove off through the clear air in her light chariot.

APPENDIX E

The Callisto Story According to Pausanias.

Lycaon had a daughter Callisto. This Callisto (I merely repeat the common Greek story) was loved by Zeus, who had an intrigue with her. When Hera found it out she turned Callisto into a bear, and Artemis, to please Hera, shot the bear down. Zeus sent Hermes with orders to save the child whom Callisto bore in her womb; and Callisto herself he changed into the stars known as the Great Bear, which Homer mentions in the return voyage of Ulysses from Calypso: –

Watching the Pleiades and late-setting Bootes,
And the Bear, which also they call the Wain.

But perhaps these stars are so called merely out of compliment to Callisto, for the Arcadians point out her grave.

* * *

Keeping to the right from Tricoloni you first ascend by a steep road to a spring called Cruni. Descending from Cruni about thirty furlongs you come to the grave of Callisto, a lofty mound of earth, on which grow trees, many of them of the cultivated sorts, and many of the kinds that bear no fruit. On the summit of the mound is a sanctuary of Artemis surnamed Calliste ('fairest'). I believe that Pamphos, the first poet who gave Artemis the epithet of Calliste, must have learnt it from the Arcadians.

APPENDIX F

from Charles Anthon: A Classical Dictionary

CALLISTO and Calisto, called also Helice, was daughter of Lycaon, king of Arcadia, and one of Diana's attendants. Jupiter saw her, and, assuming the form of Diana, accompanied the maiden to the chase, and surprised her virtue. She long concealed her shame; but at length, as she was one day bathing with her divine mistress, the discovery was made, and Diana, in her anger, turned her into a bear. While in this form she brought forth her son Arcas, who lived with her in the woods, till the herdsmen caught both her and him, and brought them to Lycaon ... Some time afterward she went into the temenus, or sacred enclosure of the Lycaean Jove, which it was unlawful to enter. A number of Arcadians, among whom was her own son, followed to kill her, but Jove snatched her out of their hands, and placed her as a constellation in the sky ... It was also fabled, that at the request of Juno, Tethys forbade the constellation of the bear to descend into her waves. This legend is related with great variety in the circumstances. According to one of these versions, Arcas, having been separated from his mother and reared among men, met her one day in the woods, and was on the point of slaying her, when Jupiter transferred the mother and son to the skies.

Notes

INTRODUCTION

1 Pratt, "The New Feminist Criticism," 877.
2 Christ, *Diving Deep and Surfacing*, 9.
3 Showalter, *The New Feminist Criticism*, 243.
4 Pratt, *Archetypal Patterns in Women's Fiction*, 5.
5 Auerbach, *Woman and the Demon*, 150.
6 de Beauvoir, *The Second Sex*, 416.
7 Brownmiller, *Against Our Will: Men, Women and Rape*, 6.
8 Rich, *Of Woman Born*, 51–2.
9 Ortner, "Is Woman to Man as Nature is to Culture?", in Rosaldo and Lamphere, *Women, Culture, and Society*, 67–87.
10 du Plessex Gray, "Nature as a Nunnery," 29.
11 Pratt, *Archetypal Patterns*, 16.
12 Ibid.
13 Auerbach, *Woman and the Demon*, 160.
14 Pratt, *Archetypal Patterns*, 19.
15 Auerbach, *Woman and the Demon*, 165–6.
16 Pratt, *Archetypal Patterns*, 142.
17 Leslie Fiedler, "Archetype and Signature," 462.
18 Lauter and Rupprecht, *Feminist Archetypal Theory*, 5.
19 Wehr, "Religious and Social Dimensions of Jung's Concept of the Archetype: A Feminist Perspective," in Lauter and Rupprecht, *Feminist Archetypal Theory*, 38.
20 Goldenberg, *Changing of the Gods*, 62.
21 Wehr, "Religious and Social Dimensions of Jung's Concept of the Archetype: A Feminist Perspective," in Lauter and Rupprecht, *Feminist Archetypal Theory*, 37.
22 Lauter and Rupprecht, *Feminist Archetypal Theory*, 13–14.

23 Lauter and Rupprecht, *Feminist Archetypal Theory*, 15.

24 Fiedler, "Archetype and Signature," 462.

25 Jung, "On the Relation of Analytical Psychology to Poetry," 83.

CHAPTER ONE

1 Hesiod, *Homeric Hymns and Homerica*, 69. See Appendix A.

2 Apollodorus, *Library of Greek Mythology*, Book III, 71. See Appendix B.

3 Hyginus, *Poetica Astronomica*, Book II, in *The Myths of Hyginus*, 181–2. See Appendix C.

4 Ovid, *Metamorphoses*, 61–4. See Appendix D.

5 Pausanias, *Description of Greece*, 419. See Appendix E.

6 Ovid, *Metamorphoses*, 61.

7 Hesiod, *Homeric Hymns and Homerica*, 69.

8 Ovid, *Metamorphoses*, 61.

9 Apollodorus, *Library of Greek Mythology*, 71.

10 Ovid, *Metamorphoses*, 61.

11 Hyginus, *Poetica Astronomica*, 181.

12 Apollodorus, *Homeric Hymns and Homerica*, 71.

13 Hesiod, *Homeric Hymns and Homerica*, 69; and Hyginus, *Poetica Astronomica*, 181.

14 Pausanias, *Description of Greece*, 376; and Apollodorus, *Library of Greek Mythology*, 71.

15 Neumann, *The Great Mother*; see also Graves, *The White Goddess*, 125.

16 J.G. Frazer, "The Magic Art and the Evolution of Kings," *The Golden Bough*, Part I (New York, 1917) I, 36, 37. Cited by Harding, *Woman's Mysteries*, 101.

17 Walker, *Woman's Encyclopedia of Myths and Secrets*, 58–60 and Gimbutas, *Gods and Goddesses of Old Europe*, 196–200.

18 Pratt, "Spinning Among Fields" in Lauter and Rupprecht, *Feminist Archetypal Theory*, 110.

19 Harding, *Woman's Mysteries*, 102.

20 Rich, *Of Woman Born*, 96; Pratt, *Archetypal Patterns*, 9; Rigney, *Madness and Sexual Politics in the Feminist Novel*, 36–6; Hinz and Teunissen, "*Surfacing*: Margaret Atwood's 'Nymph Complaining,'" 230.

21 In the earliest stages of this study (1980), I was compelled to note that heroines like Tess, Atwood's narrator, and Hester Prynne, while caught up in the fate of the mortal Callisto, were represented via the iconography of the Great Goddess. Operating purely on a hunch, I returned to the classical sources, examined the conclusions of classical scholars more closely, and widened the nets of my research in women's studies of mythology. Oddly enough, it was not difficult to prove that Callisto and Diana are identical: the facts were easily found in Pausanias, Guthrie (1954), and Fox (1964). One wonders what other truths are sitting quietly in reference rooms, waiting for someone to decide they're impor-

tant and explore their significance? While Walker's *Women's Encyclopedia* (1983) verifies my conclusion, I have left the somewhat lengthy argument describing my own discovery intact, both because our independent work lends credence to our conclusions, and because it is an intrinsic part of the inductive process of this study.

22 Pausanias, *Description of Greece*, 419.
23 Fox, *Greek and Roman*, vol. 1 of *The Mythology of All Races*, 21.
24 Harding, *Woman's Mysteries*, 149.
25 Walker, *Woman's Encyclopedia of Myths and Secrets*, 59, 134.
26 Gimbutas, *Gods and Goddesses of Old Europe*, 198.
27 Neumann, *The Great Mother*, 276–7.
28 Guthrie, *The Greeks and Their Gods*, 103.
29 Bachofen, *Myth, Religion, and Mother Right*, 74.
30 Walker, *Woman's Encyclopedia of Myths and Secrets*, 1030, 60, 233, 1031.
31 Merchant, *The Death of Nature*, 19, 25.
32 Walker, *Woman's Encyclopedia of Myths and Secrets*, 501.
33 Harding, *Woman's Mysteries*, 137.
34 Gimbutas, *Gods and Goddesses of Old Europe*, 198.
35 Walker, *Woman's Encyclopedia of Myths and Secrets*, 134.
36 Downing, *The Goddess*, 182.
37 Harding, *Woman's Mysteries*, 146.
38 Ibid., 187.
39 Ochshorn, *The Female Experience and the Nature of the Divine*, 127.
40 Harding, *Woman's Mysteries*, 144.
41 de Beauvoir, *The Second Sex*, 416.
42 Harding, *Woman's Mysteries*, 11, 29.
43 Ibid., 38.
44 Rheinhold, *Past and Present*, 326.
45 Harding, *Woman's Mysteries*, 11, 29, 38.
46 Ibid., 187.
47 Ibid., 154.
48 de Beauvoir, *The Second Sex*, 374.
49 Ibid., 275–6.
50 Brownmiller, *Against Our Will*, 4–5.
51 de Beauvoir, *The Second Sex*, 388.
52 On the chthonic nature of women, see de Beauvoir, Sanday, and Ortner, "Is Female to Male as Nature Is to Culture?", in Rosaldo and Lamphere, *Women, Culture, and Society*, 67–87.
53 MacCormack and Strathern, *Nature, Culture, and Gender*, 31–3.
54 Ibid., 61.
55 Rich, *Of Woman Born*, 116.
56 In a passage on page 85, Ortner discusses the ways in which women become the keepers of mores in patriarchal societies. For the most part, their condem-

nation of other women becomes a means of protecting their own reputations which, given the prevalence of misogyny, is important. Again and again, we find that this is what the Hera and Diana figures intend when they cast out or condemn Callisto.

57 Downing, *The Goddess*, 70.
58 Ibid., 83.
59 Bolen, *Goddesses in Everywoman*, 140, 146, 161.
60 Harvey, *Oxford Companion to Classical Literature*, 251.
61 Hamilton, *Mythology: Timeless Tales of Gods and Heroes*, 30.

CHAPTER TWO

1 Golding, *Shakespeare's Ovid*, 45–6, 11. 539–44. Subsequent page references will be given parenthetically in the text.
2 Sandys, *Ovid's Metamorphoses Englished, Mythologiz'd, and Represented in Figures*, 91–2. Subsequent page references will be given parenthetically in the text.
3 Caxton, *The Metamorphoses of Ovid*, n.p.
4 To assist readers who are not specialists in medieval and Renaissance literature, I have changed four aspects of the conventional period orthography, but have left the other spellings as they appear in the original. Printers often use ı for ȷ, u for v, v for u, and ꜰ for s; in the text I have substituted the letter we commonly expect for the one used in the originals.
5 Lefevre, *The Recuyell of the Historyes of Troy*, xxxi. Subsequent page references will be given parenthetically in the text. Punctuation has been regularized for the sake of the reader.
6 Joseph and Francis Gies, in *Woman in the Middle Ages*, remark that "Feudalism ... brought a reactionary shift in the status of women. A system by which a Lord granted land to a vassal in return for services that were primarily military, it produced a society organized for war, an essentially masculine world. Pre-feudal society was already male-biased and military, but by linking landholding to military service, feudalism meant a further disenfranchisement of women. Feudalism was theoretically grounded in the concept that land actually belonged only to the lord, who granted it to his vassals for life" (27). Mary Kinnear, however, points out in *Daughters of Time* that "indisputably some women owned both real estate, in land and buildings, and personal estate, in movable property ... Customs varied in time and place. There was frequently a distinction made between realty and personalty, with women prohibited from ownership of realty altogether, for example, in the Salic Law. The ninth-century Thuringians also made it difficult for a woman to inherit land ... The Visgothic code, on the other hand, allowed women to inherit property without priority being accorded to brothers" (70).
7 Bullough, *The Subordinate Sex*, 157.

8 Casey, "The Cheshire Cat," 224–49; esp. 239–40.

9 Martin, "Notes on Thomas Heywood's *Ages*," 23–9. In his article on Heywood, Martin compares these arguments of Jupiter in Lefevre to those that Heywood's Jupiter offers Callisto and similar passages which appear in Shakespeare's *Venus and Adonis*, finally noting "the popularity of the motif," 25.

10 Kaufman, "Spare Ribs," 139–63; esp. 161–2. Fraser, *The Weaker Vessel*, 68.

11 Kaufman notes that the necessity of threatening to excommunicate priests who had any concourse with women had the side-effect of making woman, as far as the clergy was concerned, the ultimate temptation. See 142.

12 Bullough, *The Subordinate Sex*, 119.

13 Ibid., 165.

14 Warner, *Albion's England*, 50. Subsequent page references will be given parenthetically in the text.

15 Kaufman, "Spare Ribs," 152.

16 Fraser, *The Weaker Vessel*, 163.

17 Kaufman, "Spare Ribs," 153.

18 Fraser, *The Weaker Vessel*, 4.

19 Maclean, *The Renaissance Notion of Woman*, 24.

20 Fraser, *The Weaker Vessel*, 3.

21 Castiglione, *The Book of the Courtier*, 217.

22 Heywood, *The Golden Age*, 45. Subsequent page references will be given parenthetically in the text.

23 Fraser, *The Weaker Vessel*, 70.

24 Quite possibly Heywood, in referring to the heresy of Diana's band recalls a similar condemnation by the papacy of *Beguines*, groups of unmarried or widowed women who, unable to fend for themselves as individuals, often banded together, vowing chastity, performing charitable deeds and discussing the religious issues of the day. It was the latter that disturbed the Catholic hierarchy, and a proclamation was issued which criticized their refusal to "follow the traditional role of women in religion." See Bullough, *The Subordinate Sex*, 62.

25 Neumann, *Amor and Psyche*, 63.

26 W.N., Gent. *The Barley-Breake, or a Warning for Wantons*, fol. B2. Subsequent folio references will be given parenthetically in the text.

CHAPTER THREE

1 For examples of allegorical criticism of *Comus*, see Adams, "Reading *Comus*"; Dyson, "The Interpretation of *Comus*"; Woodhouse, "*Comus* Once More"; and Tillyard, "The Action of *Comus*", in Dieckoff, *A Mask at Ludlow: Essays on Milton's "Comus"*.

2 Harding, *Milton and the Renaissance Ovid*, 58–66.

3 Osgood, *The Classical Mythology of Milton's Poems*, 18. Under the "Callisto" entry, Osgood merely catalogues Milton's reference to the "star of Arcady" in

the masque; he makes no effort to relate the reference to the whole mythic fabric of the work.

4 Milton, *A Mask Presented at Ludlow Castle*, 97, 1. 340. Subsequent page and line references will be given parenthetically in the text.

5 Sandys, *Ovid's Metamorphoses Englished, Mythologiz'd, and Represented in Figures*, 645.

6 Graves, *The White Goddess*, 448. Graves further identifies Circe with the Triple Goddess in her aspect as muse.

7 Harvey, *The Oxford Companion to Classical Literature*, 195.

8 Arthos, "Milton, Ficino, and the Charmides," 265.

9 Lawry, *The Shadow of Heaven*, 77.

10 Woodhouse, "The Argument of Milton's *Comus*," in Lovelock, *Milton: "Comus" and "Samson Agonistes*," 45, 51.

11 Tillyard, "The Action of *Comus*," in Dieckhoff, *A Maske at Ludlow: Essays on Milton's "Comus*," 50.

12 Tillyard, *Milton*, 321, 320.

13 Broadbent, *Milton: "Comus" and "Samson Agonistes*," 17.

14 Among those who consider the genre of *Comus* by comparing it, favourably or unfavourably, with masques written before Milton's are Barber, "A Mask Presented at Ludlow Castle: The Mask as a Mask," in Lovelock, *Milton: "Comus" and "Samson Agonistes"*; Demaray, *Milton and the Masque Tradition*; Martin, "Transformations in Genre in Milton's *Comus*"; and Tuve, *Images and Themes in Five Poems of Milton*.

15 Fletcher, *The Transcendental Masque*, 8, 22, xiii, 157.

16 Kelso, *Doctrine for the Lady of the Renaissance*, 24.

17 See Cox, "Poetry and History in Milton's Country Mask," 3–20.

18 Wilcher, "Milton's Masque: Occasion, Form, and Meaning," 8.

19 Fletcher, *The Transcendental Masque*, 163.

20 Wilcher, "Milton's Masque: Occasion, Form, and Meaning," 14.

21 Fletcher, *The Transcendental Masque*, 164.

22 See Ortner, "Is Female to Male as Nature is to Culture?" in Rosaldo and Lamphere, *Women, Culture, and Society*, 67–87.

23 Tillyard, "The Action of *Comus*," 54.

24 Ovid, *Metamorphoses*, 240.

25 Ibid., 244.

26 Lawrence, *The Collected Letters of D.H. Lawrence*, 2: 615.

27 Neumann, *Amor and Psyche*, 74.

28 Woodhouse, "The Argument of Milton's *Comus*," in Lovelock, *Milton: "Comus" and "Samson Agonistes"*, 61–6.

29 Tillyard, "The Action of *Comus*," 55.

30 Ibid.

31 Kelso, *Doctrine for the Lady of the Renaissance*, 24.

CHAPTER FOUR

1 Duffy, *The Erotic World of Faery*, 212.
2 Radcliffe, *The Mysteries of Udolpho*, 565. Subsequent page references will be given parenthetically in the text.
3 Poovey, "Ideology and *The Mysteries of Udolpho*," 308–9.
4 Jacobs, *Beyond the Castle: The Paradigmatic Female Story*, iv.
5 Poovey, "Ideology and *The Mysteries of Udolpho*," 311.
6 Howells, *Love, Mystery, and Misery: Feeling in Gothic Fiction*, 46.
7 Poovey, "Ideology and *The Mysteries of Udolpho*," 323.
8 Holcombe, "Victorian Wives and Property," in Vicinus, *A Widening Sphere*, 4–5.
9 Poovey, "Ideology and *The Mysteries of Udolpho*," 323–4.

CHAPTER FIVE

1 Moglen, *Charlotte Brontë*, 106–7.
2 Hellerstein, Hume, and Offen, eds., *Victorian Women*, 281.
3 Brontë, *Jane Eyre*, 96. Subsequent page references will be given parenthetically in the text.
4 Hughes, "*Jane Eyre*: The Unbaptised Dionysos," 353.
5 Hellerstein, Hume, and Offen, *Victorian Women*, 281.
6 Fulton, "*Jane Eyre*: The Development of a Female Consciousness," 433. Hughes also notes that the frames of mind which Jane must somehow integrate are Dionysian and Apollonian, two terms which are almost synonymous with the words Logos and Eros, which I use here.
7 Moglen, *Charlotte Brontë*, 129.
8 This attitude is basically Freudian, and can be attributed to Chase, "The Brontes, or Myth Domesticated," 108. Barbara Rigney, in *Madness and Sexual Politics in the Feminist Novel*, comes to similar conclusions: "Bertha is as much a doppelganger for Jane as for Rochester: she serves as a distorted mirror image of Jane's own dangerous propensities toward 'passion,' Brontë's frequent euphemism for sexuality," 16. Nevertheless, Rigney's feminist point of view touches more on ways in which Bertha's situation provides insight into Jane's. Although it is, like Chase's, psychoanalytic, Rigney's has far more sympathy for Brontë's use of this figure. In *A Literature of Their Own*, Showalter interprets Bertha's madness as symptomatic of her sexual appetite: "Bertha Mason ... is the incarnation in the flesh, of female sexuality in its most irredeemably bestial and terrifying form. Brontë's treatment of the myth of the Mad Wife is brilliantly comprehensive and reverberative, and rich with historical, medical, and sociological implications, as well as with psychological force." Showalter's subsequent treatment of Bertha Mason contains useful information on the attitudes of Brontë's contemporaries toward madwomen in general and, more specifically, the "moral

madness" which was believed to be an inevitable product of *any* degree of sexual appetite in women. See 118–22.

9 Gilbert and Gubar, *The Madwoman in the Attic*, 361–2. In exploring Jane's relationship to Mrs. Rochester, Gilbert and Gubar focus far less upon psychoanalytic parallels, than on the similarities of the situations of Jane and Bertha. Bertha acts out Jane's *anger*, not her passion.

10 Rich, *On Lies, Secrets, and Silence*, 99.

11 Mann, "Bertha Mason and Jane Eyre: The True Mrs. Rochester," 33.

12 Harvey, *The Oxford Companion to Classical Literature*, 200.

13 Mann, "Bertha Mason and Jane Eyre: The True Mrs. Rochester," 33.

14 Radcliffe, *Mysteries of Udolpho*, 624.

15 Ewbank, *Their Proper Sphere*, 196.

16 Ibid.

17 Chase, "The Brontes, or Myth Domesticated," 108.

18 Burckhart, "Another Key Word for *Jane Eyre*," 179.

19 Rich, *On Lies, Secrets, and Silence*, 101–2; also see Heilman, "Charlotte Bronte, Reason, and the Moon," 283–302; and Rigney, *Madness and Sexual Politics*, 35.

20 Heilman, "Charlotte Bronte, Reason, and the Moon," 294.

21 Ibid., 299.

22 Rich, *On Lies, Secrets, and Silence*, 102, 105.

23 Rigney, *Madness and Sexual Politics*, 35–6.

24 Rich, *On Lies, Secrets, and Silence*, 104–5.

CHAPTER SIX

1 Hawthorne, *Tanglewood Tales* and *The Wonder Book*, in *Complete Works of Nathaniel Hawthorne*, 4:212.

2 Hawthorne, *The Scarlet Letter*, 1. Subsequent page references will be given parenthetically in the text.

3 The patriarchal nature of the Custom House is indicated by much heavily-loaded language. There the narrator works for a "common Uncle" (12), "Uncle Sam" (3). Among the "patriarchal body of veterans" who are his fellow-workers (10), the narrator has a somewhat "paternal position" (13), taking care of the elderly and hence childlike men who still work there. Among them are the old general and the permanent inspector, whom the narrator considers "the father of the Custom-House" as well as "the patriarch, not only of this little squad of officials, but, I am bold to say, of the respectable body of tide-waiters all over the United States" (14). Women seem actually disallowed from the Custom-House; the "sea-flushed shipmaster" takes care of the business there even before he greets his wife, and "womankind, with her tools of magic, the broom and mop, has very infrequent access" to the "sanctuary" where the men work (5). The only flush of femininity about the place is the eagle, but "she has no great tenderness, even in the best of moods" (3).

4 Stouck, "The Surveyor of the Custom House: A Narrator for *The Scarlet Letter*," 325.

5 The ambiguity of Hawthorne's narrative has been much discussed, but three critics in particular deal with the ambiguity in terms that are related or parallel to those of this study, logos and eros. Best known, perhaps, is Ringe's "Hawthorne's Psychology of the Head and Heart," 120–32. Also important are Fogle, *Hawthorne's Fiction: The Light and the Dark*; Martin, *Nathaniel Hawthorne*; and Deamer, "Hawthorne's Dream in the Forest," 327–39.

6 Person, "*The Scarlet Letter* and the Myth of the Divine Child," 301.

7 Person also notes that the "passionate moment" in the forest is a repeat of earlier encounters, and that Dimmesdale is here reborn. See 301.

8 Abel also observes that Chillingworth "regarded his wife jealously, as a chattel, not as a person with needs and rights of her own." See "Hawthorne's Hester," 305.

9 See Ringe, "Hawthorne's Psychology of the Head and Heart," 120–32.

10 McPherson, *Hawthorne as Mythmaker*, 11.

11 Among those who notice the goddess in Hester are Lawrence, *Studies in Classic American Literature*, 88; Van Doren, *Nathaniel Hawthorne*, 154–5; and Hutchinson, "Antiquity in *The Scarlet Letter*: The Primary Sources," 101.

12 Baym, "Hawthorne's Women: The Tyranny of Social Myths," 250, 256.

13 McPherson comments, regarding the character of Hester's initiation: "In the 'pure' myth, then, the Dark Lady (Pandora, Proserpina) is blameless. It is only in the Christian tradition that she has become a figure of fear, haunted by the spectre of a 'Black Man' who will never let society forget that she knows the realm of night." See "Hawthorne's Mythology: A Mirror for Puritans," 271.

14 Person, "*The Scarlet Letter* and the Myth of the Divine Child," 304.

CHAPTER SEVEN

1 Wallace, "A Probable Source for Dorothea and Casaubon: Hester and Chillingworth," 25.

2 Eliot, *Adam Bede*, 124. Subsequent page references will be given parenthetically in the text.

3 Jones, *George Eliot*, 15.

4 Harris, "Arthur's Misuse of the Imagination: Sentimental Benevolence and Wordsworthian Realism in *Adam Bede*," 45.

5 Knoepflamacher, *George Eliot's Early Novels: The Limits of Realism*, 120. Knoepflamacher notes Arthur's camouflage of the interest in animals. Obviously, given the iconography of the myth, I would also be looking for animal imagery. Knoepflamacher, however, does not really make any use of the descriptions of Hetty which involve comparisons to animals.

6 Harvey, in *The Oxford Companion to Classical Literature*, describes the Centaurs' attempts to carry off the female wedding guests of King Pirithous. See 96.

7 Jones, *George Eliot*, 17–18.

8 Burch, "Eliot's *Adam Bede*", 27–8.

9 Gregor and Nicholas, *The Moral and the Story*, 27. Gregor's perception of Hetty is that "for all her vanity, Hetty really belongs with the wronged women of folk tale who pine away for their lost lovers." He does not, however, see her as mythic.

10 Harvey, *The Art of George Eliot*, 141. Harvey notes the structural parallels between Dinah and Hetty, but his criticism ends with this observation, concerned as he is with proving that Eliot was not a naive writer.

11 Staves, "British Seduced Maidens," 109–34.

12 Leslie Stephen, for example, was one proper Victorian gentlemen who found Hetty charming. See his *George Eliot*, 76.

13 This impression of the novel is so ubiquitous as almost not to need documentation. Nevertheless, see Gregor, *The Moral and the Story*, 15; and Harvey, *The Art of George Eliot*, 231, for examples of this opinion.

14 Gregor and Nichols, *The Moral and the Story*, 29.

15 See Appendix I: "George Eliot's History of *Adam Bede*" in the Penguin edition.

CHAPTER EIGHT

1 Kettle, "Introduction" to 1966 Harper and Row edition of *Tess of the D'Urbervilles*, in La Valley, *Twentieth Century Interpretations of "Tess of the D'Urbervilles"*, 14; Howe, *Thomas Hardy*, 111; Hyman, *Ethical Perspectives in the Novels of Thomas Hardy*, 106.

2 Eakins, "Tess, the Pagan and Christian Traditions" in Smith, *The Novels of Thomas Hardy*, 107.

3 Fertility myths in *Tess* are commented upon by Millgate, *Thomas Hardy*, 270; Brooks, *Thomas Hardy: The Poetic Structure*, 240; and Horne, "The Darkening Sun of Tess Durbeyfield," 299.

4 Kozicki, "Myths of Redemption in Hardy's *Tess of the D'Urbervilles*," 151.

5 Hardy, *Tess of the D'Urbervilles*, 150. Subsequent page references will be given parenthetically in the text.

6 Frazer, *The Golden Bough*, 166.

7 Millgate, *Thomas Hardy*, 269.

8 Harding, *Woman's Mysteries*, 45.

9 Graves, *The White Goddess*, 173–4. The many reasons include: "it is the tree that loves water most, and the Moon-goddess is the giver of dew and moisture generally; its leaves and bark, the source of salicylic acid, are sovereign against rheumatic cramps formerly thought to be caused by witchcraft. The goddess's prime orgiastic bird, the weyneck, or snake bird, or cuckoo's mate – a spring migrant which hisses like a snake, lives flat along a bough, erects its crest when angry, writhes its neck about, lays white eggs, eats ants, and has v-markings on its feathers like those on the scales of oracular serpents in Ancient Greece – always nests in willow-trees. Moreover, the *liknos*, or basket-sieve anciently used for winnowing corn, was made from willow ..."

10 Laird, *The Shaping of "Tess of the D'Urberbervilles,"* 88.

11 Frazer, *The Golden Bough*, 5.

12 Graves, *The White Goddess*, 389–91.

13 Harding, *Woman's Mysteries*, 25.

14 Neumann, *The Great Mother*, 280.

15 Harding, *Woman's Mysteries*, 24.

16 Steele, "Which Ovid in the Hay-Shed?", 430–2. Steele notes the Ovidian echoes in this scene – Hardy's description of nymphs and satyrs – but does not mention the Callisto myth.

17 Horne, "The Darkening Sun of Tess Durbeyfield," 303.

18 Graves, *The White Goddess*, 65.

19 Enstice, *Thomas Hardy: Landscapes of the Mind*, 148.

20 See Brown, "A Novel of Character and Environment," in Draper, *The Tragic Novels*, 158–64; and Kettle, *An Introduction to the English Novel*, 2:45.

21 Brown, *Thomas Hardy*, 91.

22 Hardy, "The Dorsetshire Labourer," *Longman's Magazine*, July, 1883, rpt. in *Thomas Hardy's Personal Writings*, 188.

CHAPTER NINE

1 Lawrence, "Study of Thomas Hardy," in *Phoenix: Posthumous Papers of D.H. Lawrence*, 484.

2 Moynihan, *"Lady Chatterley's Lover*: The Deed of Life," 72–92.

3 Lawrence, *Lady Chatterley's Lover*, 123. Subsequent page references will be given parenthetically in the text.

4 Sanders, *D.H. Lawrence: The World of the Five Major Novels*, 181. This argument, that the mythic aspects of *Lady Chatterley's Lover* refer to the Grail Legend, is also proposed by Hoffman in *The Mortal No: Death and the Modern Imagination*, 417.

5 Mandel, "Mediaeval Romance and *Lady Chatterley's Lover*," 25.

6 Balbert, "The Loving of Lady Chatterley: D.H. Lawrence and the Phallic Imagination," in Partlow and Moore, *D.H. Lawrence: The Man Who Lived*, 144.

7 Lawrence, "A Propos of *Lady Chatterley's Lover*," in *Phoenix II: Uncollected, Unpublished and Other Prose Works by D.H. Lawrence*, 504.

8 Gregor and Nicholas, *The Moral and the Story*, 239.

9 Black, *The Literature of Fidelity*, 180; Spilka, "On Lawrence's Hostility to Wilful Women: The Chatterley Solution," in Smith, *Lawrence and Women*, 192; and Schorer, "On *Lady Chatterley's Lover*", 154.

10 Harding, *Woman's Mysteries*, 134.

11 Descriptions of Mellors as a Green Knight or fertility figure are contained not only in the studies identified in note 7 above, but also in the following: Tedlock, *D.H. Lawrence, Artist and Rebel: A Study of Lawrence's Fiction*, 221; Stoll, *The Novels of D.H. Lawrence: A Search for Integration*; 234; and Jackson, "The 'Old Pagan Vision': Myth and Ritual in *Lady Chatterley's Lover*," 262–3.

12 We might also note that in this scene Mellors can be seen to represent the bathing Diana, and Connie, who is "hunting" for something vital and who feels that she has seen something divine, could be compared to Actaeon. Lawrence's use of myth in this novel is not, I think, limited to that of Callisto. But even understanding this scene as an image of Actaeon and Diana still identifies Mellors with the feminine, which is my main point here.

13 Balbert, "The Loving of Lady Chatterley: D.H. Lawrence and the Phallic Imagination," in Partlow and Moore, *D.H. Lawrence: The Man Who Lived*, 143.

14 Rossman, "'You are the Call and I am the Answer': D.H. Lawrence and Woman," 255. Although they do not use the term "psychological virginity," there are a number of critics who discuss Lawrence's preoccupation with his character's paradoxical achievement of independence through a union with another. See, for example, Vivas, *D.H. Lawrence, The Failure and Triumph of Art*, 126; and Schorer, "On *Lady Chatterley's Lover*," 160.

15 See Sagar, *The Art of D.H. Lawrence*, 183; Moynihan, "*Lady Chatterley's Lover*: The Deed of Life," 76, and Hoffman, *The Mortal No: Death and the Modern Imagination*, 418. Hinz describes the union between Connie and Mellors as a hierogamy in "Hierogamy versus Wedlock: Types of Marriage Plots and Their Relationship to Genres of Prose Fiction," 908.

16 Sanders, *D.H. Lawrence: The World of the Five Major Novels*, 201.

17 Smith's anthology, *Lawrence and Women*, provides an interesting starting point for this kind of discussion of Lawrence's attitudes toward women. Rossman provides a very lucid and balanced view of the development of Lawrence's attitude toward women in his works. Of course a number of readers have been less sympathetic, have ignored the impact of the whole canon and consequently have ignored Lawrence's attempts to come to grips with his position *vis à vis* the women in his life. Others have suggested that Lawrence's hostility toward women simply comes out of his homosexuality: see specifically Carolyn Heilbrun in *Toward a Recognition of Androgyny*. The important point to be made is that Lawrence is often very wrong about women. When he is working on his difficult and somewhat anomalous relationship with Frieda, he is often jealous, spiteful, defensive. But in these moments he expresses those feelings which many modern men who endeavour to become "liberated" also experience. On the other hand, it must also be recognized that the "feminine" was strong in Lawrence, and that he understood and was often very perceptive about women's issues.

CHAPTER TEN

1 du Plessex Gray, "Nature as a Nunnery," 3, 29.

2 See, for example, Campbell, "The Woman as Hero in Margaret Atwood's *Surfacing*," 17–28.

3 Davidson and Davidson, "The Anatomy of Margaret Atwood's *Surfacing*," 50. On the inadequacy of Frye's and Campbell's theories, see Christ, *Diving Deep and Surfacing*.

4 Hinz and Teunissen, "*Surfacing*: Margaret Atwood's 'Nymph Complaining,'" 230.
5 Pratt, *Archetypal Patterns*, 160.
6 Atwood, *Surfacing*, 52. Subsequent page references will be given parenthetically in the text.
7 Davidson and Davidson, "The Anatomy of Margaret Atwood's *Surfacing*," 42.
8 Christ, "Margaret Atwood: The Surfacing of Women's Spiritual Quest and Vision," 320
9 In *Of Woman Born*, Adrienne Rich explores the ways in which the patriarchy did manage to limit woman's power in motherhood, as well as the ways in which woman managed to circumlocute those imposed limitations.
10 Hinz, "The Masculine/Feminine Psychology of American/Canadian Primitivism: *Deliverance* and *Surfacing*," 94.
11 For a discussion of the shamanistic aspects of the narrator's dive, see Ross, "Nancy Drew as Shaman: Atwood's *Surfacing*," 7-17.
12 McLay, "The Divided Self: Theme and Pattern in Margaret Atwood's *Surfacing*," 87.
13 Hinz and Teunissen, "*Surfacing*: Margaret Atwood's 'Nymph Complaining,'" 230.
14 Pratt, *Archetypal Patterns*, 159.
15 Rubenstein, "*Surfacing*: Margaret Atwood's Journey to the Interior," 393.
16 See Ortner, "Is Female to Male as Nature is to Culture?" in Rosaldo and Lamphere, *Women, Culture and Society*, 67-87.
17 See Rich, *Of Woman Born*.

CHAPTER ELEVEN

1 Contemporary perspectives on rape are provided by Brownmiller, *Against Our Will: Men, Woman and Rape*; Griffin, *Made from This Earth*; Medea and Thompson, *Against Rape*; Morgan, "Theory and Practice: Pornography and Rape," in *Going Too Far*, 163-9; and Rowland, *The Ultimate Violation*. The basic information on rape provided in the next few pages is a synthesis of these women's findings and opinions.
2 Rowland, *The Ultimate Violation*. The old cliche, "a woman with her dress up can run faster than a man with his pants down" actually seems true to people; they do not realize, until an expert is placed on the stand, that people in this situation are frozen with fear, and obey their attacker out of terror for their lives.
3 Ibid., 115.
4 Ibid., 164.
5 Brownmiller, *Against Our Will*, 283.
6 Reeves Sanday, *Female Power and Male Dominance*. Griffin, in *Made from This Earth*, discusses Margaret Mead's studies of societies where rape is unthinkable, 42.
7 Morgan, "Theory and Practice: Pornography and Rape," in *Going too Far*, 167.
8 Griffin, *Made from This Earth*, 41, quotes the study *Patterns of Forcible Rape* by Menachem Amir: "Studies indicate that sex offenders do not constitute a uni-

que or psychopathological type; nor are they as a group invariably more disturbed than the control groups to which they are compared." Alan Taylor, a parole officer who has worked with rapists in the prison facilities at San Luis Obispo, California, says the same thing in plainer language: "Those men were the most normal men there. They had a lot of hang-ups, but they were the same hang-ups as men walking out on the street."

9 Rowland quotes Nicholas Groth's study *Men Who Rape* at great length in chapter 15. On the subject of averting rape, Groth reports: "In discussing the issue of deterrence with convicted offenders, three common qualities emerged in those cases in which the victim had an opportunity to confront her assailant and to resist the assault successfully. First, she managed to keep self-control and refused to be intimidated. Second, she did not counter-attack; she was assertive without being aggressive. And third, she said or did something that registered with the offender and communicated to him that she was a real person and not just an object." Rowland, p. 301. Dr. Pauline Bart reported similar findings to Rowland, 282.

10 Auerbach, *Woman and the Demon*, 7.

11 Kinnear, *Daughters of Time*, 151, quotes Gladstone on the virtues of women.

12 Eco, *The Role of the Reader*, 49.

13 Steiner, *Antigones*.

14 Edwards, *Psyche as Hero*, 237–8.

15 Katterman, "Uncovering the Secrets of a Mystery Goddess," 16.

16 Edwards, *Psyche as Hero*, 145.

17 Lauter, *Women as Mythmakers*, 149.

Bibliography

PRIMARY SOURCES

Apollodorus. *The Library of Greek Mythology*. Trans. Keith Adlrich. Lawrence: Coronado Press 1975, Book 3: 71.

Atwood, Margaret. *Surfacing*. Toronto: McClelland and Stewart 1972.

Brontë, Charlotte. *Jane Eyre*. Harmondsworth: Penguin 1966.

Caxton, William, ed. and trans. 1480. *The Metamorphoses of Ovid. The Phillips Manuscripts*. New York: George Braziller 1968, vol. 1.

Eliot, George. *Adam Bede*. Harmondsworth: Penguin 1980.

Golding, Arthur, trans. *Shakespeare's Ovid*. Ed. W. H. D. Rouse. 1567. Reprint. London: Centaur Press 1961.

Hardy, Thomas. *Tess of the D'Urbervilles*. Harmondsworth: Penguin 1978.

Hawthorne, Nathaniel. *The Scarlet Letter*. Ed and intro. Austin Warren. 1947. Reprint. New York: Holt, Rinehart 1963.

Hesiod. *The Homeric Hymns and Homerica*. Trans. Hugh G. Evelyn-White. New York: Macmillan 1914, 69.

Heywood, Thomas. *The Golden Age*. In *The Dramatic Works of Thomas Heywood*. 1874. Reprint. New York: Russell and Russell 1964, vol 3.

Hyginus. *Poetica Astronomica*, In *The Myths of Hyginus*, trans. and ed. Mary Grant. Lawrence: University of Kansas 1960, 181–2.

Lawrence, D.H. *Lady Chatterley's Lover*. 1928. Reprint. Harmondsworth: Penguin 1983.

Lefevre, Raoul. *The Recuyell of the Historyes of Troye Translated and Printed by William Caxton*. 1503. Ed. H. Oskar Sommer. 1894. Reprint. London: AMS Press 1973.

Milton, John. *A Mask Presented at Ludlow Castle*. In *The Works of John Milton*, ed. Frank Allen Peterson. New York: Columbia University Press 1931, vol. 1, part 1: 85–123.

Ovid. *Metamorphoses*. Trans. Mary M. Innes. Harmondsworth: Penguin 1955.

Pausanias. *Description of Greece*. Trans. J.G. Frazer. London: Macmillan and Co. 1913, vol. 1.

Radcliffe, Anne. *The Mysteries of Udolpho*. 1794. Ed. Bonamy Dobrée. Oxford: Oxford University Press 1966.

Sandys, George, trans. *Ovid's Metamorphoses Englished, Mythologiz'd, and Represented in Figures*. 1632. Ed. Karl K. Hulley and Stanley T. Vandersall. Lincoln: University of Nebraska Press 1970.

W.N., Gent. *The Barley-Breake, or a Warning for Wantons*. London: Simon Stafford 1607. Reprinted in *Early English Books, 1475-1640*. Ann Arbor Mich.: University Microfilms 1957.

Warner, William. *Albion's England*. 1612. Reprint. New York: George Olms Verlag 1971.

SECONDARY SOURCES

Abel, Darrell. "Hawthorne on the Strong Division-Lines of Nature." *American Transcendental Quarterly* 14 (1972): 23–31.

– "Hawthorne's Dimmesdale: Fugitive from Wrath." *Nineteenth-Century Fiction* 2 (1956) 81–105.

– "Hawthorne's Hester." *College English* 13 (1952): 302–9.

Adam, Ian. "The Structure of Realisms in *Adam Bede*." *Nineteenth-Century Fiction* 30 (1975–76), 127–49.

Adams, Maurianne. "*Jane Eyre*: Woman's Estate." In *The Authority of Experience*, ed. Arlyn Diamond and Lee R. Edwards. Amherst: University of Massachusetts Press 1977.

Alcott, Miriam. *Charlotte Brontë: Jane Eyre and Villette: a Casebook*. London: Macmillan 1973.

Anthon, Charles. *A Classical Dictionary*. 4th. Ed. New York: Harper 1848.

Arthos, John. "Milton, Ficino, and the *Charmides*." *Studies in the Renaissance* 6 (1959): 261–74.

Askew, Melvin. "Hawthorne, the Fall, and the Psychology of Maturity." *American Literature* 34 (1962): 335–43.

Artz, Frederick B. *The Mind of the Middle Ages*. 3rd ed., rev. New York: Alfred A. Knopf 1962.

Atwood, Margaret. *Survival*. Toronto: Anansi 1972.

Auerbach, Nina. *Woman and the Demon: The Life of a Victorian Myth*. Cambridge: Harvard University Press 1982.

Auster, Henry. *Local Habitations: Regionalism in the Early Novels of George Eliot*. Cambridge: Harvard University Press 1970.

Austin, Allen. "Satire and Theme in *The Scarlet Letter*." *Philological Quarterly* 41 (1962): 508–11.

Bachofen, J.J. *Myth, Religion, and Mother Right*. Trans. Ralph Manheim. Princeton, N.J.: Princeton University Press 1967.

Baker, Derek, ed. *Medieval Women*. Oxford: Basil Blackwell 1978.

Balakian, Anna. "'... and the pursuit of happiness': *The Scarlet Letter* and *A Spy in the House of Love*." *Mosaic* 11, no. 2 (1977-8): 163-70.

Barber, Richard. *The Knight and Chivalry*. Ipswich, England: The Boydell Press 1974.

Basket, Sam. "*The* (Complete) *Scarlet Letter*." *College English* 22 (1961): 321-8.

Baym, Nina. "Hawthorne's Women: the Tyranny of Social Myths." *Centennial Review* 15 (1971): 250-72.

Beal, Anthony, *D.H. Lawrence*. New York. Grove Press 1961.

Beards, Richard D. "D. H. Lawrence and the *Study of Thomas Hardy*, His Victorian Predecessor." *D.H. Lawrence Review* 2 (1969): 210-29.

Beaty, Jerome. "*Jane Eyre* and Genre." *Genre* 10 (1977): 619-54.

Bedient, Calvin. "The Radicalism of *Lady Chatterley's Lover*." *Hudson Review* 19 (1966): 407-16.

Bell, Michael Davitt. *Hawthorne and the Historical Romance of New England*. Princeton, N.J.: Princeton University Press 1971.

Beach, Joseph Warren. *The Technique of Thomas Hardy*. New York: Russell and Russell 1962.

Beauvoir, Simone de. *The Second Sex*. 1952. Trans. and ed. H.M. Parshley. New York: Vintage Books 1974.

Bennett, Joan. *George Eliot: Her Mind and Her Art*. Cambridge: Cambridge University Press 1948.

Björk, Harriet. *The Language of Truth: Charlotte Brontë, the Woman Question, and the Novel*. Lund: Gleerup 1974.

Black, Michael. *The Literature of Fidelity*. New York: Barnes and Noble 1975.

Blom, Margaret Howard. *Charlotte Brontë*. Boston: Twayne Publishers 1977.

Bodenheimer, Rosemarie. "*Jane Eyre* in Search of Her Story." *Papers on Language and Literature* 16 (1980): 387-402.

Bolen, Jean Shinoda. *Goddesses in Everywoman: A New Psychology of Women*. San Francisco: Harper and Row 1984.

Brantl, Ruth, ed. *Medieval Culture*. New York: George Braziller 1966.

Broadbent, J. B. *Milton: Comus and Samson Agonistes*. London: Edward Arnold 1961.

Brooks, Jean R. *Thomas Hardy: The Poetic Structure*. Ithaca, N. Y.: Cornell University Press 1971.

Brown, Douglas. "A Novel of Character and Environment." In *The Tragic Novels*, ed. R. P. Draper. London: Macmillan 1975, 158-64.

- *Thomas Hardy*. London: Longmans, Green 1961.

Brownmiller, Susan. *Against Our Will: Men, Women and Rape*. New York: Bantam 1975.

Bullough, Vern L. *The Subordinate Sex*. Chicago: University of Illinois Press 1974.

Burch, Beth. "Eliot's *Adam Bede*." *Explicator* 40, no. 1 (1981): 27-8.

Burkhart, Charles. "Another Key Word for *Jane Eyre*." *Nineteenth-Century Fiction* 16 (1961): 177-9.

- *Charlotte Brontë: A Psychosexual Study of Her Novels*. London: Victor Gollancz 1973.
Bush, Douglas. *John Milton*. London: Weidenfeld and Nicolson 1965.
- *Mythology and the Renaissance Tradition in English Poetry*. New York: Pageant 1957.
- *Mythology and the Romantic Tradition in English Poetry*. Cambridge, Mass.: Harvard University Press 1937.
Butery, Karen Ann. "Jane Eyre's Flights from Decision." *Literary Review* 24, no. 2 (1981): 222–51.
Calder, Jenni. *Women and Marriage in Victorian Fiction*. New York: Oxford University Press 1976.
Campbell, Joseph. *Flight of the Wild Gander*. New York: Viking 1969.
Campbell, Josie P. "The Woman as Hero in Margaret Atwood's *Surfacing*." *Mosaic* 11, no. 3 (1978): 17–28.
Casey, Kathleen. "The Cheshire Cat: Reconstructing the Experience of Mediaeval Woman." In *Liberating Women's History*, ed. Berenice A. Carroll. Urbana: University of Illinois Press 1976. 224–49.
Castiglione, Baldesar. *The Book of the Courtier*. Trans. Charles S. Singleton. New York: Anchor, Doubleday 1959.
Cavitch, David. *D. H. Lawrence and the New World*. New York: Oxford University Press 1969.
Chase, Richard. "The Bontës, or, Myth Domesticated." In *Forms of Modern Fiction*, ed. William Van O'Connor. Minneapolis: The University of Minnesota Press 1948, 102–19.
Christ, Carol P. *Diving Deep and Surfacing*. Boston: Beacon Press 1980.
- "Margaret Atwood: The Surfacing of Women's Spiritual Quest and Vision." *Signs* 2, no. 2 (1976): 316–30.
Christ, Carol T. "Imaginative Constraint, Feminine Duty, and the Form of Charlotte Brontë's Fiction." *Women's Studies* 6 (1979): 287–96.
Christopher, Georgia B. "The Virginity of Faith: *Comus* as a Reformation Conceit." *Journal of English Literary History* (ELH) 43 (1976): 479–99.
Clark, Lorenne, and Debra Lewis. *Rape: The Price of Coercive Sexuality*. Toronto: The Women's Press 1977.
Connors, Patricia E. "A Mythic Analysis of *Adam Bede*". PHD diss., University of Detroit, 1978. Ann Arbor Mich.: University Microfilms.
Cox, John D. "Poetry and History in Milton's Country Mask." *ELH* 44 (1977): 622–40.
Critical Inquiry (Special Issue: "Writing and Sexual Difference") 8 (1981).
Cronin, Morton. "Hawthorne on Romantic Love and the Status of Women." *Publications of the Modern Language Association* (PMLA) 69 (1954): 89–98.
Crow, Duncan. *The Victorian Woman*. New York: Stein & Day 1972.
Daleski, H.M. *The Forked Flame*. London: Faber & Faber 1965.
Dauber, Kenneth. *Rediscovering Hawthorne*. Princeton, N.J.: Princeton University Press 1977.
Davidson, Arnold E., and Cathy N. Davidson. "The Anatomy of Margaret Atwood's

Surfacing." ArielE 10, no. 3 (1979): 38–54.

Davidson, Cathy. "Chopin and Atwood: Woman Drowning, Woman Surfacing." *Kate Chopin Newsletter* 1, no. 3 (1975–6): 6–10.

Deamer, Robert Glen. "Hawthorne's Dream in the Forest." *Western American Literature* 13 (1979): 327–39.

Demaray, John G. *Milton and the Masque Tradition*. Cambridge: Harvard University Press 1968.

Dessner, Lawrence. *The Homely Web of Truth*. The Hague: Mouton 1975.

Deutsch, Helene. *A Psychoanalytic Study of the Myth of Dionysus and Apollo: Two Variants of the Son-Mother Relationship*. New York: International Universities Press 1969.

Dieckhoff, John, ed. *A Maske at Ludlow: Essays on Milton's Comus*. Cleveland: The Press of Case Western Reserve University 1968.

Downing, Christine. *The Goddess: Mythological Images of the Feminine*. New York: Crossroad 1981.

Drabble, Margaret, ed. *The Genius of Thomas Hardy*. New York: Knopf 1976.

Duffy, Maureen, *The Erotic World of Faery*. Toronto: Hodder and Stoughton 1972.

du Plessex Gray. "Nature as Nunnery." In *New York Times Book Review*, 17 July 1977: 3, 29.

Eakin, John Paul. "Hawthorne's Imagination and the Structure of 'The Custom House.'" *American Literature* 43 (1971): 346–58.

Eakins, Rosemary L. "Tess: the Pagan and Christian Traditions." In *The Novels of Thomas Hardy*, ed. Anne Smith. London: Vision Press 1979, 107–25.

Eastman, Donald R. "Myth and Fate in the Characters of *Women in Love*." *D.H. Lawrence Review* 9 (1976): 177–93.

Ebbatson, J. R. "Thomas Hardy and Lady Chatterley." *ArielE* 8, no. 2 (1977): 85–95.

Eco, Umberto. *The Role of the Reader*. Bloomington: Indiana University Press 1979.

Edwards, Lee R. *Psyche as Hero: Female Heroism and Fictional Form*. Middleton, CT: Wesleyan University Press 1984.

Enstice, Andrew. *Thomas Hardy: Landscapes of the Mind*. New York: St. Martin's Press 1979.

Erasmus, Desiderius. *The Colloquies*. Trans. Craig R. Thompson. Chicago: University of Chicago Press 1965.

Ewbank, Inga-Stina. *Their Proper Sphere: A Study of the Brontë Sisters as Early Victorian Female Novelists*. London: Edward Arnold 1966.

Fairbanks, Carol. "Margaret Atwood: A Bibliography of Criticism." *Bulletin of Bibliography* 36 (1979): 85–90, 98.

Fairbanks, Henry G. "Sin, Free Will, and 'Pessimism' in Hawthorne." *PMLA* 71 (1956): 975–89.

Ferguson, Mary Anne. "The Female Novel of Development and the Myth of Psyche." In *The Voyage In: Fictions of Female Development*, ed. Elizabeth Abel, Marianne Hirsh, and Elizabeth Langland. Hanover: University Press of New England 1983, 228–43.

Fiedler, Leslie A. "Archetype and Signature." In *Art and Psychoanalysis*, ed. William

Phillips. Cleveland: World Publishing 1963, 454–72.

Fletcher, Angus. *The Transcendental Masque*. Ithaca, N.Y.: Cornell University Press 1971.

Fogle, Richard Harter. *Hawthorne's Fiction: The Light and the Dark*. Rev. ed. Norman: University of Oklahoma Press 1964.

– *Hawthorne's Imagery*. Norman: University of Oklahoma Press 1969.

Ford, George H. *Double Measure: A Study of the Novels and Stories of D. H. Lawrence*, New York: Holt, Rinehart, Winston 1965.

Foster, Charles Howell. "Hawthorne's Literary Theory." *PMLA* 57 (1942): 241–54.

Fox, William Sherwood. *Greek and Roman*. Vol. 1 of *The Mythology of All Races*, ed. Louis Herbert Gray. New York: Cooper Square Publishers, 1964, 21.

Fraser, Antonia. *The Weaker Vessel*. London: Methuen 1985.

Frazer. J. G. *The Golden Bough*. 1922. Reprint. London: Macmillan 1951.

– *Pausanias's Description of Greece*. London: Macmillan 1913, vols. 4 and 6.

Frye, Northrop. *Anatomy of Criticism*. Princeton, N.J.: Princeton University Press 1957.

Fulton, E. Margaret. "Jane Eyre: The Development of a Female Consciousness." *English Studies in Canada* 5 (1979): 432–47.

Garebian, Keith. "*Surfacing*: Apocalyptic Ghost Story." *Mosaic* 9, no. 3 (1976): 1–9.

Gates, Barbara. "'Visionary Woe' and its Revision: Another Look at Jane Eyre's Pictures." *ArielE* 7, no. 4 (1976): 36–49.

Gerber, Charles C., ed. *Twentieth Century Interpretations of The Scarlet Letter*. Englewood Cliffs, N.J.: Prentice-Hall 1968.

Gies, Francis and Joseph Gies. *Women in the Middle Ages*. New York: Barnes-Noble 1978.

Gilbert, Allan. "Milton on the Position of Woman." *Modern Language Review* 15 (1920): 7–27, 240–64.

Gilbert, Sandra M. "Patriarchal Poetry and Woman Readers: Reflections on Milton's Bogey." *PMLA* 93 (1978): 368–82.

– , and Susan Gubar. *The Madwoman in the Attic*. New Haven: Yale University Press 1979.

Gimbutas, Marija. *The Gods and Goddesses of Old Europe*. Berkeley: University of California Press 1974.

Goldenberg, Naomi. "A Feminist Critique of Jung." *Signs* 2 (1976): 343–9.

Gombrich, E.H. *Symbolic Images: Studies in the Art of the Renaissance*. London: Phaidon 1972.

Gottlieb, Lois C., and Wendy Keitner. "Colonialism as Metaphor and Experience in *The Grass is Singing* and *Surfacing*." In *Awakened Conscience: Studies in Commonwealth Literature*, ed. C.D. Narasimhaiah. New Dehli: Sterling Publishers 1978, 307–14.

Grace, William J. *Ideas in Milton*. Notre Dame: University of Notre Dame Press 1968.

Graves, Robert. *The White Goddess*. 1948. Rev. and enl. ed. New York: Farrar, Strauss and Giroux 1966.

Gregor, Ian and Brian Nicholas. *The Moral and the Story*. London: Faber and Faber 1962.

Griffin, Susan. *Made from This Earth*. New York: Harper 1982.

Grudin, Peter. "Jane and the Other Mrs. Rochester: Excess and Restraint in *Jane Eyre*." *Novel* 10 (1977): 145 – 57.

Guthrie, W.K.C. *The Greeks and Their Gods*. Boston: Beacon Press 1955.

Gutierrez, Donald. *Lapsing Out: Embodiments of Death and Rebirth in the Last Works of D. H. Lawrence*. Toronto: Associated University Presses 1980.

Haegert, John W. "D.H. Lawrence and the Ways of Eros." *D.H. Lawrence Review* 11 (1978): 199–233.

Haight, Gordon S. *A Century of George Eliot Criticism*. Boston: Houghton Mifflin 1965.

Hamilton, Edith. *Mythology: Timeless Tales of Gods and Heroes*. Boston: Little, Brown 1940.

Hansen, Elaine Tuttle. "Ambiguity and the Narrator of *The Scarlet Letter*." *Journal of Narrative Technique* 5 (1975): 147–63.

Harcourt, Joan. "Atwood Country." *Queens Quarterly* 80 (1973): 278–81.

Harding, Davis P. *Milton and the Renaissance Ovid*. Urbana: University of Illinois Press 1966.

Harding, Mary Esther. *Woman's Mysteries, Ancient and Modern*. 1935. Reprint. New York: G. P. Putnam's Sons 1971.

Hardwick, Elizabeth. *Seduction and Betrayal*. New York: Random House 1970.

Hardy, Barbara. *The Appropriate Form: An Essay on the Novel*. London: Athlone Press 1964.

– *The Novels of George Eliot: a Study in Form*. London: University of London, The Athlone Press 1959.

Hardy, Thomas. "The Dorsetshire Labourer." *Longman's Magazine* July, 1883. Reprint. *Thomas Hardy's Personal Writings*. Ed. Harold Orel. Lawrence, Kansas: University of Kansas Press 1966, 168–91.

Harris, Mason. "Arthur's Misuse of the Imagination: Sentimental Benevolence and Wordsworthian Realism in *Adam Bede*." *English Studies in Canada* 4 (1978): 41–59.

Harrison. James. "The 20,000,000 Solitudes of *Surfacing*." *Dalhousie Review* 59 (1979): 74–81.

Harrison, Jane Ellen. *Ancient Art and Ritual*. New York: Holt 1913.

Harvey, Sir Paul. *The Oxford Companion to Classical Literature*. London: Oxford 1969.

Harvey, W.J. *The Art of George Eliot*. London: Chatto and Windus 1961.

– "George Eliot and the Omniscient Author Convention." *Nineteenth-Century Fiction* 13 (1958): 81–108.

Hawthorne, Nathaniel. *Tanglewood Tales* and *The Wonder Book*. In *Complete*

Works of Nathaniel Hawthorne, ed. George Parsons Lathrop. Boston: Houghton-Mifflin 1882–1883, vol. 4.

Heilbrun, Carolyn. *Towards a Recognition of Androgyny*. New York: Knopf 1973.

Heilman, Robert B. "Charlotte Brontë, Reason, and the Moon." *Nineteenth-Century Fiction* 14 (1960): 283–302.

Hellerstrom, Erna Olafson, Leslie Parder Hume, and Karen M. Offen, eds. *Victorian Women*. Stanford, CA: Stanford University Press 1981.

Herbert, Christopher. "Preachers and the Schemes of Nature in *Adam Bede*. *Nineteenth-Century Fiction* 29 (1974–5): 412–27.

Hilgers, Thomas L. "The Psychology of Conflict Resolution in *The Scarlet Letter*: A Non-Freudian Perspective." *American Transcendental Quarterly* 43 (1979): 211–24.

Hinz, Evelyn J. "*Ancient Art and Ritual* and *The Rainbow*." *Dalhousie Review* 58 (1978–9) 617–37.

– "D.H. Lawrence's Clothes Metaphor." *D.H. Lawrence Review* 1 (1968): 87–113.

– "Hierogamy versus Wedlock: Types of Marriage Plots and their Relationship to Genres of Prose Fiction." *PMLA* 91 (1976): 900–13.

– "The Masculine/Feminine Psychology of American/Canadian Primitivism: *Deliverance* and *Surfacing*." In *Other Voices, Other Views*, ed. Robin Winks. *Contributions in American Studies*, no. 34. Westport, CT: Greenwood, 1978, 75–96.

– "Pornography, Novel, Mythic Narrative: The Three Versions of *Lady Chatterley's Lover*." *Modernist Studies, Literature, and Culture* 3 (1979): 35–47.

– "*Sons and Lovers*: The Archetypal Dimensions of Lawrence's Oedipal Tragedy." *D.H. Lawrence Review* 5 (1972): 26–53.

– and John J. Teunissen. "*Surfacing*: Margaret Atwood's 'Nymph Complaining.'" *Contemporary Literature* 20 (1979): 221–36.

– and John J. Teunissen. "The Attack on the Pieta: An Archetypal Analysis." *Journal of Aesthetics and Art Criticism* 33 (1974): 43–50.

– and John J. Teunissen. "The Pieta as Icon in *The Golden Notebook*." *Contemporary Literature* 14 (1973): 457–70.

Hoffman, Frederick J. *The Mortal No: Death and the Modern Imagination*. Princeton, N.J.: Princeton University Press 1964.

Homer. *The Odyssey*. Trans. Samuel Butler, ed. Louise Ropes Loomis. New York: Walter J. Black 1944.

Horne, Lewis B. "The Darkening Sun of Tess Durbeyfield." *Texas Studies in Language and Literature* 13 (1971): 299–311.

Hough, Graham. *The Dark Sun*. London: Gerald Duckworth 1956.

Howe, Irving. *Thomas Hardy*. New York: Macmillan 1967.

Howe, Marguerite Beede. *The Art of the Self in D. H. Lawrence*. Athens, Ohio: Ohio University Press 1977.

Howells, Coral Ann. *Love, Mystery, and Misery: Feeling in Gothic Fiction*. London: The Athlone Press 1978.

Hughes, R. E. "*Jane Eyre*: The Unbaptised Dionysos." *Nineteenth-Century Fiction* 18 (1964): 347–64.

Hussey, Maurice. "Structure and Imagery in *Adam Bede*." *Nineteenth-Century Fiction* 10 (1955): 115–29.

Hutchinson, Earl R., Sr. "Antiquity in *The Scarlet Letter*: The Primary Sources." *University of Hartford Studies in Literature* 13, no. 2 (1981): 99–110.

Hyman, Virginia R. *Ethical Perspective in the Novels of Thomas Hardy*. New York: Kennikat Press 1975.

Jackson, Dennis. "The 'Old Pagan Vision': Myth and Ritual in *Lady Chatterley's Lover*." *D.H. Lawrence Review* 11 (1978): 260–71.

Jacobs, Maureen Shuhan. "Beyond the Castle: The Development of the Paradigmatic Female Story." PHD diss. The American University 1980. Ann Arbor Mich.: University Microfilms.

Jacobus, Mary. "Tess: The Making of a Pure Woman." In *Tearing the Veil: Essays on Femininity*, ed. Susan Lipshitz. London: Routledge and Kegan Paul 1978, 77–92.

James, William C. "Atwood's *Surfacing*." *Canadian Literature* 91 (1981): 174–81.

Johnson, Bruce. "'The Perfection of the Species' and Hardy's Tess." In *Nature and the Victorian Imagination*, ed. U. C. Knoepflamacher and G.B. Tennyson. Berkeley: University of California Press 1977, 259–77.

Johnson, Claudia D. *The Productive Tension of Hawthorne's Art*. Birmingham: University of Alabama Press 1981.

Jones, R. T. *George Eliot*. Cambridge: Cambridge University Press 1970.

Jung, Carl G. *Man and His Symbols*. New York: Dell 1964.

– "Women in Europe." In *Contributions to Analytical Psychology*. Trans. Gary F. Baynes and H. G. Baynes. London: Kegan Paul 1928, 164–88.

Kahane, Claire. "Gothic Mirrors and Feminine Identity." *Centennial Review* 24 (1980): 43–64.

Katterman, Lee. "Research Update: Uncovering the Secrets of a Mystery Goddess." *The Research News* 36, no. 3–4 (1985): 16.

Kaufman, Michael W. "Spare Ribs: The Conception of Woman in the Middle Ages and the Renaissance." *Soundings* 56 (Summer 1973): 139–63.

Kelso, Ruth. *Doctrine for the Lady of the Renaissance*. Urbana: University of Illinois Press 1956.

Kennard, Jean E. *Victims of Convention*. Hamden, CT: Archon Books 1978.

Keife, Robert. *Charlotte Brontë's World of Death*. Austin: University of Texas 1979.

Kerényi, C. *Eleusis: Archetypal Image of Mother and Daughter*. Trans. Ralph Manheim. New York: Schocken Books 1977.

– and C.G. Jung. *Essays on a Science of Mythology: the Myth of the Divine Child and the Mysteries of Eleusis*. Trans. R.F.C. Hull. Princeton, N.J.: Bollinger 1950.

Kermode, Frank. "Lawrence and the Apocalyptic Types." *Critical Quarterly* 10 (1968): 14–38.

Kettle, Arnold. *An Introduction to the English Novel*. 1953. Reprint. London: Hutchinson University Library 1969, vol. 2.

Kiely, Robert. *The Romantic Novel in England*. Cambridge: Harvard University Press 1972.

Kinnear, Mary. *Daughters of Time*. Ann Arbor: University of Michigan Press 1982.

Kinkead-Weekes, Mark. "Lawrence on Hardy." In *Thomas Hardy after Fifty Years*, ed. Lance St. John Butler. Totowa, N.J.: Rowman and Littlefield 1977, 90–103.

Knies, Earl A. *The Art of Charlotte Brontë*. Athens, Ohio: Ohio University Press 1969.

Knoepflamacher, U. C. *George Eliot's Early Novels: The Limits of Realism*. Berkeley: University of California Press 1968.

Kozicki, Henry. "Myths of Redemption in Hardy's *Tess of the D'Urbervilles*." *Papers on Language and Literature* 10 (1974): 150–8.

Laird, J. T. *The Shaping of Tess of the D'Urbervilles*. Oxford: Clarendon Press 1975.

Laser, Marvin. "'Head,' 'Heart', and 'Will' in Hawthorne's Psychology." *Nineteenth-Century Fiction* 10 (1955): 130–40.

Lauter, Estella. *Women as Mythmakers: Poetry and Visual Art by Twentieth-Century Women*. Bloomington: Indiana University Press 1984.

Lauter, Estella, and Carol Schreier Rupprecht. *Feminist Archetypal Theory: Interdisciplinary Re-Visions of Jungian Thought*. Knoxville: University of Tennessee Press 1985.

La Valley, Albert J., ed. *Twentieth Century Interpretations of "Tess of the D'Urbervilles"*. New Jersey: Prentice-Hall 1966.

Lawrence, D.H. *The Collected Letters of D.H. Lawrence*, ed. Harry T. Moore. New York: Viking 1962.

– *The Escaped Cock*. Los Angeles: Black Sparrow Press 1973.

– *The First Lady Chatterley*. London: Heinemann 1944.

– *John Thomas and Lady Jane*. London: Heinemann 1972.

– *Phoenix: Posthumous Papers of D.H. Lawrence*. Ed. Edward D. McDonald. New York: Viking 1936.

– *Phoenix II: Uncollected, Unpublished and Other Prose Works by D.H. Lawrence*. Ed. Warren Roberts and Harry T. Moore. New York: Viking 1968.

– *Studies in Classic American Literature*. New York: Viking 1966.

Lawry, Jon S. *The Shadow of Heaven*. Ithaca, N. Y.: Cornell University Press 1968.

Levin Harry. *The Power of Blackness*. New York: Knopf 1958.

Lewis, Paul. "Mournful Mysteries: Gothic Speculation in *The Scarlet Letter*." *American Transcendental Quarterly* 44 (1979): 279–93.

Liddell, Robert. *The Novels of George Eliot*. London: Duckworth 1977.

Linder, Cynthia A. *Romantic Imagery in the Novels of Charlotte Brontë*. New York: Harper and Row, Barnes and Noble Import Division 1978.

Lodge, David. *The Language of Fiction*. London: Routledge and Kegan Paul 1966.

Lovelock, Julian, ed. *Milton: "Comus" and "Samson Agonistes": A Casebook*. London: Macmillan 1975.

Lyons, Bonnie. "'Neither Victims nor Executioners' in Margaret Atwood's Fiction." *World Literature Written in English* 17 (1978): 181–7.

MacAndrew, Elizabeth. *The Gothic Tradition in Fiction*. New York: Columbia University Press 1979.

MacCormack, Carol, and Marilyn Strathern, eds. *Nature, Culture, and Gender*. Cambridge: Cambridge University Press 1980.

MacShane, Frank. "The House of the Dead: Hawthorne's 'Custom House' and *The Scarlet Letter*." *New England Quarterly* 35 (1962): 93–101.

Maclean, Ian. *The Renaissance Notion of Woman*. London: Cambridge University Press 1930.

Malahat Review (Special Atwood Issue) 41 (1977).

Male, Roy R., Jr. "From the Innermost Germ: The Organic Principle in Hawthorne's Fiction." *ELH* 20 (1953): 218–36.

Mandel, Eli. "Atwood Gothic." *Malahat Review* 41 (1977): 165–74.

Mandel, Jerome. "Mediaeval Romance and *Lady Chatterley's Lover*." *D.H. Lawrence Review* 10 (1977): 20–33.

Mann, Karen. "Bertha Mason and Jane Eyre: The True Mrs. Rochester." *Ball State University Forum* 19, no. 1 (1978): 31–4.

Mansbridge, Francis. "Search for Self in the Novels of Margaret Atwood." *Journal of Canadian Fiction* 22 (1978): 106–17.

Margalioth, Daniel. "Passion and Duty: A Study of Charlotte Brontë's *Jane Eyre*." *Hebrew University Studies in Literature* 7 (1979): 212–13.

Marotta, Kenny. "*Adam Bede* as Pastoral." *Genre* 9 (1976): 59–72.

Martin, Jeanne S. "Transformations in Genre in Milton's *Comus*." *Genre* 10 (1977): 195–213.

Martin, R.G. "Notes on Thomas Heywood's *Ages*." *Modern Language Notes* 33 (1918): 23–9.

Martin, Robert Bernard. *The Accents of Persuasion: Charlotte Brontë's Novels*. London: Faber and Faber 1966.

Martin, Robert K. "*Jane Eyre* and the World of Faery." *Mosaic* 10, no. 4 (1977): 85–95.

Matthiessen, F. O. *American Renaissance*. New York: Oxford University Press 1941.

McCall, Dan. "The Design of Hawthorne's 'Custom House.'" *Nineteenth-Century Fiction* 21 (1967): 349–58.

McCombs, Judith. "Atwood's Nature Concepts: An Overview." *Waves* 7, no. 1 (1978): 68–77.

McLay, Catherine. "The Divided Self: Theme and Pattern in Margaret Atwood's *Surfacing*." *Journal of Canadian Fiction* 4, no. 1 (1975): 82–95.

McPherson, Hugo. *Hawthorne as Mythmaker*. Toronto: University of Toronto Press 1969.

– "Hawthorne's Major Source for his Mythological Tales." *American Literature* 30 (1958): 364–5.

– "Hawthorne's Mythology: A Mirror for Puritans." *University of Toronto Quarterly* 28 (1959): 267–78.

Medea, Andrea, and Kathleen Thompson. *Against Rape*. New York: Farrar, Straus and Giroux 1974.

Merchant, Carolyn. *The Death of Nature: Women, Ecology, and the Scientific Revolution*. San Francisco: Harper and Row 1980.

Mews, Hazel. *Frail Vessels: Woman's Role in Woman's Novels from Fanny Burney to George Eliot*. London: Athlone Press 1969.

Miko, Stephen J. *Toward Women in Love*. New Haven: Yale University Press 1971.

Miller, Hugh. "Surfacing to No Purpose: Margaret Atwood's Apparent Survival." *Antigonish Review* 24 (1976): 59–61.

Millgate, Michael. *Thomas Hardy*. London: The Bodley Head 1971.

Mills, Barriss. "Hawthorne and Puritanism." *New England Quarterly* 21 (1948): 78–102.

Milton, John. *Animadversions upon the Remonstrants Defense, Against Smectymnuus*, In *The Works of John Milton*, ed. Harry M. Ayres. New York: Columbia University Press 1931, vol 3, part 1, 105–79.

Moglen, Helene. *Charlotte Brontë: The Self Conceived*. New York: Norton 1976.

Momberger, Philip. "Self and World in the Works of Charlotte Brontë." *ELH* 32 (1965): 349–69.

Moore, Harry T. "*Lady Chatterley's Lover* as Romance." In *A D.H. Lawrence Miscellany*, ed. Harry T. Moore. Carbondale: Southern Illinois University Press 1959, 262–4.

Morewedge, Rosemarie Thee, ed. *The Role of Woman in the Middle Ages*. Albany: SUNY Press 1975.

Morgan, Robin. "Theory and Practice: Pornography and Rape." In *Going Too Far*, ed. Robin Morgan. New York: Vintage Books 1978, 163–9.

Moynahan, Julian. "*Lady Chatterley's Lover*: The Deed of Life." *ELH* 26 (1959): 66–90. Reprinted in *D. H. Lawrence: A Collection of Critical Essays*, ed. Mark Spilka. Englewood Cliffs, N.J.: Prentice-Hall 1963, 72–92.

– *The Deed of Life: The Novels and Tales of D. H. Lawrence*. Princeton, N.J.: Princeton University Press 1963.

Müller, Max. "Solar Myths." *Nineteenth Century* (18 December, 1885): 900–22.

Mundy, John H. *Europe in the High Middle Ages*. New York: Basic Books 1973.

Neumann, Erich. *Amor and Psyche: The Psychic Development of the Feminine: A Commentary on the Tale by Apuleius*. Trans. Ralph Manheim. New York: Pantheon Books for the Bollinger Found. 1956.

– *The Great Mother: An Analysis of the Archetype*. Trans. Ralph Manheim. Bollingen Series 47, 1955. 2nd Ed. Princeton: Princeton University Press 1963.

Newton, K.M. *George Eliot: Romantic Humanist: A Study of the Philosophical Structure of Her Novels*. New Jersey: Barnes and Noble 1981.

Ochshorn, Judith. *The Female Experience and the Nature of the Divine*. Bloomington: Indiana University Press 1981.

Osgood, Charles Grosvenor. *The Classical Mythology of Milton's English Poems*. Vol. 8 of *Yale Studies in English*, New York: Henry Holt 1900.

Paris, Bernard J. *Experiments in Life: George Eliot's Quest for Values*. Detroit: Wayne State University Press 1965.

Parker, David. "Lawrence and Lady Chatterley: the Teller and the Tale." *Critical Review* 20 (1978): 31–41.

Partlow, Robert B., and Harry T. Moore. *D. H. Lawrence: The Man Who Lived.*
D. H. Lawrence Conference at Southern Illinois University, Carbondale, Ill. April,
1979. Carbondale: Southern Illinois University Press 1980.

Paterson, John. "Lawrence's Vital Source: Nature and Character in Thomas Hardy."
In *Nature and the Victorian Imagination,* ed. U.C. Knoepflmacher and G.B. Tennyson. Berkeley: University of California Press 1977, 455-69.

Pattison, Joseph C. "Point of View in Hawthorne." *PMLA* 82 (1967): 363-9.

Pearce, T. S. *George Eliot.* London: Evans Bros. 1973.

Pell, Nancy. "Resistance, Rebellion and Marriage: The Economics of *Jane Eyre.*"
Nineteenth-Century Fiction 31 1976-1977: 397-420.

Person, Leland S., Jr. "*The Scarlet Letter* and the Myth of the Divine Child."
American Transcendental Quarterly 44 (Fall 1979): 279-93.

Poole, Adrian. "'Men's Words' and Hardy's Women." *Essays in Criticism* 31, no. 4
(1981): 328-45.

Poovey, Mary. "Ideology and *The Mysteries of Udolpho.*" *Criticism* 21 (1979):
307-30.

Power, Elaine. *Mediaeval Women.* Cambridge: Cambridge University Press 1975.

Pratt, Annis. *Archetypal Patterns in Women's Fiction.* Bloomington: Indiana University Press 1981.

- "The New Feminist Criticism." *College English* 32 (1971): 872-8.

- "*Surfacing* and the Rebirth Journey." In *The Art of Margaret Atwood,* ed. Arnold
E. Davidson and Cathy N. Davidson. Toronto: House of Anansi Press 1981.

- "Women and Nature in Modern Fiction." *Contemporary Literature* 13 (1972):
476-90.

Putzell, Sara Moore. "Rights, Reason, and Redemption: Charlotte Brontë's Neo-
Platonism." *Victorian Newsletter* 55 (1979): 5-7.

Rheinhold, Meyer. *Past and Present.* Toronto: Hakkert 1972.

Rich, Adrienne. *Of Woman Born: Motherhood as Experience and Institution.* New
York: Bantam 1976.

- *On Lies, Secrets, and Silence: Selected Prose, 1966-1978.* New York: W.W. Norton 1979.

Rigney, Barbara Hill. *Madness and Sexual Politics in the Feminist Novel: Studies
in Brontë, Woolf, Lessing and Atwood.* Madison: University of Wisconsin Press
1978.

Ringe, Donald L. "Hawthorne's Psychology of the Head and Heart." *PMLA* 65
(1950): 120-32.

Roberts, Doreen. "*Jane Eyre* and 'The Warped System of Things.'" In *Reading the
Victorian Novel: Detail into Form,* ed. Ian Gregor. London: Vision 1980, 131-49.

Roberts, Neil. *George Eliot: Her Beliefs and Her Art.* Pittsburgh: University of
Pittsburgh Press 1975.

Rogers, Katherine. *The Troublesome Helpmate: A History of Misogyny in
Literature.* Seattle: University of Washington Press 1966.

Rosaldo, Michelle Zimbalist, and Louise Lamphere, eds. *Women, Culture, and*

Society. Stanford: Stanford University Press 1974.

Rosenberg, Jerome H. "Women as Everyman in Atwood's *Surfacing*: Some Observations on the End of the Novel." *Studies in Canadian Literature* 3 (1978): 127–32.

Ross, Catherine Sheldrick. "A Singing Spirit: Female Rites of Passage in *Klee Wyck*, *Surfacing* and *The Diviners*." *Atlantis* 4, no. 1 (1978): 86–94.

– "Nancy Drew as Shaman: Atwood's *Surfacing*." *Canadian Literature* 84 (1980): 7–17.

Rossman, Charles. "'You are the Call and I am the Answer': D.H. Lawrence and Women." *D.H. Lawrence Review* 8 (1975): 255–328.

Rowland, Judith. *The Ultimate Violation*. Garden City, N.Y.: Doubleday 1985.

Rubenstein, Roberta. "*Surfacing*: Margaret Atwood's Journey to the Interior." *Modern Fiction Studies* 22 (1976): 387–99.

Rule, Jane. "Life, Liberty and the Pursuit of Normalcy." *Malahat Review* 41 (1977): 42–9.

Sadoff, Dianne F. "Nature's Language: Metaphor in the Text of *Adam Bede*." *Genre* 11 (1978): 411–26.

Sagar, Keith. *The Art of D.H. Lawrence*. Cambridge: Cambridge University Press 1966.

Sanday, Peggy Reeves. *Female Power and Male Dominance: On the Origins of Sexual Inequality*. Cambridge: Cambridge University Press 1981.

Sanders, Scott. *D.H. Lawrence: The World of the Five Major Novels*. New York: The Viking Press 1973.

Schreiber, Annette. "The Myth in Charlotte Brontë." *Literature and Psychology* 18 (1968): 48–67.

Schaeffer, Susan F. "'It Is Time that Separates Us': Margaret Atwood's *Surfacing*." *Centennial Review* 18 (1974): 319–37.

Schorer, Mark. "On *Lady Chatterley's Lover*." *Evergreen Review* 1, no. 1 (1957): 149–78.

Seznec, Jean. *The Survival of the Pagan Gods*. Trans. Barbara F. Sessions. New York: Pantheon Books for the Bollinger Found. 1953.

Showalter, Elaine. *A Literature of Their Own: British Women Novelists from Brontë to Lessing*. New Jersey: Princeton University Press 1977.

Smith, Anne, ed. *Lawrence and Women*. London: Vision Press 1978.

Smith, George William, Jr. "Milton's Revisions and the Design of *Comus*." *ELH* 46 (1979): 56–80.

Smith, Nelson C. "Sense, Sensibility, and Anne Radcliffe." *Studies in English Literature* 13 (1973): 577–90.

Solomon, Eric. "*Jane Eyre*: Fire and Water." *College English* 25 (1963): 215–17.

Spilka, Mark. "Lawrence's Quarrel with Tenderness." *Critical Quarterly* 9 (1967): 363–77.

– "Post-Leavis Lawrence Critics." *Modern Language Quarterly* 25 (1964): 212–17.

Squires, Michael. "New Light on the Gamekeeper in *Lady Chatterley's Lover*." *D.H. Lawrence Review* 11 (1978): 234–45.

- "Scenic Construction and Rhetorical Signals in Hardy and Lawrence." *D.H. Lawrence Review* 8 (1975): 125–46.

Staves, Susan. "British Seduced Maidens." *Eighteenth Century Studies* 14, no. 2 (1980–81): 109–34.

Steadman, John M. "Milton's Haemony: Etymology and Allegory." *PMLA* 77 (1962): 200–7.

Steele, Jeremy. "Which Ovid in the Hay-Shed?" *Notes and Queries* 24 (1977): 430–2.

Steiner, George. *Antigones*. New York: Oxford University Press 1984.

Stephen, Leslie. *George Eliot*. London: Macmillan 1907.

Stoll, John E. *The Novels of D. H. Lawrence: a Search for Integration*. Columbia: University of Missouri Press 1971.

Stouck, David. "The Surveyor of the Custom House: A Narrator for *The Scarlet Letter*." *Centennial Review* 15 (1971): 309–29.

Stubbs, John C. *The Pursuit of Form: A Study of Hawthorne and the Romance*. Urbana: University of Illinois Press 1970.

Stump, Reva. *Movement and Vision in George Eliot's Novels*. Seattle: University of Washington Press 1959.

Sulivan, Paula. "Fairy Tale Elements in *Jane Eyre*." *Journal of Popular Culture* 12 (1978): 61–74.

Sullivan, Rosemary. "Breaking the Circle." *Malahat Review* 41 (1977): 30–41.

- "*Surfacing* and *Deliverance*." *Canadian Literature* 67 (1976): 6–20.

Sweetapple, Rosemary. "Margaret Atwood: Victims and Survivors." *Southern Review* 9 (1976): 50–69.

Taylor, J. Golden. *Hawthorne's Ambivalence Toward Puritanism*. Utah State University Press Monograph Series, vol. 12, no. 1. Logan, Utah: Utah State University Press, 1965.

Tedlock, E. W., Jr. *D. H. Lawrence, Artist and Rebel: A Study of Lawrence's Fiction*. Albuquerque: University of New Mexico Press 1963.

Thompson, G.R., ed. *The Gothic Imagination: Essays in Dark Romanticism*. Washington: Washington State University Press 1974.

Thurley, Geoffrey. *The Psychology of Hardy's Novels*. Queensland: University of Queensland Press 1975.

Tillyard, E. M. W. *Milton*. London: Chatto and Windus 1966.

Tuve, Rosamund. *Images and Themes in Five Poems of Milton*. Cambridge, Mass.: Harvard University Press 1962.

Updike, John. "On Hawthorne's Mind." *New York Review of Books* 28, no. 4 (1981): 41–2.

Van Doren, Mark. *Nathaniel Hawthorne*. New York: William Sloan Associates 1949.

Van Duesen, Marshall. "Narrative Tone in 'The Custom House' and *The Scarlet Letter*." *Nineteenth-Century Fiction* 21 (1966): 61–71.

Van Ghent, Dorothy. "On *Tess of the D'Urbervilles*." In *Hardy: A Collection of Critical Essays*, ed. Albert J. Guerard. New Jersey: Prentice-Hall 1964, 77–90.

Vicinus, Martha, ed. *A Widening Sphere*. Bloomington: Indiana University Press 1977.

Vigar, Penelope. *The Novels of Thomas Hardy: Illusion and Reality*. London: University of London, The Athlone Press 1974.

Vivas, Eliseo. *D. H. Lawrence: The Failure and Triumph of Art*. Evanston, Ill.: Northwestern University Press 1960.

Voelker, Joseph C. "The Spirit of No-Place: Elements of the Classical Ironic Utopia in D. H. Lawrence's *Lady Chatterley's Lover*." *Modern Fiction Studies* 25 (1979): 223–40.

Walker, Barbara G. *The Woman's Encyclopedia of Myths and Secrets*. San Francisco: Harper and Row 1983.

Wallace, Robert K. "A Probable Source for Dorothea and Casaubon: Hester and Chillingworth." *English Studies* 58 (1977): 23–5.

Weathers, Winston. "Mythology in Modern Literature." *D.H. Lawrence Review* 6 (1973):201–13.

Weiss, Daniel A. "D. H. Lawrence's Great Circle: From *Sons and Lovers* to *Lady Chatterley*." *Psychoanalytic Review* 50 (1963): 112–38.

Wickham, Anna. "The Spirit of the Lawrence Women: A Posthumous Memoir." *Texas Quarterly*, 9 (Autumn 1966): 31–50.

Widmer, Kingsley. "The Pertinence of Modern Pastoral: The Three Versions of *Lady Chatterley's Lover*." *Studies in the Novel* 5 (1973): 298–313.

Wiesenfarth, Joseph. "George Eliot's Notes for *Adam Bede*." *Nineteenth-Century Fiction* 32 (1977–78): 127–66.

Williams, Merryn. *Thomas Hardy and Rural England*. New York: Columbia University Press 1972.

Wilcher, Robert, "Milton's Masque: Occasion, Form, and Meaning." *Critical Quarterly* 20, no. 1 (1978): 3–20.

Wind, Edgar. *Pagan Mysteries of the Renaissance*. New York: Norton 1968.

Woodcock, George. "Surfacing to Survive: Notes of the Recent Atwood." *ArielE* 4, no. 3 (1973): 16–28.

Wollstonecraft, Mary. "A Vindication of the Rights of Women with Strictures on Political and Moral Subjects." 1792. Reprinted in *A Mary Wollstonecraft Reader*, ed. Barbara H. Solomon and Paula S. Berggren. New York: Mentor 1983.

Worthen, John. *D. H. Lawrence and the Idea of the Novel*. Totowa, N.J.: Rowman and Littlefield 1979.

Ziff, Larzer. "The Ethical Dimension of 'The Custom House.'" *Modern Language Notes* 73 (1958): 338–44.

Index